CW01651394

Mental Health: Tribunal Procedure

Mental Health: Tribunal Procedure

Second Edition

Larry Gostin
JD
Executive Director, American Society of Law and Medicine
Professor of Health Law and Policy Harvard University

Phil Fennell
BA, MPhil (Kent)
Lecturer Cardiff Law School
Member of the Mental Health Act Commission 1983–1989

LONGMAN

ISBN 0 85121 4304

Second Edition 1992

Published by
Longman Law, Tax and Finance
Longman Group UK Ltd
21–27 Lamb's Conduit Street
London WC1N 3NJ

Associated Offices
Australia, Hong Kong, Malaysia, Singapore, USA

A CIP catalogue record for this book is available from the British Library

Printed and bound in Great Britain by
Biddles of Guildford Ltd, Surrey

Contents

Preface

A person is compulsorily detained in a psychiatric hospital for his own health or safety or for the protection of other persons. Nevertheless, it is one of the few situations where the law of England and Wales permits a person to be held against his will without prior access to a court. Mental Health Review Tribunals provide a check on the use of this power. The tribunal is an independent body which examines the justification for continuing a patient's detention and is normally the only form of independent review having the power to discharge the detained patient.

It is difficult to find a more pressing case for representation: the client is usually ill and receiving medication such as the major tranquillisers. Moreover, the tribunal has the power in some circumstances to withhold crucial case papers from the patient and to exclude him from much of the proceedings. Why, therefore, have lawyers until recently known so little about the tribunals? There are two main reasons. Firstly, prior to the Mental Health Act 1983 only a small proportion of detained patients had the right to apply to the tribunal and, of those who were eligible, only a few exercised that right. There were less than a thousand tribunals a year; most of those were concerned with patients in the four special hospitals. Secondly, until recently there has been no public funding for representation. This has effectively prevented most solicitors from providing their services.

Law reform in the last few years has changed this situation. The report of the Butler Committee on Mentally Abnormal Offenders in 1975 and the publication by MIND of *A Human Condition* in the same year began a campaign to reform the Mental Health Act 1959. The Mental Health (Amendment) Act was passed in 1982 and the provisions were consolidated in the Mental Health Act 1983. This Act, which came into operation on 30 September 1983, brought important changes for Mental Health Review Tribunals. Many more patients are eligible to apply to a tribunal (including patients who are detained for 28 days only). Patients who do not apply to the tribunal of their own accord may be referred automatically. It is estimated that there will be a five-fold increase in the number of tribunals under the 1983 Act. The Act also expands the tribunal's powers, enabling it to discharge restricted patients and to give a wider range of directions in all cases.

While the Act was being revised an interdepartmental committee set about revising the procedural rules. The Mental Health Review Tribunal Rules 1983 strengthen the rights of the representative and the patient in respect to the receiving of documents available to the tribunal, the conduct of the proceedings and the receiving of reasoned decisions. For the lawyer, a crucial reform was the extension of the 'assistance by way of representation' provisions to Mental Health Review Tribunals in December 1982. This enabled the solicitor to cover the costs of representation before the tribunal, costs that formerly he might well have had to bear himself.

It is impossible at present to predict the precise effects of these reforms. Nevertheless, it can confidently be said that there will be much greater call on the legal profession for their services. This book is written as a guide to the law and practice of Mental Health Review Tribunals. Is such a guide necessary? Could a solicitor or barrister not obtain the same information from the Act and statutory instruments? In the preparation of this book we discussed the contents with members of the legal profession. It became clear to us that a guide is essential. Representation before the Mental Health Review Tribunals requires a unique and rather daunting mixture of professional expertise: the issues are not simply legal, but psychiatric and social in nature. The lawyer must not only know the law but must have an appreciation of psychiatric concepts and treatment and the problems of caring for a person following discharge from a psychiatric hospital. Few lawyers feel comfortable in this field without some form of training or guidance. This book is intended to provide such guidance.

We should point out that the book was written prior to the implementation of the 1983 Act and Rules. Over the years practices will develop which the authors may not have predicted; nevertheless we have made all possible attempts to discover how the provisions are intended to operate in practice and have drawn on our considerable experience of Mental Health Review Tribunals and their operation under the 1959 Act.

We are indebted to MIND and the Law Society for their help, and in particular, to William Bingley, Laura Jacobs, Hazel Burke, Professor Derek Russell Davis and Simon Hillyard. Our thanks also go to Jenny Levin and the Legal Action Group which, together with MIND, has provided for the training of lawyers in this field. We would also like to thank the officers of the Department of Health and Social Security, the Home Office, the Lord Chancellor's Department and the Mental Health Review Tribunal Office, Oliver Thorold and Jill Peay who have provided helpful information, criticised our drafts and pondered long and hard with us on obscure points of interpretation. A special thanks to our families for coping with the added domestic burdens while we wrote this book.

Larry Gostin, Elaine Rassaby and Andrew Buchan
November, 1983

Preface to the Second Edition

Since the publication of the first edition of this book in 1983, there has been an unprecedented growth in the case load of MHRTs, in the case law governing their operation, and in the number of lawyers and others who have undertaken training to provide representation. In 1982 there were 1,006 applications or references and 858 cases were dealt with. In 1988, there were 5,834 applications or references and 3,327 cases were disposed of during the year. Whilst under the Mental Health Act 1959 there had been one appeal by case stated from a MHRT to the High Court (*Re VE* [1973] 1 QB 452), since 1983 there have been over 20 cases resulting in rulings affecting the powers and functioning of MHRTs. There has also been a remarkable increase in legal representation before MHRTs.

The impact of the European Convention on Human Rights in this area has continued to grow, and the Code of Practice on the Mental Health Act 1983 (Department of Health 1990) has spelt out important principles governing the care and treatment of mentally disordered people. This edition has been completely revised in the light of these developments. There is a new chapter (chapter 5) which concentrates on the requirements of the European Convention regarding the review of detention on psychiatric grounds and the possibilities which exist to review psychiatric detention in the ordinary courts.

The increase in interest in the legal rights of mentally disordered people to seek review of their detention has directed attention towards the other legal needs of mentally disordered people in general. The Law Society established a Mental Health Subcommittee with the initial task of overseeing the selection of competent representatives for patients whose cases had been referred to MHRTs under the new arrangements in the 1983 Act. The Mental

Health and Disability Subcommittee now keeps under review the legal needs and legal rights of all mentally disordered and disabled people. It has been instrumental in securing the passage of the Criminal Procedure (Insanity and Unfitness to Plead) Act 1991, which mitigates many of the draconian consequences of being found not guilty by reason of insanity or unfit to plead. The provisions of that Act are discussed in chapters 2, 4 and 7. The Subcommittee has also prompted the Law Commission to take on a review of the law governing decision-making on behalf of mentally incapacitated adults.

This guide is intended not only for those who provide representation before tribunals, but also for tribunal members, Responsible Medical Officers (RMOs), independent psychiatrists, and social workers.

Our gratitude is due to David Burnet, Melvin Crawford, Nigel Lowe, John Sturrock, Peter Edwards, Malcolm Hurwitt, Penny Letts, and Shirley Turner, who have read and criticised our drafts. Their help has been invaluable. Out thanks are due too, to the staff at the Tribunal Offices and the Special Hospitals Service Authority, who have responded very patiently to our many inquiries. We should also like to thank Susan Marshall and Tara Walsh of Longmans for their patience and hard work in keeping us in line.

Definitions and Abbreviations

Definitions

Approved Social Worker
An officer of the local social services authority who is appointed by the authority to carry out functions specified in s 114 of the Act (s 145(1)). No social worker can be appointed as an approved social worker unless the authority is satisfied that he is competent to deal with persons suffering from mental disorder.

Hospital
Any health service hospital within the meaning of the NHS Act 1977 (including special hospitals), any hospital vested in a National Health Service Trust and any accommodation provided by a local authority and used as a hospital by or on behalf of the Secretary of State for Health under that Act (s 145(1)). For the purposes of compulsory admission under Parts II or III of the Act, hospital includes mental nursing home registered under the Registered Homes Act 1984, s 23(5) to accept patients who are liable to be detained (ss 34(2) and 55(5)).

Hospital managers
1 In relation to a NHS hospital, the district or special health authority responsible for the administration of the hospital, or in relation to a hospital vested in a NHS trust, the directors of the trust.
2 In relation to a special hospital, the special hospital services authority.
3 In relation to a mental nursing home, the persons who are registered as managers in respect of that home in pursuance of the Registered Homes Act 1984.

Hospital order
An order by a court directing the admission of an offender to hospital in accordance with s 37 of the Act.

Medical treatment
Includes nursing care, care, habilitation and rehabilitation under medical supervision (s 145(1)).

Mental Health Act Commission
A special health authority established under s 11 of the NHS Act 1977 (s 121(1)). Its functions include the investigation of complaints relating to powers and duties under the Act or complaints in respect of detained patients (ss 121(2)(*b*); 120(1), (4)); appointing doctors and other persons for the purposes of providing second opinions and verifying consent in accordance with the provisions of Part IV of the Act relating to consent to treatment (s 121(2)(*a*)); reviewing, upon request, a decision to withhold correspondence from a special hospital patient (ss 121(7); 134); and monitoring the operation of the Mental Health Act Code of Practice published by the Department of Health and the Welsh Office (ss 118; 121(2)(*a*)). The Commission reports biennially to Parliament.

Mental nursing home
Any premises, apart from a hospital, used or intended to be used for the reception of, and the provision of nursing or other medical treatment for, one or more mentally disordered patients, whether exclusively or in common with other persons (Registered Homes Act 1984, s 22).

Nominated medical attendant
A doctor appointed by a private guardian to act as a medical attendant for a person subject to guardianship (ss 34(1), 9(2); SI 1983 No 893, reg 12).

Non-restricted patient
A detained patient who is not subject to a restriction order or a restriction direction. This includes all patients detained under Part II of the Act, patients detained under a hospital order without a restriction order or transferred to hospital from prison without a restriction direction, and patients subject to guardianship.

Parties
The applicant to a MHRT, the patient, the responsible authority, and any person who has been given notice of the tribunal proceedings or who is added as a party by the tribunal (r 2).

Patient

Except in Part VII of the Act (which relates to the Court of Protection), a person who is, or appears to be, suffering from mental disorder.

Registration authority

The district health authority exercising the functions of the Secretary of State under the Registered Homes Act 1984. The registration authority of a mental nursing home has the power to discharge a detained patient under s 23 of the Act.

Responsible authority

1 In relation to a detained patient, the hospital managers or managers of the mental nursing home where the patient is detained.
2 In relation to a patient subject to guardianship, the responsible local social services authority.

Responsible medical officer

The registered medical practitioner in charge of the treatment of the patient (s 34(1)(*a*)). In the case of a patient subject to guardianship, the registered medical practitioner appointed by the responsible social services authority (s 34(1)(*b*)).

Restricted patient

A patient who is subject to a restriction order (s 41) or a restriction direction, or an order or direction having the same effect as a restriction order or direction (s 79(1)). The special restrictions applicable to these patients are set out in s 41(3) of the Act.

Restriction direction

A direction by the Home Secretary in respect of a patient who has been transferred from hospital. A restriction direction has the same effect as a restriction order, except in relation to the MHRT's powers (s 49).

Restriction order

An order by a court in addition to a hospital order made in accordance with s 41 of the Act. The order has the effect of requiring the Home Secretary's consent before the RMO or hospital managers can discharge a patient, grant leave of absence or transfer him to another hospital (s 41(3)). However, a discharge order can be made by a MHRT (s 73).

Special hospital
Hospitals for the treatment of detained patients who, because of their dangerous violent or criminal propensities require conditions of special security (NHS Act 1977, s 4). There are three special hospitals in England: Ashworth (near Liverpool—formerly Moss Side and Park Lane); Broadmoor (near Reading) and Rampton (near Nottingham).

Abbreviations

ABWOR	Assistance by way of representation
ASW	Approved Social Worker
CPN	Community Psychiatric Nurse
DHA	District Health Authority
DH	Department of Health
ECT	Electroconvulsive therapy
LAG	Legal Action Group
MENCAP	Royal Society for Mentally Handicapped Children and Adults
MHA	Mental Health Act 1983
MHRT	Mental Health Review Tribunal
MIND	National Association for Mental Health
NHS	National Health Service
RHA	Regional Health Authority
RMO	Responsible Medical Officer
RSC	Rules of the Supreme Court
RSU	Regional Secure Unit
SHSA	Special Hospitals Service Authority
VIA	Values into Action

Table of Cases

Table of Statutes

Table of Statutory Instruments

Introduction

The absence of any 'typical' case makes representation before Mental Health Review Tribunals difficult, frustrating and challenging. Patients arrive in hospital by numerous routes: eg, a person may be taken from his home during some family crisis and detained for 28 days; he may be admitted on an informal basis and subsequently detained because he has refused to take medication or has threatened to discharge himself; or he may be sent to hospital by the court following the commission of an offence which may be trivial or serious. The patient may be suffering from an acute psychotic illness and may appear to the representative to live in an incomprehensible world; or he may be learning disabled and unable to understand what is happening to him or why he is appearing before the tribunal; or he may appear completely sane and be capable of giving clear and rational instructions. He may have a supportive family who visit him regularly and would offer him all the support they could if he were to be discharged, or he may have no person outside the hospital to whom he can turn. He may apply to the tribunal in anger at what he sees to be an unjust admission or may apply as a matter of course during each eligibility period. A patient who is referred to the tribunal may not have applied of his own accord because of fear of disapproval from hospital staff or because, after years in hospital, he is frightened of leaving. There is no typical case and no standard solution.

This book is a guide to representation before Mental Health Review Tribunals. A patient may be represented by any person except another detained patient or a person receiving treatment for a mental disorder at the same hospital. In the vast majority of cases the representative is a lawyer. Legal argument and examination of witnesses may be complex and require the skill of the trained advocate. The availability of legal aid finance now allows the lawyer to meet the sometimes substantial costs involved in preparing a case. So this book is addressed primarily to the lawyer. However, we emphasise that lay representation can be effective and we encourage able people outside of the legal profession to take an interest in this work.

This book starts with the admission of patients to hospital. Part I of the text concerns the admission of patients and their discharge by means other than as a result of the decision of a tribunal. The provisions concerning civil admission are described in chapter 1. Most patients are admitted to hospital on an informal basis. Detention under the civil provisions may be for a period ranging from up to 72 hours to six months, subject to powers of renewal. Only patients detained for up to 28 days or more are eligible to apply to the Mental Health Review Tribunal. Chapter 2 concerns the admission of mentally disordered offenders. This includes not only those who are sent to hospital directly from the courts but also prisoners who are transferred to hospital because of mental disorder. For quick reference the procedures concerning the admission of patients under civil and criminal provisions are summarised in Appendix 5.

For many patients, applying to the Mental Health Review Tribunal is the final step when other methods of obtaining discharge have failed. The lawyer may be instructed at any stage of the process—soon after admission, before an application has been made to the tribunal or just prior to the hearing. He should therefore be acquainted with other ways in which a patient may obtain his discharge—eg, the nearest relative may have the power to discharge the patient. Chapter 3 is concerned with the discharge of non-offender patients and chapter 4 with the discharge of patients who have been involved in criminal proceedings. Chapter 5 concentrates on the requirements of the European Convention on Human Rights regarding the review of psychiatric detentions and the possibilities which exist for review in the ordinary courts. The division between patients detained under the civil process and through the criminal courts is a logical one. But often a more important distinction is between restricted and non-restricted patients. In general, the provisions for discharge are similar for all non-restricted patients; restricted patients can be discharged only by a tribunal or the Home Secretary.

Part II of the text concerns the legal provisions relating to Mental Health Review Tribunals and practical issues arising from those provisions. Chapter 6 describes the structure of the tribunals and their administration. Chapter 7 provides in tabular form a comprehensive account of the periods when a patient may apply to the tribunal, the times when a nearest relative may apply and the times when a patient's case will be referred automatically to the tribunal.

The 1983 Act significantly expands the tribunal's powers, enabling it to deal much more flexibly with the patient's needs. Where a patient is not subject to a restriction order the tribunal may discharge him; delay his discharge (if, eg, accommodation must be arranged); recommend that he is transferred to another hospital or given leave of absence as a trial for discharge; or reclassify the form of mental disorder from which he is considered to be suffering. The expansion of the tribunal's powers in relation to restricted patients was a response to the decision of the European Court in *X v United Kingdom*, judgment given 5 November 1981, which held that a tribunal which had advisory powers only (as it did under the 1959 Act) did not constitute a judicial body as required by Art 5(4) of the European Convention on Human Rights. The 1983 Act gives the tribunal the power to discharge a restricted patient either absolutely or subject to conditions. The tribunal has the power to vary the conditions imposed on a conditionally discharged patient or to lift a restriction order. It is only in relation to patients who have been transferred from prison that the tribunal's role is limited to an advisory one only. The tribunal's powers and the criteria which it must consider in exercising those powers are the subject of chapter 8.

Chapters 9 and 10 concern the pre-hearing and hearing procedures which apply to applications other than assessment applications (ie, applications by patients admitted for 28 days only). The special provisions which apply to assessment applications and reference cases are discussed in chapter 11.

There are two features which are striking to lawyers looking for the first time at MHRT proceedings. They are the positioning of the burden of proof, and the fact that the rules allow limitations to be placed on the patient's access to the documents which form the basis of the case for continued detention.

Although with patients who are not subject to Home Office restrictions Mental Health Review Tribunals have a general discretion to discharge the patient, in all cases the formal burden of proof is on the patient to satisfy the tribunal that he is *not then* suffering from mental disorder so as to make detention appropriate (*Perkins v Bath District Health Authority*, *The Times*,

29 August 1989), *or* that his detention is not necessary in the interests of his health or safety or for the protection of others. For this reason an independent medical opinion concerning not only the presence or absence of mental disorder, but also the general clinical management of the case may well be an essential part of a patient's case, and guidance is given on this question.

Lawyers operating under the Mental Health Act 1959 were often taken aback by the secrecy which could surround the tribunal's proceedings. There are few, if any, other legal proceedings where the case papers which form the basis of the case against the applicant may be withheld from him, where the applicant can be excluded from parts of the proceedings and where the representative is privy to information about his client which he cannot disclose to him. Where these provisions are applied, they upset the traditional lawyer-client relationship and can create tensions and sometimes distrust between the lawyer and his client. Moreover, they make it difficult to prepare a case properly. In fact, since the reforms in the 1983 Act and Rules there has been much greater openness. Tribunals have been much more willing to disclose information and reports to patients which previously would have been withheld. Nevertheless, the representative is advised to question critically any requirement of non-disclosure to his client, or the exclusion of his client from any part of the proceedings. Another major issue in the procedural chapters is the means available to the tribunal to obtain further information, if the information provided is inadequate.

Chapter 12 concerns finance. It contains an up-to-date guide to the availability of financial support via the green form and assistance by way of representation (ABWOR) schemes, and the directive which enables the tribunal to meet the expenses of witnesses and others in certain circumstances.

The decision as to whether or not a patient should be discharged rests on a variety of factors, such as his state of health, his need for continuing treatment, his ability to take care of himself in the community and the threat that he might pose to the public, the availability of facilities in the community to give him any necessary care, treatment or supervision, and the support he would receive from family and friends. Hence the case rests on opinions from psychiatrists and reports from social workers as well as legal factors. The lawyer's effectiveness depends on his ability to understand and, if necessary to challenge, the reports and opinions given by these professionals. Chapter 13 provides a basic introduction to psychiatric concepts and methods of treatment. The intention is not to produce amateur psychiatrists but to give the lawyer confidence and skill to put constructive questions to psychiatrists and others. Independent psychiatric opinion may be helpful in appropriate cases.

There are many problems in locating suitable accommodation and care in the community for psychiatric patients. Not least of these is the scarcity of resources. There is a multitude of legislation and government directives which concern this issue. Chapter 14 provides a brief guide. In appropriate cases an independent social enquiry report may be obtained; often it will be necessary for the lawyer to investigate the facilities himself.

Patients in special hospitals form a large proportion of applicants to Mental Health Review Tribunals. For the majority, discharge will be via transfer to a local hospital or regional secure unit (RSU). Yet transfer represents one of the most difficult problems facing the mental health system. The refusal by local hospitals to accept special hospital patients has left hundreds of patients in special hospitals who do not require conditions of special security. The tribunal's role is a limited one, but skilful representation may assist the tribunal in persuading the authorities that a transfer is appropriate. Chapter 15 is devoted to this issue.

Finally, in the appendices the representative will find a copy of the relevant provisions of the 1983 Act and the tribunal rules (cross-referenced to the appropriate passages in the text), a summary of the provisions for compulsory admission, a list of who may be a 'nearest relative', a list of useful addresses including those of the tribunal offices, a model application form and a chart summarising the steps in representation. A selected bibliography is also provided for further reading.

Part I

Admission to Hospital, and Discharge other than by Mental Health Review Tribunals

Chapter 1

Admission of Non-Offender Patients

1.1 Mental disorder

A person cannot be detained under the Mental Health Act unless he is suffering from mental disorder. Section 1(2) of the Act defines mental disorder as mental illness, arrested or incomplete development of mind, psychopathic disorder, and any other disorder or disability of mind. A person may not be dealt with under the Act as suffering from mental disorder by reason *only* of promiscuity, immoral conduct, sexual deviancy, drug or alcohol dependence (s 1(3)).

For the purposes of the provisions of the Act which authorise 'long term' detention, ie, for more than 28 days, the person must be classified as suffering from one of the following categories of mental disorder:

(1) *mental illness*: not defined in the Act;

(2) *psychopathic disorder*: a persistent disorder or disability of mind (whether or not including significant impairment of intelligence) which results in abnormally aggressive or seriously irresponsible conduct (s 1(2));

(3) *mental impairment*: a state of arrested or incomplete development of mind (not amounting to severe mental impairment) which includes significant impairment of intelligence and social functioning and is associated with abnormally aggressive or seriously irresponsible conduct (s 1(2)).

(4) *severe mental impairment*: as above, except that there is severe, as opposed to significant, impairment of intelligence and social functioning (s 1(2)).

For conceptual purposes mental illness and severe mental impairment can be thought of as major disorders and mental impairment and psychopathic disorder as minor disorders; significant legal consequences flow from this distinction.

The representative is referred to chapter 13 for a more detailed discussion of the legal definitions of mental disorder and their relation to clinical diagnoses. For a summary of the criteria and procedures for compulsory admission, *see* Appendix 5.

1.2 Informal admission (s 131; Code, para 2.7)

The 1983 Act is based on the principle that, wherever possible, patients should be admitted to hospital on an informal basis and that powers of compulsion should be used as a last resort. Section 131 states:

> Nothing in this Act shall be construed as preventing a patient who requires treatment for mental disorder from being admitted to any hospital or mental nursing home ... without any application, order or direction rendering him liable to be detained under this Act ...

Approximately 90 per cent of all admissions to mental illness and mental handicap hospitals and units are informal. Informal admission is to be distinguished from voluntary admission, which is not mentioned in the Act, in that under the former the person need not positively consent to the admission. Thus patients who are too ill or are unable, because of handicap, to raise any objection to admission may be admitted informally. There is nothing in the Act which forces a hospital to accept a patient; for example, some hospitals refuse to accept patients on an informal basis if they have a history of discharging themselves against the doctor's advice. The Code states that where a patient is willing to be admitted informally, this should in general be arranged. However, compulsory admission should be considered where the patient's current mental state, together with reliable evidence of past experience, indicates a strong likelihood that he will change his mind about informal admission prior to his actual admission to hospital with a resulting risk to his health or safety or that of other persons (para 2.7).

The informal patient is free to leave hospital at any time (he need not seek permission from his doctor or anyone else although it is desirable to inform the hospital staff) unless a holding power under s 5 is invoked (*see* **1.3** below).

1.2.1 Children

Any minor aged 16 or above can make arrangements for his informal admission to hospital, notwithstanding any right of custody or control vested by law in his parent or guardian (s 131(2)). It is likely that a child under 16 would need the consent of his parent or guardian before being admitted informally to hospital. There is, however, a persuasive view that under the common law a child under 16 can consent to treatment and care if he has the necessary understanding and intelligence to enable him to understand fully what is proposed. (See *Gillick v West Norfolk and Wisbech Area Health Authority* [1986] AC 112.) This view is reflected in ss 22(4), (5), 43, 49 and 100 of the Children Act 1989, the *Mental Health Act Code of Practice*, para 29.7, and the *Children Act 1989 Guidance and Regulations. Volume 4 Residential Care*, para 2.32 (cf *Re R (a minor) (wardship: medical treatment)* [1991] 4 All ER 177).

1.3 Holding powers

The Act provides doctors and nurses with powers to detain an informal patient so that an application for compulsory admission under Part II of the Act can be made. These powers apply only to those who are already in-patients and not to people who are receiving treatment on an out-patient basis.

1.3.1 Doctor's holding power (s 5(2); Code, paras 8.1–8.16)

Maximum duration of detention: 72 hours.

Criteria: The doctor in charge of the patient's treatment (or a doctor nominated by him) considers that an application should be made for admission under Part II of the Act.

Procedural requirement: The doctor must furnish a report to that effect to the hospital managers on Form 12 (Mental Health (Hospital, Guardianship and Consent to Treatment) Regulations 1983, (SI No 893), Sched 1; Code, paras 8.9–8.11).

The purpose of the doctor's holding power is to prevent the patient from discharging himself before the necessary application and medical recommendations are completed for his admission for assessment or treatment. The holding power ceases when the application and medical recommendations are completed or at the expiry of 72 hours, whichever is the earlier. Section 5(3) authorises the doctor to nominate one (but only one) doctor in the hospital to exercise the holding power in his absence (Code, paras 8.13–8.16). The power may be exercised in respect of any in-patient, including a patient in a general hospital who is not being treated for mental disorder. The Code defines an informal in-patient for the purposes of s 5 as 'one who has understood and accepted the offer of a bed, who has freely appeared on the ward, and who has co-operated in the admission procedure. The section . . . cannot be used for an out-patient attending the hospital's accident and emergency department' (para 8.4).

1.3.2 Nurse's holding power (s 5(4); Code, paras 9.1–9.10)

Maximum duration of detention: Six hours or until the earlier arrival of a doctor who can exercise the holding power under s 5(2).

Criteria: It appears to a registered mental nurse or a registered nurse of mentally handicapped people (Mental Health (Nurses) Order 1983, SI No 891) that:

(1) the patient is suffering from mental disorder to such a degree that it is necessary for his health or safety or for the protection of others that he be immediately restrained from leaving hospital; and
(2) that it is not practicable to secure the immediate attendance of the doctor for the purpose of exercising his holding power under s 5(2).

Procedural requirement: The nurse must record in writing on statutory Form 13 (Mental Health (Hospital, Guardianship and Consent to Treatment) Regulations 1983, (SI No 893), Sched 1) the fact that the above criteria are satisfied, and must deliver the completed form to the managers or their appointed officer as soon as possible after completion (s 5(5); Code, para 9.4). Paragraph 9.4 of the Code requires that the reasons for invoking the power must be entered in the patient's nursing and medical notes and that a local incident report form should be sent to the managers. If, following the exercise of the nurse's holding power, the doctor exercises his holding power under s 5(2), the 72-hour period (see above) runs from the time of exercise of the nurse's holding power (s 5(5)). It is worth noting that this power can be used only where an informal patient is receiving treatment as an in-patient for mental disorder; it cannot, for example be used on a general hospital ward where the patient is receiving treatment for a physical disorder.

1.4 Compulsory admission for periods not exceeding 72 hours

1.4.1 Admission for assessment in cases of emergency (s 4; Code, paras 6.1–6.8)

Maximum duration of detention: 72 hours.

Criteria: The patient must be suffering from mental disorder of a nature or degree which warrants detention in hospital for assessment with or without medical treatment, and it must be certified that he ought to be detained in the interests of his own health or safety or for the protection of others. It must be of urgent necessity that the patient is admitted for assessment. Emergency admission may only take place if compliance with the provisions for admission for assessment under s 2 of the Act would involve undesirable delay, ie, if there is not enough time to get a second medical recommendation (s 4(2); Code, para 6.1).

Procedural requirements: An application by an approved social worker (ASW) or by the patient's nearest relative (*see* Appendix 6) supported by one medical recommendation.

Where it appears that a patient should be admitted urgently under s 2 (admission for assessment; *see* **1.5** below) but that compliance with the provisions of s 2 would involve undesirable delay, he may be admitted under an emergency application (s 4(1),(2)). The application may be made by an ASW (*see 1.5.1* below, for requirements as to applications) or by the patient's nearest relative, and must be supported by one medical recommendation, preferably given by a doctor who has had previous acquaintance with the patient (this is usually the patient's general practitioner). The application must state that the patient should be urgently admitted and that compliance with the full procedures for admission for assessment would involve undesirable delay; this statement must also be verified in the medical recommendations (s 4(2),(3)). The applicant must have seen the patient within the 24-hour period prior to the making of the application (ss 4(5),11(5)). The patient must be admitted to hospital within 24 hours of the medical examination or the application, whichever was the earlier (s 6(1)(*b*)). The authority to detain expires after 72 hours unless a second medical recommendation (which, together with the first recommendation, complies with the requirements for admission under s 2) is received by the managers within that period (s 4(4)).

Admission under s 4 should only be used in cases of genuine emergency where admission under s 2 is regarded as necessary. The Code states that s 4 should never be used for administrative convenience, and that those involved in the process of admission are entitled to expect 'second doctors' to be available so that they do not have to consider using s 4 other than in genuine emergencies (Code, para 6.2). It should not be used as a short 'cooling off' period for patients who clearly do not require admission under s 2.

1.4.2 Detention by police (s 136)

Maximum duration of detention: 72 hours.

Criteria: It appears to a constable that a person in a public place is suffering from mental disorder and needs immediate care and control.

Procedural requirements: If a constable finds a person in a public place who appears to be mentally disordered and to require immediate care and control, he may, if he thinks it is necessary in that person's interests or for the protection of others, take the person to a place of safety (s 136(1)). A place of safety is defined in s 135(6) as residential accommodation provided by a local social services authority, a hospital, a police station, a mental nursing home or residential home for mentally disordered persons, or any other suitable place the occupier of which is willing temporarily to receive the patient. The Code states that the identification of preferred places of safety is a matter for local agreement between the local social services authority, district health authority and the Chief Officer of Police, whose task it is jointly to establish a clear local policy (paras 10.1, 10.5). In formulating such a policy, regard is to be had to the impact different types of place of safety may have on the person and on the outcome of the assessment. There is no legal obligation for a hospital to accept the patient, who may be detained for no longer than 72 hours. Section 136 is not an emergency admission section. The purpose of the detention is to enable a doctor and an approved social worker to assess the patient, to decide whether he should be admitted to hospital, either informally or under compulsion, and to make any other necessary arrangements for his care and treatment. The authority for detention under s 136 expires when these arrangements have been made or after 72 hours, whichever is the earlier.

Note that the person need not be mentally disordered; the constable need only have a reasonable belief that this is the case. The police have a wide discretion under s 136; see *Carter v Commissioner of Police for the Metropolis* [1975] 1 WLR 507.

The Code states that a record of the person's time of arrival must be made immediately he reaches the place of safety, and that as soon as he is no longer detained under s 136 he must be advised of the fact. It also advises that it is good practice, where the hospital is the place of safety, for the managers to devise and use a form for recording the end of a person's detention under this section (para 10.7). Where an individual has been arrested by the police under s 136 he is entitled to have another person informed of his arrest and whereabouts, and where he is in police detention he has a right of access to legal advice (Police and Criminal Evidence Act 1984, ss 56, 58; Code, para 10.9).

1.4.3 Warrant to search for and remove patients

Maximum duration of detention: 72 hours.

Criteria: There is reasonable cause to suspect that a person believed to be suffering from mental disorder:

(1) is being, or has been, ill-treated, neglected or kept otherwise than under proper control; or

(2) is living alone and is unable to care for himself.

Procedural requirements: A justice of the peace issues a warrant on the basis of information on oath laid by an ASW.

Section 136 provides the authority to remove a person believed to be suffering from mental disorder from a public place to a place of safety. Where such a person is on private premises and access is being denied, the Code states that consideration should be given to the implementation of s 135 and that local social services authorities should issue guidance to ASWs on the exercise of this power. If an ASW has reasonable cause to suspect the criteria above apply, he may apply to a justice of the peace for a warrant which authorises any constable to enter, if necessary by force, the premises where the person is believed to be and to remove him to a place of safety (defined in s 135(6); *see 1.4.2* above). The person may be detained for a maximum of 72 hours. As with removal by the police under s 136 (*see 1.4.2* above), the purpose of removal is to enable the patient to be assessed so that he may be admitted to hospital if necessary or so that other arrangements can be made for his care and treatment. The authority for detention expires when those arrangements have been made or after 72 hours, whichever is the sooner (s 135(1)). Section 135(4) requires the constable to be accompanied by an ASW or a doctor.

1.5 Admission for assessment (s 2; Code, paras 5.1–5.4)

Maximum duration of detention: 28 days.
Criteria:

(1) the patient is suffering from mental disorder of a nature or degree which warrants his detention in hospital for assessment or for assessment followed by medical treatment for at least a limited period; and
(2) he ought to be so detained in the interests of his health or safety or for the protection of other persons.

Procedural requirements: An application by an ASW or the nearest relative (*see* Appendix 6) supported by two medical recommendations.

Where the above criteria are satisfied a patient may be admitted to hospital for a maximum of 28 days (s 2(1)–(4)). Note that, unlike those admitted for treatment (s 3; *see* **1.6** below), patients need not be classified as suffering from a particular form of mental disorder (see the broad definition of mental disorder in **1.1** above). Thus they can be admitted if they are suffering from arrested or incomplete development of mind or any other disorder or disability of mind. Patients detained for assessment are subject to the provisions of Part IV of the Act and may, under certain circumstances, be given treatment for mental disorder without their consent (s 56(1)).

1.5.1 The application

The application must be made either by an ASW or by the patient's nearest relative (*see* Appendix 5) (s 11(1)).

Where an ASW makes the application he must:

(1) interview the patient and satisfy himself that detention in hospital is the most appropriate way of providing the care and treatment which the patient needs (s 13(2));
(2) take all reasonable steps to inform the nearest relative of the application either before it is made or within a reasonable time thereafter (s 11(3)). (When applying for admission for treatment the ASW must consult the nearest relative, unless to do so would not be reasonably practicable or would involve unreasonable delay); the detention under s 3 may not take place if the nearest relative objects, although an unreasonable objection may lead to the displacement of the nearest relative (ss 11(4); 29); and

(3) inform the nearest relative of his power to discharge the patient (s 11(3)). For the nearest relative's power of discharge *see 3.3.2.*

The Act places a duty on the local social services authority, at the request of the patient's nearest relative, to send an ASW to interview the patient and to consider the case with a view to making an application for his admission. If, in such a case, the ASW does not make an application, he must give the nearest relative written reasons (s 13(4)). Paragraph 2.33 of the Code says that local authorities should issue ASWs with guidance as to what amounts to a 'request' under s 13(4), and give guidance as to whether nearest relative requests can be accepted by way of general practitioners (GPs) or other professionals. Such requests should be accepted, provided the GP or other professional has acted pursuant to a request by the nearest relative.

Where the nearest relative makes the application, the hospital managers must inform the responsible local social services authority which must arrange for a social worker to interview the patient and report on his social circumstances (s 14). This provision ensures that, in every case of admission for assessment or treatment, there is a social report available to the managers and to the MHRT.

The applicant, whether an ASW or the nearest relative, must personally have seen the patient within the 14-day period prior to the application (s 11(5)).

Once it is decided that compulsory detention is appropriate, the Code of Practice offers guidance to professionals on the choice between detention under s 2 and s 3. It identifies six pointers to detention under s 2. They are:

(1) where the diagnosis and prognosis of the patient's condition are unclear;

(2) where there is a need to carry out an in-patient assessment in order to formulate a treatment plan;

(3) where a judgment is needed as to whether the patient will accept treatment on a voluntary basis following admission;

(4) where a judgment has to be made as to whether a particular treatment proposal, which can only be administered under Part IV of the Act, is likely to be effective;

(5) where a patient who has already been assessed, and who has been previously admitted compulsorily under the Act, is judged to have changed since the previous admission and needs further assessment; and

(6) where the patient has not previously been admitted to hospital either compulsorily or informally (para 5.2).

The Code emphasises that decisions should not be influenced by:

(1) wanting to avoid consulting the nearest relative;
(2) the fact that a proposed treatment will last less than 28 days; or
(3) the fact that a patient detained under s 2 will get quicker access to a MHRT than one detained under s 3 (para 5.4).

1.5.2 Medical recommendations

The application must be supported by medical recommendations given by two doctors, one of whom must be approved by the Secretary of State for Health as having special experience in the diagnosis or treatment of mental disorder. Where possible one recommendation should be given by a doctor who has had previous acquaintance with the patient (s 12(2)). The two doctors must have examined the patient either together or within five days of each other (s 12(1)). Generally only one of the recommendations can come from a doctor on the staff of the hospital to which the patient is to be admitted (s 12(3)) although there are certain exceptions to this rule (s 12(4)). Section 12(5) defines those doctors who are precluded from making a recommendation in respect of a patient; eg, a doctor who has a specified close relationship to the patient or a doctor who stands to make a financial gain from the maintenance of the patient.

1.6 Admission for treatment (s 3; Code, paras 2.1–2.39; 5.1–5.4)

Maximum duration of detention: Six months, renewable for a further six months, and then for further periods of 12 months at a time.

Criteria:

(1) the patient is suffering from mental illness, severe mental impairment, psychopathic disorder or mental impairment of a nature or degree which makes it appropriate for him to receive medical treatment in a hospital; and
(2) in the case of psychopathic disorder or mental impairment, such treatment is likely to alleviate or prevent deterioration of his condition; and
(3) it is necessary in the interests of his health or safety or for

the protection of other persons that he should receive such treatment and that it cannot be provided unless he is detained under this section.

Procedural requirements: Where the above criteria are satisfied a patient may be admitted to hospital for treatment. Under criterion (1) a patient who is classified as suffering from 'arrested or incomplete development of mind or any other disorder or disability of mind' cannot be admitted for treatment (cf admission for assessment in **1.5** above). The treatability criterion (2) does not apply to the major disorders (mental illness and severe mental impairment) at the time of admission, but a 'modified' treatability criterion is relevant at the time of renewal of detention (s 20(4) *1.6.1* below). The requirement in (3), that the treatment which the patient needs cannot be provided unless he is detained under s 3, was considered in *R v Hallstrom ex parte W (No 2)* [1986] 2 All ER 306. McCullough J said (at p 315b) that:

> Admission for treatment under s 3 is intended for those whose mental condition is believed to require a period of treatment as an in-patient. It may be that such patients will also be thought to require a period of out-patient treatment thereafter, but the concept of 'admission for treatment' has no applicability to those whom it is intended to admit and detain for a purely nominal period, during which no necessary treatment will be given.

The criteria for admission for treatment are further considered in **8.1** in relation to the tribunal's criteria for discharge.

The application may be made by an ASW or by the patient's nearest relative (s 11(1)). The provisions relating to making an application in relation to admission for assessment (*see* **1.5** above) apply to admission for treatment, except that when applying for admission for treatment the ASW must consult the nearest relative unless to do so would not be reasonably practicable or would involve unreasonable delay. Detention under s 3 may not take place if the nearest relative objects (s 11(4)). If the approved social worker considers that the nearest relative's objection is unreasonable he may apply to the county court for an order appointing someone else to act as nearest relative in his place (s 29).

Once compulsory detention has been decided to be appropriate, the Code describes three factors pointing towards detention under s 3 rather than s 2. They are:

(1) where a patient has been admitted in the past, is considered to need compulsory admission for the treatment of a mental

disorder which is already known to his clinical team, and has been assessed in the recent past by that team;

(2) where a patient already admitted under s 2 is assessed as needing further treatment in hospital at the end of 28 days and is unwilling to remain in hospital informally and to consent to medical treatment; and

(3) where a patient is detained under s 2 and assessment indicates a need for treatment under the Act beyond the 28 days (para 5.3; See also *R v Wessex Mental Health Review Tribunal ex parte Wiltshire County Council*, *The Times*, 29 August 1989).

In case (3) the Code advises that an application for detention under s 3 should be made at the earliest opportunity and should not be delayed until the end of the s 2 detention. Since this action may deprive the patient of the opportunity to appeal to a MHRT against detention under s 2, the Code advises the managers in such a case to consider themselves reviewing the patient's detention quickly (para 5.3c).

The provisions relating to medical recommendations are fuller than as those which apply to admission for assessment (*see* **1.5** above); each recommendation must state the grounds of the doctor's opinion and each must state whether there are other methods for dealing with the patient and, if so, why they are not appropriate (s 3(3)).

1.6.1 Renewal of detention

The patient may be detained under s 3 for up to six months (s 20(1)). The authority for detention may be renewed for six months and thereafter for periods of a year at a time (s 20(2)).

The grounds for renewal are similar to those which apply to admission except that the treatability requirement applies to all four categories of mental disorder (s 20(4); treatability is discussed in **13.6**). However, in the case of mental illness and severe mental impairment, even if the patient is untreatable, the authority to detain may be renewed if he would be unlikely, if discharged, to be able to care for himself, to obtain the care he needs or to guard against serious exploitation (s 20(4)). In *R v Gardner ex parte L* [1986] 2 All ER 306, it was held to be unlawful for the managers to renew the authority to detain whilst the patient was on leave in the community, since he could not be said to require to be detained in order to receive the treatment which he needed.

1.7 Reception into guardianship (s 7; Code, paras 13.1–13.10)

Maximum duration of guardianship: Six months, renewable for a further six months, and then for further periods of 12 months at a time.

Criteria:

(1) the patient is suffering from mental illness, severe mental impairment, psychopathic disorder or mental impairment of a nature or degree which warrants his reception into guardianship; and

(2) it is necessary in the interests of the patient's welfare or for the protection of other persons that he should be received into guardianship.

Procedural requirements: Application by an ASW or the nearest relative supported by two medical recommendations.

A person of 16 years or more may be received into guardianship if the above criteria are satisfied (s 7(1),(2)). It may be observed that under criterion (2) a patient may be received into guardianship if it is in the interests of his welfare; this is wider than the interests of the *health or safety* criteria which applies to admission for treatment and may refer to situations where a person is unable to manage his financial affairs or is being exploited financially or socially by others.

The provisions relating to the application are the same as those that apply to applications in respect of admission for treatment (*see* **1.6** above) with the following exceptions. First, the application must state the age of the patient or, if it is unknown, that the patient is believed to be 16 or over (s 7(4)). Secondly, it must name the guardian, who may be either a local social services authority or another person (including the applicant himself); if the latter, he must be acceptable as a guardian to the local social services authority in whose area he lives, and a personal statement of his willingness to act as guardian must accompany the application (s 7(5)).

The provisions relating to medical recommendations are the same as those that apply to admissions for treatment (*see* **1.6** above).

The guardian has the following powers only (s 8(1)):

(1) to require the patient to reside at a specified place;

(2) to require the patient to attend specified places at specified times for the purpose of medical treatment, occupation, education or training;

(3) to require that any doctor, approved social worker or other person specified by the guardian is given access to the patient at the place where he is living.

It should be observed that although the guardian may under (2) above, require a patient to attend a place for medical treatment, he cannot force him to receive treatment; patients under guardianship are not included in the consent to treatment provisions in Part IV of the Act, and are therefore in the same position under common law as an informal patient as regards consent to treatment (s 56).

Section 126(2) states that it is an offence for a guardian to ill-treat or wilfully to neglect a patient in his care (these are separate offences—See *R v Newington*, *The Times*, 27 February 1990).

Where the guardian is someone other than a local authority he must inform the local social services authority of both his address and that of the patient, and give the authority the name and address of a doctor appointed by him to act as the patient's nominated medical attendant (*see* Definitions) and any further reports or particulars that it may require (s 9; Mental Health (Hospital, Guardianship and Consent to Treatment) Regulations 1983 (SI No 893), reg 12). The responsible social services authority must arrange for the patient to be visited at intervals of not longer than three months, and at least one visit per year must be by a doctor approved by the Secretary of State for Health as having special experience in the diagnosis and treatment of mental disorder (reg 13).

The authority for guardianship expires after six months but may be renewed for a further six months and thereafter for periods of a year at a time (s 20(2)).

It is worth noting that whilst there is a power to return the patient to the specified place of residence, there is no power forcibly to take and convey the patient there in the first place, as exists for compulsory admission to hospital under s 6(1). The Code states that guardianship must not be used to require a patient to reside in hospital, except in very rare circumstances where it is necessary for a very short time to provide shelter whilst a place in the community is being obtained; nor should it ever be used to transfer an unwilling person into residential care (Code, para 13.9).

Under the 1959 Act little use was made of guardianship. It was generally felt that the guardian's powers were too wide and imposed too great a responsibility upon the guardian. The Code of Practice states that 'The purpose of guardianship is to enable patients to receive community care where it cannot be provided without the use of compulsory powers. It enables the establishment of an authoritative framework for working with the patient with a minimum of constraint to achieve as independent a life as possible within the community' (para 13.1). However, the experience with guardianship under the 1983 Act has been disappointing. Its use with mentally handicapped people who might otherwise benefit from such supervision is limited by the fact that a person must be 'mentally impaired' which requires abnormally aggressive or seriously irresponsible conduct (see P Fennell, 'The Beverley Lewis Case: Was the Law to Blame?' (1989) Vol 139 New LJ 1557–8). The Law Commission is currently conducting an examination of decision-making on behalf of mentally incapacitated adults, and their review will involve consideration of reform of guardianship (The Law Commission, *Mentally Incapacitated Adults and Decision-Making: An Overview* (Consultation Paper No 119) (1991) paras 3.24–3.34; 6.36–6.37).

Chapter 2

Admission of Mentally Disordered Offenders

2.1 Patients concerned in criminal proceedings

Traditionally, mentally disordered offenders have been exempt from ordinary penal measures on the grounds that they are not criminally responsible for their behaviour (not guilty by reason of insanity) or they are unable to understand the course of the proceedings at their trial and contribute to their defence (unfit to plead).

Since the Mental Health Act 1959, the use of hospital orders has virtually replaced these traditional measures, although the Criminal Procedure (Insanity and Unfitness to Plead) Act 1991 (which came into force on 1 January 1992, and is discussed at *2.2.1* and *2.3.1* below) may lead to an increase in their use. In making a hospital order the court is not concerned with criminal responsibility or the defendant's fitness to participate in the trial; the person has usually already been tried and convicted. The only relevant considerations are his mental condition and the need for psychiatric treatment in hospital at the time of sentencing. The 1959 Act also provided for the transfer of mentally disordered prisoners (whether on remand or serving a sentence) from prison to hospital on the authority of a Home Secretary's warrant.

The 1983 Act introduced three further powers with regard to mentally disordered offenders:

(1) the power to remand an accused person for reports on his mental condition (s 35);
(2) the power to remand for psychiatric treatment (s 36); and
(3) the power to impose an interim hospital order (s 38).

The Code of Practice asserts that 'Those subject to criminal proceedings have the same right to psychiatric assessment and treatment as other citizens. The aim should be to ensure that everyone in prison or police custody who is in need of medical treatment which can only satisfactorily be given in a hospital . . . is admitted to such a hospital' (para 3.1). Moreover, the Code makes it clear that a prison hospital is not a hospital within the meaning of the 1983 Act (para 3.2). The Home Office has issued Circular 66/90 'Provision for Mentally Disordered Offenders' to encourage a policy of diversion of mentally disordered offenders from custody (see P Fennell 'Diversion of Mentally Disordered Offenders from Custody' [1991] Crim LR 333–48).

Broadly speaking, there are four points at which an offender's mental condition can become relevant: at the time of the offence, the trial, sentencing, or whilst the offender is in custody on remand or serving a sentence. The relevant orders and procedures are described briefly below.

2.2 Mental disorder at the time of the offence

2.2.1 The insanity defence (Trial of Lunatics Act 1883, s 2; Criminal Procedure (Insanity) Act 1964, s 1; Criminal Procedure (Insanity and Unfitness to Plead) Act 1991)

Criteria: That, at the time of committing the act, the accused was labouring under such a defect of reason from disease of the mind that he did not know the nature and quality of the act, or that he did not know that what he was doing was wrong (*McNaghten's* Case [1843] X Clark and Finnelly 200, 201).

Burden of proof: If the defendant raises the issue, the burden is on him to satisfy the jury on the balance of probabilities. If the issue is raised by the prosecution, the prosecution must satisfy the jury beyond reasonable doubt that the defendant was insane at the time of the offence.

Procedural requirements: The Criminal Procedure (Insanity and Unfitness to Plead) Act 1991, s 1 requires that a jury shall not return a special verdict except on the written or oral evidence of two medical practitioners, one of whom must be approved under s 12.

Effects: The insanity defence, or the special verdict, has been very little used in recent years, partly because of the fact that s 5 of the Criminal Procedure (Insanity) Act 1964 required that the automatic consequence of a special verdict must be the imposition of a hospital order and a restriction order without limit of time (see RD Mackay 'Fact and Fiction about the Insanity Defence' [1990] Crim LR 247–55). For a discussion of the distinction between the defence of non-insane automatism and the insanity defence see *R v Sullivan* [1983] 2 All ER 673 (HL) and *R v Burgess* [1991] 2 All ER 769 (CA).

The Criminal Procedure (Insanity and Unfitness to Plead) Act 1991 came into force on 1 January 1992 (The Criminal Procedure (Insanity and Unfitness to Plead) Act 1991 (Commencement) Order 1991, SI No 2488). A Crown Court which finds a defendant not guilty by reason of insanity is no longer bound to impose a restriction order without limit of time. Instead Crown Courts have the power to impose:

(1) a hospital order with or without restrictions;
(2) a guardianship order;
(3) a supervision and treatment order under Schedule 2 to the 1991 Act; or
(4) an order for the defendant's absolute discharge (Criminal Procedure (Insanity) Act 1964, s 5, as amended by the Criminal Procedure (Insanity and Unfitness to Plead) Act 1991, s 3 and Sched 1).

Where the sentence for the offence is fixed by law, the 1991 Act provides that there must be a restriction order without limit of time (Criminal Procedure (Insanity and Unfitness to Plead) Act 1991, Sched 1, para 2(2)).

2.2.2 Diminished responsibility (The Homicide Act 1957, s 2)

Criteria: The accused must be suffering from such abnormality of mind (whether arising from a condition of arrested or incomplete development of mind or any inherent cause or induced by disease or injury) as substantially impaired his mental responsibility for his acts or omissions in doing or being a party to the killing (1957 Act, s 2).

Decision-maker: The jury (but the court will accept pleas of guilty to manslaughter except in cases where medical opinion is divided or is open to challenge; see *R v Cox* (1968) Cr App R 130; *R v Vinagre* (1979) 69 Cr App R 104).

Burden and standard of proof: The defence must prove on the balance of probabilities.

Effect: The defendant will be convicted of manslaughter instead of murder, hence avoiding the mandatory life sentence. A successful plea of diminished responsibility gives the judge discretion in sentencing. This does not necessarily mean that a hospital order will be made.

2.3 Mental disorder at the time of trial

2.3.1 Unfitness to plead (Criminal Procedure (Insanity) Act 1964, s 4; Criminal Procedure (Insanity and Unfitness to Plead) Act 1991)

Criteria: That the defendant is unable to plead to the indictment, and unable to understand the proceedings so as to be able to challenge jurors, understand and give evidence, and to make a proper defence (*R v Pritchard* (1836) 7 C & P 303).

Decision-maker: The jury.

Burden of proof: If the defendant raises the issue, the burden is on him to satisfy the jury on the balance of probabilities. If the issue is raised by the prosecution, the prosecution must satisfy the jury beyond reasonable doubt that the defendant is under disability in relation to his trial ('unfit to plead').

Effect: In recent years the plea that the defendant is unfit to plead is little used; See DH Grubin, 'Unfit to plead in England and Wales 1976–1988: A Survey' (1991) *British Journal of Psychiatry* 540. This is because under the Criminal Procedure (Insanity) Act 1964, the automatic consequence of a finding that a defendant was unfit to plead was that the trial was halted and the Crown Court imposed a restriction order without limit of time. The defendant might have been returned to court to face trial if, at a later date, his RMO advised that he was fit to do so.

The Criminal Procedure (Insanity and Unfitness to Plead) Act 1991 (the 1991 Act) provides for 'a trial of the facts' to take place where a defendant is found to be unfit to plead. A full trial will not take place, but a jury will be required to hear evidence to determine whether they are satisfied that the defendant did the act or made the omission charged against him as an offence. If they are satisfied that the defendant did the act or made the omission charged, they must make a finding to that effect; if they are not so satisfied, they will be obliged to return a verdict of acquittal. The defendant's intent (*mens rea*) should not normally be taken into account.

Under the 1991 Act, where a finding of unfitness to plead is followed by a finding that the defendant did the act or made the omission, Crown Courts will have the power to impose:

(1) a hospital order with or without restrictions (Criminal Procedure (Insanity) Act 1964, s 5, as amended by the Criminal Procedure (Insanity and Unfitness to Plead) Act 1991, s 3 and Sched 1);
(2) a guardianship order under s 37 of the 1983 Act;

(3) a supervision and treatment order under Sched 2 to the 1991 Act; or

(4) an order for the defendant's absolute discharge.

Where the sentence for the offence is fixed by law the court will be required to impose a restriction order without limit of time (Criminal Procedure (Insanity and Unfitness to Plead) Act 1991, Sched 1, para 2(2)).

2.3.2 Remand for a psychiatric report (s 35; Code, paras 17.1–17.5)

Maximum duration of detention: 28 days with further periods of 28 days for not more than 12 weeks in all.

Criteria: The court must be satisfied:

(1) that there is reason to suspect that the accused person is suffering from mental illness, psychopathic disorder, severe mental impairment or mental impairment; and

(2) that it would be impracticable for a report to be made on his mental condition if he were remanded on bail.

Procedural requirements: Remand by a Crown Court or a magistrates' court on the evidence of one doctor, who must be approved by the Secretary of State as having special experience in the diagnosis or treatment of mental disorder (s 54(1)). The court cannot make a remand order unless it is satisfied, on the evidence of the doctor who would be responsible for making the report or some other person representing the hospital managers, that arrangements have been made for the patient's admission to hospital within a period of seven days after the remand order has been made (s 35(4)).

The court can further remand the accused in his absence (as long as he is represented in court), if it is satisfied on the evidence of the doctor preparing the report, that a further remand is necessary in order to complete the psychiatric assessment (s 35(5),(6)).

A person remanded for reports is entitled to commission an independent report at his own expense, and to apply to the court for his remand to be terminated (s 35(8)), but has no right to apply for discharge to a MHRT. He is not subject to the consent to treatment provisions in Part IV of the Act (s 56(1)(*b*)) and therefore retains his common law right to refuse treatment.

The Code of Practice advises that where a patient remanded under s 35 is thought to be in need of medical treatment for mental disorder under Part IV of the Act, consideration ought to be given to referring the patient back to court with an appropriate recommendation, and with an assessment of whether the patient is in a fit state to attend court. It goes on to suggest that if there is delay in securing a court date, and depending on the patient's mental condition, consideration should be given to whether the patient meets the criteria of s 3 (para 17.3). It is submitted that the use of s 3 to admit a patient already admitted compulsorily under remand powers is contrary to the spirit of the 1983 Act (see P Fennell, 'Double Detention under the Mental Health Act 1983—A Case of Extra-Parliamentary Legislation' (1991) *J Social Welfare and Family Law* 194–208).

2.3.3 Remand for treatment (s 36)

Maximum duration of detention: 28 days with further periods of 28 days for not more than 12 weeks in all.

Criteria: The court must be satisfied that the accused is suffering from mental illness or mental impairment of a nature or degree which makes it appropriate for him to be detained in hospital for medical treatment (s 36(1)).

Procedural requirements: A remand order under s 36 may only be made by the Crown Court on the evidence of two doctors, one of whom must be approved by the Secretary of State as having special experience in the diagnosis or treatment of mental disorder (s 54(1)). The court cannot make a remand order unless it is satisfied, on the evidence of the doctor who would be in charge of his treatment or some other person representing the hospital managers, that arrangements have been made for the patient's admission to hospital within a period of seven days after the remand order has been made (s 36(3)).

As with accused persons remanded for reports, a person remanded for treatment is entitled to commission an independent medical report and apply for the remand to be terminated (s 36(7)). However, a person remanded for treatment is subject to the second opinion provisions in Part IV of the Act (s 56(1)). An accused person remanded for treatment has no right to apply for discharge to a MHRT.

2.3.4 Mental condition of those accused of murder

A person accused of murder, because the sentence is fixed by law, cannot be remanded for treatment under s 36 (s 36(2)). However, s 3(6A) of the Bail Act 1976 (as amended by s 34(2) of the Mental Health (Amendment) Act 1982) allows the court to impose the following conditions of bail:

(1) that the accused must undergo examination by two doctors for psychiatric reports to be prepared; and
(2) that he must attend an institution or place as the court directs for that purpose and comply with any other directions from the doctors.

2.4 Mental disorder at the time of sentence

When s 4 of the Criminal Justice Act 1991 comes into force, courts will be under a duty, where they are considering a custodial sentence, where the offender appears to be mentally disordered and where they consider it necessary, to obtain and consider a medical report. This duty does not apply to offences the sentence for which is fixed by law or to offences triable only on indictment.

2.4.1 Interim hospital order (s 38)

Maximum duration of detention: 12 weeks in the first instance, renewable for 28-day periods up to a maximum of six months in all.

Criteria: The court must be satisfied that:

(1) the offender is suffering from mental illness, psychopathic disorder, severe mental impairment or mental impairment; and
(2) there is reason to suppose that the mental disorder is such that it may be appropriate for a hospital order to be made.

Procedural requirements: An order may be made by the Crown Court or a magistrates' court on the evidence of two doctors (one of whom must be approved under s 12) that the relevant criteria are met (s 38(1)).

The court must be satisfied on the evidence of the RMO or hospital managers that arrangements have been made for the patient's admission to hospital within 28 days (s 38(4)). The court can renew the interim order or make a full hospital order in the absence of the patient, provided he is represented in court (s 38(2),(6)). A patient on an interim hospital order is subject to the consent to treatment provisions in Part IV of the Act (s 56(1)), but is not entitled to apply to a Mental Health Review Tribunal for discharge (s 40(3)).

2.4.2 Hospital order (s 37)

Maximum duration of detention: Six months, renewable for a further six months and then for periods of one year at a time.

Criteria: The court must be satisfied that:

(1) the offender is suffering from mental illness, psychopathic disorder, severe mental impairment or mental impairment of a nature or degree which makes it appropriate for him to be detained for medical treatment; and

(2) in the case of psychopathic disorder or mental impairment such treatment is likely to alleviate or prevent deterioration in his condition; and

(3) the court is of the opinion, having regard to all the circumstances, including the nature of the offence and the character and antecedents of the offender and to other methods of dealing with him, that the most suitable method of disposing of the case is by means of a hospital order.

Procedural requirements: The Crown Court can make an order if the person is convicted of an offence punishable with imprisonment, except in the case of murder (for which the sentence is fixed by law) (s 37(1)). A magistrates' court can make a hospital order without recording a conviction if the person is suffering from mental illness or severe mental impairment, and the court is satisfied that he committed the act with which he is charged (s 37(3)). One of the two doctors giving evidence must be approved under s 12.

A hospital order cannot be made unless the court is satisfied, on the evidence of the RMO or the hospital managers, that arrangements have been made for the patient's admission to hospital within 28 days (s 37(4)). Note that the Secretary of State for Health has been given the power by statutory instrument to reduce the 28-day period specified in ss 37(4),(5), and s 38(4) (Mental Health Act 1983, s 54A as inserted by the Criminal Justice Act 1991, s 27(2)). Thus the hospital has the discretion to decide whether to admit an offender; in some cases under the 1959 Act, mentally disordered people were sentenced to imprisonment because hospitals refused to accept them. Section 39 of the 1983 Act therefore empowers a court considering making a hospital order, or an interim hospital order, to require a representative of the regional health authority (or the Welsh Office in Wales) to provide information about the hospital or hospitals within its region or elsewhere where arrangements could be made for the admission of the offender.

The Code of Practice states that the regions and the Welsh Office should appoint a named person to respond to these requests and, if the patient is to be accommodated outside the region, the funding arrangements should be clarified (para 3.4).

The effect of a hospital order is similar to that of an admission for treatment under s 3 (s 40(4)) with some exceptions; the most important and that a hospital order patient cannot be discharged by his nearest relative (*see* **4.2**), and the patient may not apply tothe MHRT within the first six months of the order. A patient under a hospital order is subject to the consent to treatment provisions in Part IV of the Act.

A hospital order can be made with or without restrictions on discharge (*see 2.4.4* below).

2.4.3 Guardianship order (s 37)

Maximum duration of guardianship: Six months, renewable for a further six months and then for periods of one year at a time.

Criteria: The offender must be at least 16 years of age and suffering from one of the four forms of mental disorder of a nature or degree which warrants his reception into guardianship. The court must be of the opinion, having regard to all the circumstances, including the nature of the offence and the character and antecedents of the offender and to other methods of dealing with him, that the most suitable method of disposing of the case is by means of a guardianship order.

Procedural requirements: The procedural requirements for making a guardianship order are virtually the same as for making a hospital order. The effect is the same as that of a guardianship application under Part II of the Act (s 40(2); *see* **1.7**). A patient subject to a guardianship order is not subject to the consent to treatment provisions in Part IV of the Act because he is not 'liable to be detained.'

When s 27 of the Criminal Justice Act 1991 is brought into force, a court considering making a guardianship order will be empowered to request the local social services authority (or any other social services authority considered by the court to be appropriate):

(1) to inform the court whether it, or any person authorised by it, is prepared to receive the patient into guardianship; and
(2) if so, to give such information as it reasonably can about how it, or the other person, could be expected to exercise the powers conferred by s 40(2) of the 1983 Act.

2.4.4 Restriction order (s 41)

Maximum duration of detention: Without limit of time, or for a period specified by the court.

Criterion: A hospital order having been made, it appears to the court, having regard to the nature of the offence, the antecedents of the offender, and the risk of his committing further offences if set at large, that a restriction order is necessary for the protection of the public from *serious* harm. The court is required to assess the seriousness of the risk not that he will re-offend, but the risk that if he does, the public will suffer serious harm. The harm in question need not be limited to personal injury, nor need it relate to the public in general, but the potential harm must be serious, and a high possibility of the recurrence of minor offences will not be sufficient (*R v Birch* (1990) 90 Cr App R 78).

Procedural requirements: A restriction order may only be made by the Crown Court where a hospital order has been made. The evidence of one of the two doctors must have been given orally. A magistrates' court has no power to make a restriction order, but if the criteria are met, it may commit an offender over 14 years of age to the Crown Court where a restriction order can be made (s 43(1)).

A restriction order is usually made without limit of time unless doctors can confidently assert that recovery will take place within a certain period (see *R v Gardiner* [1967] 1 All ER 895).

The effect of a restriction order is that a patient cannot be granted leave of absence, transferred or discharged by the RMO or hospital managers without the consent of the Home Secretary (s 41(3)(*c*)); the nearest relative does not have the power to discharge the patient (ss 41(3), 40(4), Part II of Sched 1, paras 2, 7). However, in order to implement the judgment of the European Court of Human Rights in *X v United Kingdom* (Judgment of 5 November 1981 Series A: Judgments and Decisions of the European Court of Human Rights No 46, (1982) 4 EHRR 188), the 1983 Act does authorise a MHRT to discharge restricted patients (*see* **8.5**).

A restriction order patient can be discharged by the Home Secretary or a MHRT either absolutely or subject to conditions. If the patient is given an absolute discharge, both the hospital and restriction orders cease to have effect, and he cannot be recalled to hospital (ss 42(2), 73(3)). If a patient's discharge is conditional, he may, for example, be directed to live in a specified place or to attend for treatment. A conditionally discharged restricted patient may be recalled to hospital by the Home Secretary at any time whilst the restriction order is in force (s 42(3); see *R v Secretary of State for the Home Department ex parte K* (QBD) [1990] 1 All ER 703 and **4.4**); under a procedure introduced as a result of the decision in *X v United Kingdom*, he must be given reasons for his recall (see DHSS Circular LASSL (80)7, and RM Jones, *Mental Health Act Manual* (3rd Edn) Sweet and Maxwell (1991), p 107). The case of a conditionally discharged restricted patient who is recalled to hospital must be referred to a MHRT within a month of his return to hospital (s 75(1)).

2.4.5 Psychiatric probation order (Powers of the Criminal Courts Act 1973, s 3; see also Criminal Justice Act 1991, Sched 1, para 5, which inserts a new Sched 1A in the 1973 Act and is in substantially the same terms as s 3 of the 1973 Act)

Maximum duration of detention: As specified in the order, being not less than six months and not more than three years.

Criteria: The offender must be over 17 years of age. His mental condition must be 'such as requires and may be susceptible to treatment but is not such as to warrant his detention in hospital' (Powers of the Criminal Courts Act 1973, s 3(1); Criminal Justice Act 1991, Sched 1, para 5(1)(*a*)(*b*))

Procedural requirements: The court must have received evidence that the criteria are met from a doctor approved under s 12 of the 1983 Act. The court must have explained all the effects of the order to the offender and he must consent to the order (s 2(6)).

The offender must attend hospital for psychiatric treatment, either as an in-patient or an out-patient, or must accept treatment from a specified medical practitioner. Psychiatric probation orders are generally encouraged by the courts for mentally disordered offenders, provided there is no significant risk of injury to the public as a result (*R v Ballester* [1971] Crim LR 111). Although the offender must consent to the order, the offender cannot be dealt with for breach of the probation order for refusal to consent to surgical, electrical or other treatment, if the court decides that the refusal is reasonable in all the circumstances (1973 Act, s 6(7)).

2.5 Mental disorder whilst a prisoner is in custody

2.5.1 Transfer to hospital of sentenced prisoners (s 47; Code, paras 3.12–3.13)

Maximum duration:

(1) if no restriction direction is made, six months, renewable for six months and then for periods of one year at a time;

(2) if a restriction direction is made, it expires on the earliest date on which the offender would have been released from prison (the earliest release date); thereafter, the patient is detained as if he were a patient under a hospital order without restrictions.

Criteria: The Home Secretary must be satisfied that:

(1) the prisoner is suffering from one of the four forms of mental disorder;

(2) the mental disorder is of a nature or degree which makes it appropriate for him to be detained in hospital for medical treatment;

(3) in the case of psychopathic disorder or mental impairment, treatment is likely to alleviate or prevent deterioration in his condition; and

(4) having regard to the public interest and to all the other circumstances, a transfer is expedient.

Procedural requirements: Direction by the Home Secretary based on two medical reports, one from a doctor approved under s 12 (s 54(1)). The Code of Practice states that the need for in-patient treatment of a prisoner must be identified and acted on swiftly, and contact made urgently between the prison doctor and the hospital doctor. It also emphasises that the transfer of a prisoner to hospital should not be delayed until close to his release date, since a transfer in such circumstances may well be seen by the prisoner as being primarily intended to extend his detention (paras 3.12–3.13).

Where the Secretary of State thinks fit, he may attach a restriction direction to a transfer direction, which has the same effect as a restriction order (s 49(1)). If a restriction direction is not given, or once it expires because the prisoner's earliest release date has passed, the offender is detained as if under a hospital order. The eligibility of patients transferred from prison to hospital to make applications or to have their cases referred to MHRTs is considered in **7.2**. If the Home Secretary is notified by the RMO, another doctor, or the MHRT that the offender no longer requires treatment in hospital, he has two options:

(1) he can either discharge an offender who would have been eligible for release on parole had he remained in prison; or

(2) he can direct that he be returned to prison to serve the remainder of his sentence (s 50(1); *see 8.6.3*).

2.5.2 Transfer of other prisoners to hospital (s 48)

Provision is made under s 48 of the Act for the transfer of civil prisoners, remand prisoners and prisoners detained under immigration legislation to a psychiatric hospital.

Criteria: The Home Secretary must be satisfied:

(1) that the person is suffering from mental illness or severe mental impairment of a nature or degree which makes it appropriate for him to be detained in hospital for medical treatment; and

(2) that he is in urgent need of such treatment.

Procedural requirements: The same procedural requirements apply as apply to a transfer direction under s 47 (s 48(1); *see 2.5.1* above). A transfer direction under s 48 must be made subject to a restriction direction (s 48(2)). The patient may make an application to a MHRT within six months of the making of the direction (s 69(2)(*b*)). For the powers of tribunals with regard to patients transferred under s 48 (*see 8.6.1*).

Chapter 3

Discharge of Non-Offender Patients

3.1 Duty to give information to detained patients (s 132; Code, paras 14.1–14.12)

Under s 132 of the Act the hospital managers must give specified information to every detained patient, as soon as practicable, after compulsory admission. The duty is to take such steps as are practicable to ensure that the patient understands under which of the provisions of the Act he is for the time being detained, the effect of that provision, the nearest relative's right of discharge, his own rights to apply to a MHRT, his right to a second opinion under Part IV, his right to complain to the Mental Health Act Commission (MHAC), and his rights regarding the interception of mail (if applicable). The Department of Health and the Welsh Office publish leaflets about the information to be given under s 132 and translations are available in various languages.

It is not enough simply to deliver the information to the patient. The hospital managers must take all practical steps to ensure that the patient understands the information provided, and these steps include giving the patient a rights leaflet as prepared by the Department of Health and an oral explanation. Thus, if the patient is too disturbed at admission to absorb the information, steps should be taken to explain it to him at a later time when he is more receptive.

Copies of the information must also be given to the patient's nearest relative unless the patient has objected—the patient must be asked before any information is given to the nearest relative (s 132(4); Code, para 14.3). The Code of Practice advises that the managers should, as far as practicable, ensure that an interpreter service is set up which would invite staff members with appropriate skills to offer their assistance and to undergo appropriate training to enable them to undertake the task of explaining to patients whose first language is not English their rights under the Act (para 14.7).

Where it appears to the legal representative that a patient or nearest relative has forfeited a right of application to a tribunal because the necessary information was not given to him or was not properly explained to him, he should ask the Secretary of State to refer the case to the tribunal under his discretionary power (ss 67 and 71; *see* **7.7**). A failure by the hospital managers to take all practicable steps to ensure that a patient understands the above information may be referred to the MHAC for investigation (ss 120(1)*(b)*(i) and (ii); *see* Definitions).

3.2 Patients held under the 72-hour detention powers (ss 4, 5, 135, 136)

3.2.1 Discharge on expiry of the 72-hours

Patients detained in hospital in accordance with s 4 (emergency admission for assessment), s 5 (detention of patients already in hospital), and persons removed to a place of safety under s 135 or s 136 (*see 1.4.2* and *1.4.3*) cannot be detained for more than 72 hours, unless before the expiry of that period, the necessary application and recommendations are completed for the patient's detention under another provision of the Act. The Code of Practice recommends that if a patient is admitted under s 4 he should be seen as soon as possible by an appropriate second doctor (para 6.8)

3.2.2 Discharge when the purpose of the order has been served

The purpose of taking a person to a place of safety (s 135 or s 136) is to provide social workers and doctors with an opportunity to assess the patient and, if necessary, to implement procedures for the patient's further detention. Once this purpose has been served the order must be discharged. Thus, for example, if within the 72-hour period a social worker and a doctor assess someone who has been removed to a place of safety and decide that an application for admission to hospital is inappropriate, the authority to detain ceases (Code, para 10.8).

3.2.3 Discharge by the RMO or the hospital managers

A patient admitted for assessment in an emergency under s 4 may be discharged by the RMO or by the hospital managers (s 23(2)(*a*)).

3.3 Patients admitted for assessment (s 2) or treatment (s 3)

3.3.1 Discharge on expiry of the authority to detain

A patient admitted for assessment under s 2 cannot be detained for more than 28 days unless, before that period has expired, he becomes liable to detention by virtue of an application for admission for treatment. The 28-day period of detention for assessment cannot be renewed. It has been known, however, for an application of admission for assessment to be made immediately after the expiry of a previous one. This is not regarded as proper practice. If it occurs the representative should consider referring the matter to the Mental Health Act Commission. If, after the expiry of 28 days, the patient has not been detained under an application for admission for treatment, he may remain in hospital as an informal patient or may discharge himself.

A patient admitted for treatment under s 3 cannot be detained for more than six months unless the order for his detention is renewed in accordance with s 20 of the Act. If the order is renewed he may be detained for a further six months; thereafter the order may be renewed at yearly intervals (s 20(1),(2); *see* **1.6**).

3.3.2 Discharge by the nearest relative

The nearest relative (*see* Appendix 6) of a patient detained under s 2 or s 3 of the Act may order the discharge of the patient (s 23(2)(*a*)). To do so, the nearest relative must give at least 72 hours' written notice to the hospital managers of his intention to discharge the patient. (The address of the hospital managers is normally given in the information provided to the patient and nearest relative following admission (*see* **3.1** above); it may also be obtained from the hospital staff or a telephone directory under the name of the district health authority or the National Health Service Trust.) There is a form which may be used by a nearest relative wishing to discharge a detained patient, which should be available on request from the hospital staff (Mental Health (Hospital, Guardianship and Consent to Treatment) Regulations 1983, r 15 and Form 34). It is not, however, obligatory that this form be used (r 15).

The hospital managers will inform the RMO of the nearest relative's intention to discharge the patient. The RMO may, within the 72-hour period, issue a report to the managers stating that, if released, the patient would be likely to act in a manner dangerous to other persons or to himself. The effect of such a report known as a 'barring certificate', is to bar the order for discharge by the nearest relative (s 25(1) (*a*)). Once the report has been issued, the nearest relative may not order the patient's discharge for another six months (s 25(1)(*b*)); this is so even if the patient is discharged and re-admitted under a fresh application.

Where such a report has been issued in the case of a patient admitted for assessment (s 2), the nearest relative may ask the hospital managers to consider the patient's case with a view to discharging him (*see 3.3.3* below); the nearest relative cannot apply to a MHRT himself but the patient may do so within the first 14 days of admission (*see* **7.2**). In the case of a patient admitted for treatment, the hospital managers have a duty to inform the nearest relative that a barring certificate has been issued (s 25(2)). The nearest relative then has a right to apply to the tribunal within 28 days of receiving notice that the barring certificate has been issued. There are distinct advantages if the nearest relative first exercises his right to discharge the patient before applying to the tribunal (*see* **7.4**).

If a nearest relative has exercised his power of discharge 'without due regard for the welfare of the patient or the interests of the public', the county court may appoint someone to act as nearest relative in his place (s 29). The displaced relative cannot then exercise the powers of the nearest relative under the Act (eg, to order the patient's discharge a second time or to block a subsequent application for the patient's admission for treatment). A displaced relative may, however, apply to the tribunal (s 66(1)(*g*); *see* **7.2**).

If the nearest relative of a patient detained under s 2 seeks to object to the admission of that patient under s 3, an application may be made for his displacement under s 29 if his objection is unreasonable. The effect of such an application is to extend the authority to detain under s 2 beyond the 28-day maximum until the county court has disposed of the displacement application and, if the court displaces the nearest relative, for seven days thereafter (s 29(4)). If such a process begins after the expiry of 14 days following admission under s 2, the patient loses his right to a tribunal, yet his detention may be prolonged for a significant period. This was a matter which caused concern to the court in *Perkins v Bath District Health Authority, The Times*, 29 August 1989 (per Lord Donaldson MR).

3.3.3 Discharge by the RMO or the hospital managers

A patient may be discharged by the RMO or by the hospital managers (s 23(2)(*a*).

The RMO may discharge the patient at any time during his detention and on any grounds. The decision as to whether the patient should be discharged normally rests on a combination of clinical and behavioural factors and the availability of appropriate aftercare facilities (*see* Chapters 13 and 14). When, and how often, the patient is assessed by the RMO depends on the practices of the individual doctor and the size of his case load. However, when the patient is admitted for treatment (s 3) the RMO has a statutory duty to examine the patient within the two-month period before the order is due to expire, and to report to the hospital managers as to whether the authority for the patient's detention should be renewed (s 20(3)).

The power of the hospital managers to discharge the patient may also be exercised at any time during the patient's detention and on any grounds. The process by which the managers decide whether to exercise this power is described in the Code of Practice as a Managers' Review. The Code declares that managers must undertake a review:

(1) when the patient requests it (unless there has been a recent review and there is no evidence that the patient's condition has changed);
(2) where the patient's RMO makes a report to the managers under s 20 that the authority to detain should be renewed; or
(3) where a patient's RMO issues a report barring the nearest relative's exercise of his power of discharge (Code, para 22.3).

The power of the managers to discharge a patient may be exercised by any three or more members appointed by them (s 23(4)).

The Code of Practice acknowledges that it is for the managers themselves to decide how to review, but stipulates that the patient must always be offered the opportunity of speaking to the managers alone and that the following steps are necessary:

(1) to strike a balance between informality and 'the gravity of the task';
(2) to help the patient to explain why he wishes to be discharged;
(3) to allow the patient to be accompanied by a member of staff, friend, or other representative of his choosing, to help to put his point of view;
(4) to ensure that the patient's RMO and other members of staff are actively and positively questioned by the managers;
(5) to ensure (subject to the patient agreeing that they be informed of the Review) that the patient's nearest/most

concerned relatives are given the opportunity to give their point of view or have it represented through an ASW, nurse, or other person;

(6) if the patient so wishes, to enable the patient and other parties to the review to hear each other's accounts to the managers, and to put questions to each other.

Where the representative asks the hospital managers to discharge the patient, although he has no statutory rights with respect to this hearing, he should nevertheless ask for copies of the admission papers, medical reports and any other relevant documents.

The Code emphasises that the Managers' Review is a different procedure from the MHRT, and that managers are responsible for ensuring that patients understand the difference. In particular it is important to ensure that no impression is given to patients that any application to a MHRT must be preceded by a Managers' Review, nor that a Managers' Review negates the patient's right to apply to a MHRT (Code, para 22.1). Where the patient or his nearest relative is eligible to apply to the tribunal he should do so, irrespective of any pending decision by the hospital managers (*see* **7.5** on the timing of an application).

In addition to the foregoing methods of discharge (ie, by the RMO, hospital managers or nearest relative) a patient detained in a mental nursing home may also be discharged by the Secretary of State and, if he is maintained under contract with a health authority, by that authority (s 23(3)).

3.3.4 Discharge during authorised leave of absence

The RMO may grant a patient leave to be absent from hospital for a specified or an indefinite period and subject to such conditions as he considers necessary (s 17(1),(2)). Leave of absence is often used as a means of assessing a patient's readiness for discharge; by imposing conditions, the patient's progress may be monitored, treatment may be given under supervision and, if necessary, the patient may be recalled to hospital. The RMO may recall the patient if it is necessary to do so in the interests of his health or safety or for the protection of other persons (s 17(4)). If, however, the patient remains absent (ie, without returning to hospital) for a continuous period of six months, he ceases to be liable to detention at the end of that period (s 17(5)). This provision is based on the rationale that a patient who is able to live in the community for six months without being recalled no longer requires detention. It had been the practice in some hospitals to recall a patient for one night before the expiry of the six-month period, thereby preventing the authority for detention from lapsing. This practice, which was aimed at achieving an equivalent of a community treatment order, was declared unlawful in *R v Hallstrom ex parte Waldron* (No 2) [1986] 2 All ER 306. If it occurs, the representative should inform the hospital managers and the Mental Health Act Commission. The managers should be asked to hold an immediate Managers' Review. If the patient is not discharged, consideration should be given to making an application for judicial review of the renewal of the detention and the decision of the Managers' Review not to direct discharge. The patient should also apply immediately to the MHRT. If the patient is not eligible to make an application, he may ask the Secretary of State to refer his case to a tribunal under s 67 of the Act (*see* **7.8**), or he can ask for a managers' hearing (*see 3.3.3* above and *8.1.2*).

If the authority for the patient's detention expires while he is on authorised leave of absence, he cannot be recalled to hospital and he ceases to be liable to be detained (s 17(5)).

3.3.5 Discharge during unauthorised leave of absence

Where a patient is absent without leave (this includes a patient who does not return to hospital following a period of authorised leave of absence) he may be taken into custody and returned to hospital (s 18(1)).

If a patient admitted for assessment under s 2 (for 28 days) is absent without leave on the day on which the authority for his detention would have expired, he cannot be taken into custody after that day (s 18(5)) and ceases to be liable to detention (s 21(1)(*a*)). If he is absent without leave in the week before his detention is due to end, and if he returns (or is returned) to hospital before the expiry of his order then, in theory, he may be detained for a further week from the day of his return (s 21(1)(*b*)). However, the application of this provision to patients admitted for assessment was probably unintentional and it is unlikely that the period of detention under s 2 will be extended in this way. In practice, the patient would either be discharged or admitted for treatment under s 3 before or upon expiry of the 28 days.

In the case of a patient admitted for treatment (s 3), if he remains absent without leave for 28 days, he cannot be taken into custody and ceases to be liable to be detained at the end of that period (s 18(4)). This provision is based on the rationale that a patient who remains absent for 28 days without being taken into custody or returned to hospital has 'proved' that he is able to care for himself, and thus does not require detention. Unlike a patient admitted for assessment, a patient admitted for treatment who is absent without leave on the day on which the authority for his detention would have expired does not cease to be liable to detention on that date. Rather, he remains liable to detention until the 28-day period has expired or until he returns (or is returned) to hospital, whichever is the earlier (s 21(1)(*a*)). If he returns to hospital before the expiry of the 28 days he remains liable to detention for a further week from the day of his return (s 21(1)(*b*)). The purpose of extending the period of detention in this way is to allow the authorities to renew the patient's detention where necessary (s 21(2)).

Being absent without leave is not an offence, but while there are no statutory penalties, the hospital might impose its own sanctions such as confining the patient to a closed ward or refusing to grant weekend or other short periods of leave. It is, however, an offence for a person to induce, or knowingly assist, a detained patient to absent himself without leave or to harbour him or to give him any help to avoid return to hospital (s 128(1),(3)). A person who is guilty of such an offence is liable on summary conviction to imprisonment for a maximum of six months or a fine not exceeding the statutory maximum or to both, or, on conviction on indictment, to imprisonment for up to two years or to any fine, or to both (s 128(4)).

3.4 Patients under guardianship (s 7)

A patient under guardianship under Part II of the Act may be discharged by his RMO, the responsible social services authority or by the nearest relative (s 23(2)(*b*)). The power of the social services authority to discharge the patient may be exercised by three or more members appointed by it (s 23(4)) and is similar to the hospital managers' power to discharge a detained patient (*see 3.3.3* above). Form 35 may be used by the nearest relative to exercise the power of discharge from guardianship (Mental Health (Hospital, Guardianship and Consent to Treatment) Regulations 1983, r 15 and Form 34). Its use is not obligatory. It should be available on request from the social services authority. In contrast to patients admitted for treatment (*see 3.3.2* above), there is no restriction on the nearest relative's power to discharge a patient under guardianship. Thus a discharge order by the nearest relative cannot be barred by the RMO or by anyone else. However, the county court may appoint an acting nearest relative if the nearest relative exercises or is likely to exercise his power to discharge without regard to the patient's welfare or the interests of the public (s 29(3)).

The provisions for discharge at the expiry of the term of guardianship are the same as for a patient admitted for treatment (s 20; *see 3.3.1* above). It should be noted that the criteria for renewing a guardianship are different from the criteria for renewing the authority for detention of a person in hospital (s 20(4),(7)).

The provisions for expiry of guardianship during unauthorised leave of absence (*see 3.3.5* above) apply to a patient subject to guardianship who, without his guardian's permission, absents himself from the place where his guardian requires him to live (s 18(3),(4),(6)). However, unlike a patient admitted for treatment, a patient subject to guardianship is not automatically discharged following a specified period of authorised leave.

Chapter 4

Discharge of Offender Patients

4.1 Remand to hospital and interim hospital orders (ss 35, 36, 38; Code, para 17.1)

In the case of someone who is remanded to hospital for a report on his medical condition (s 35) or for treatment (s 36) or detained in hospital under an interim hospital order (s 38) there are no provisions for him to be discharged by the RMO, the hospital managers or by the nearest relative. The RMO, however, may advise the court as to whether further detention in hospital is necessary. An accused person remanded under s 35 or s 36 may obtain, at his own expense, an independent psychiatric report and use the report as the basis for an application to terminate the remand (ss 35(7)–(8), 36(6)–(7)).

4.2 Hospital order without restrictions (s 37)

The provisions relating to the discharge of a patient at the expiry of the order, discharge by the RMO or the hospital managers, and expiry of the order during authorised or unauthorised leave of absence apply to a patient detained under a hospital order as they do to patients admitted for treatment. However, unlike the nearest relative of a patient admitted for treatment, the nearest relative of a patient detained under a hospital order does not have the power to discharge him (s 40(4), Sched 1, Part I, paras 1, 2, 4, 6, 8; *3.3.2*).

4.3 Guardianship order (s 37)

Like patients subject to guardianship under Part II of the Act, a patient subject to a guardianship order under Part III may be discharged by his RMO or the responsible social services authority. However, the nearest relative does not have the power to order the patient's discharge. The provisions relating to discharge at the expiry of the order and after 28 days unauthorised leave of absence apply to a patient subject to guardianship under Part III of the Act as they do to a patient subject to guardianship under Part II (s 40(4), Sched 1, Part I, paras 1, 2, 4, 6, 8; **3.4**).

4.4 Restricted patients

Restricted patients have usually committed serious offences. The purpose of a restriction order or restriction direction is to ensure that special precautions are taken in discharging the patient. Thus the nearest relative cannot discharge a restricted patient and the RMO and hospital managers may only do so with the consent of the Home Secretary (ss 41(3), 40(4), Sched 1, Part II, paras 2, 7). There are three ways in which a restricted patient may be discharged:

(1) by the Home Secretary (s 42(2));
(2) by the RMO or hospital managers with the consent of the Home Secretary (see above);
(3) in the case of patients subject to a *restriction order*, by a MHRT. In the case of patients subject to a *restriction direction*, a patient can only be discharged by a tribunal with the Home Secretary's consent (ss 73(1)–(3), 74(1), (2); *8.5.1, 8.5.2, 8.6.1*).

A restricted patient may be discharged either absolutely or subject to conditions which are determined by the tribunal or by the Home Secretary. Where a patient has been conditionally discharged he remains subject to the restriction order or direction until it is removed by the Home Secretary (s 42(1)), or by the tribunal (s 75(3), (1)(*b*)). A conditionally discharged patient may be recalled to hospital at any time while the restriction order or direction remains in force.

Unlike non-restricted patients a restricted patient who is granted leave of absence remains liable to be recalled by the Home Secretary irrespective of how long he has been absent from hospital (ss 41(3)(*c*), 40(4), Sched 1, Part II, paras 2, 4; cf non-restricted patients in *3.3.4* and *3.3.5*). A restriction order may remain in force even if the patient is subsequently imprisoned for any offence committed after his conditional discharge, and the patient may be recalled to hospital on the expiry of the prison sentence (see

R v Mersey Mental Health Review Tribunal ex parte K (CA) [1990] 1 All ER 694 and *R v Secretary of State for the Home Department ex parte K* (QBD) [1990] 1 All ER 703).

4.5 The Advisory Board on Restricted Patients (the Aarvold Board)

On 28 June 1972 a committee chaired by Sir Carl Aarvold was instructed by the Home Secretary to advise on whether the procedures for the discharge and supervision of patients subject to restrictions should be modified within the existing law (*Report on the Review of Procedures and Supervision of Psychiatric Patients Subject to Special Restrictions* Cmnd 5191, 1975). At the same time the Butler Committee was asked to examine the wider question of possible changes in the law (*Report of the Committee on Mentally Disordered Offenders* Cmnd 6244, 1975). The Aarvold report made a number of recommendations which were accepted and implemented by the Home Secretary. The changes were announced by Lord Harris, the Minister of State, on 22 March 1978 (*Hansard*, HL Debs, cols 1879–1881).

Where the risk of a patient re-offending is considered particularly difficult to assess, the case for transfer or discharge is considered by the Advisory Board on Restricted Patients (the Aarvold Board), which then advises the Home Secretary. The Board has eight members: two lawyers (one of whom, a judge, is the chairman); two experienced forensic psychiatrists; two senior social work representatives (one from social services, the other from the probation service); and two members with special experience of the criminal justice system (Home Office Memorandum, *Restricted Patients Detained in the Special Hospitals: Information for the Special Hospitals Service Authority* (1990), Annex C).

The Board meets once a month and deals with about four or five cases each meeting. It is the practice for a Board member to visit the hospital where the patient is detained to discuss his case with him, his doctor, and, if necessary, with others concerned with his care. This is not intended to be a clinical examination, the aim being 'solely to provide the Board with the fullest possible information about the case, and to give the patient himself the opportunity to make any points which he wishes the Board to take into account' (Home Office Memorandum, *Restricted Patients Detained in the Special Hospitals: Information for the Special Hospitals Service Authority* (1990), Annex C, paras 3–4). The patient does not appear in person before the full Board, but the visiting member prepares a written report of the visit which is distributed to the other members prior to the meeting, and offers his views in the light of discussion with the patient and others responsible for his case.

The Board is an extra-statutory body. Its task is to advise the Home Secretary on the exercise of his discretion. It has no power to take decisions on its own, and for that reason has been held not to be amenable to judicial review (see *R v Secretary of State for the Home Department ex parte Powell* (unreported) QBD 21 December 1978, reproduced in L Gostin and E Rassaby, *Representing the Mentally Ill and Handicapped* (MIND/LAG, Quatermaine 1980), in which the court held that in consequence of its status the Board is not subject to a duty to act judicially or fairly).

4.6 Appeal against sentence

Hospital orders and interim hospital orders are forms of sentence (Criminal Appeal Act 1968, s 50(1)). They are therefore appealable. The offender may appeal against sentence from a magistrates' court by giving notice within 21 days of conviction (Crown Court Rules (S I 1982 No 1109), r 7). Appeal lies from the Crown Court to the Court of Appeal by giving notice to the Registrar of Criminal Appeals within 28 days of the sentence being passed (Criminal Appeal Act 1968, s 18(2)). An appellant may abandon his appeal, or application for leave to appeal, by serving notice on the Registrar of Criminal Appeals; it is then treated as having been dismissed or refused by the court. The appellant may withdraw his notice of abandonment only where it can be regarded as a nullity. This will arise only exceptionally where, for example, some vital mistake of fact or fraud has resulted in an unintentional decision to abandon (see *R v Medway* [1976] QB 779 and *R v Keating* [1982] Crim LR 228). A mistake as to the prospects of success is not sufficient (Criminal Appeal Rules 1968, r 10; *R v Peters* (1973) 58 Cr App R 328, CA).

If the court hears an appeal it can take into account changes which have occurred since the date of the trial. In particular the court can hear up-to-date medical evidence which was not available at the time of the trial (*R v Bennett* [1968] 1 WLR 988; cf Criminal Appeal Act 1968, s 23(2)).

On an appeal by the defendant the court cannot deal with the appellant more severely than the court below (Criminal Appeal Act 1968, s 11(3)). A hospital order, being therapeutic in purpose, is not regarded as more severe than imprisonment (see *R v Bennett* above). The Attorney General is empowered under the Criminal Justice Act 1988, ss 35 and 36 to refer a sentence to the Court of Appeal if he considers it unduly lenient. For the purposes of the Criminal Justice Act 1988 'sentence' excludes interim hospital orders, so the Attorney General may not refer an interim hospital order as an unduly lenient sentence (s 35(6)).

Where a restriction order is imposed by the Crown Court the offender may appeal on the grounds that the restrictions are not necessary to protect the public from *serious* harm (s 41(1); *see 2.4.4* above, *R v Birch* (1990) 90 Cr App R 78).

4.7 Appeal against a special verdict or a finding of unfitness to plead

Since the Criminal Procedure (Insanity and Unfitness to Plead) Act 1991 came into force, a Crown Court which finds a defendant unfit to plead, or not guilty by reason of insanity, is no longer bound to impose a restriction order without limit of time, unless the offence is murder. The court may impose a hospital order with or without restrictions, a guardianship order, a supervision and treatment order, or an order for absolute discharge. There is no express provision for appeal against a decision of the Crown Court to choose one of these options rather than another. This raises the question, which is not explicitly addressed in the 1991 Act, of whether these dispositions count as sentences for the purposes of the provisions of the Criminal Appeal Act relating to appeals against sentence. Section 50(1) of the Criminal Appeal Act provides that 'sentence', in relation to an offence, includes any order made by a court in dealing with an offender and this includes a hospital order with or without a restriction order under Part III of the Mental Health Act 1983. Section 9 of the 1968 Act states that a person 'who *has been convicted of an offence on indictment* may appeal to the Court of Appeal against any sentence . . .'. Defendants found not guilty by reason of insanity are not 'convicted'. Although a hospital order with or without restrictions may be 'a sentence' if imposed on an offender who has been found or pleaded guilty, it would appear not to be an appealable sentence for the purposes of s 9 of the 1968 Act where there has been a special verdict. Where a defendant has been found to be unfit and the jury is satisfied that he did the act or made the omission charged, the question is whether he can be said to have been *convicted of an offence on indictment*. The effect of a trial of the facts where the defendant is found to have committed the act or made the omission is of the nature of a conviction, the jury finding the *actus reus* proved but not the mental element. The same may be said of a special verdict, except that the defendant is expressly found not guilty by reason of insanity. There is some authority to the effect that the term sentence should be construed widely for the purposes of appeal provisions (see *R v Hayden* [1975] 1 WLR 852 (CA)), where it was decided that an order that a convicted defendant pay a sum towards the cost of the prosecution is open to appeal under the Criminal Appeal Act 1968, as it is a sentence within the meaning of s 50(1). Some express provision on this point would have been welcome in the 1991 Act.

Whether the choice of disposition would be open to judicial review depends on whether it could be said to be 'a matter relating to trial on indictment' within the meaning of s 29(3) of the Supreme Court Act 1981. This provides that 'In relation to the jurisdiction of the Crown Court, other than its jurisdiction in relation to matters relating to trial on indictment, the High Court shall have all such jurisdiction to make orders of *mandamus*, prohibition or *certiorari* as the High Court possesses in relation to the jurisdiction of an inferior court.' The leading authority on this question is in *Re Smalley* ([1985] AC 622; [1985] 2 WLR 538; [1985] 1 All ER 769) where the House of Lords held that an order estreating recognisance of a surety for a defendant who failed to surrender to his bail could not affect the conduct of any trial on indictment in any way. Lord Bridge, who gave the leading judgment, said that the words of s 29(3) expressly excluded appeal or judicial review in respect of the verdict given, or sentence passed, at the conclusion of a trial on indictment, and also the 'trial' of a defendant who pleaded guilty on arraignment. If the defendant was aggrieved, he said, he would have his remedy by way of appeal against sentence or conviction under the Criminal Appeal Act 1968. The purpose of the provision excluding judicial review was to prevent serious delay to the trial. Lord Bridge went on to state that he could see no discernible legislative purpose which would be served by giving to the word 'relating to trial on indictment' a wider operation than that indicated above.

The implication of Lord Bridge's reasoning is that if a defendant has an alternative remedy (eg, appeal against sentence) judicial review will be excluded, but the courts will hesitate before applying the exclusion of judicial review so as to leave an aggrieved defendant completely without a remedy (see also *R v Maidstone Crown Court ex parte Gill* [1986] 1 WLR 1405).

4.7.1 Appeal against a special verdict

A person found not guilty by reason of insanity may appeal against the verdict to the Court of Appeal on any ground involving a question of law or, with the leave of the Court of Appeal or a certificate from the trial judge, on a question of fact, or a mixed question of law and fact (Criminal Appeal Act 1968, s 12).

The appeal must be allowed if the Court of Appeal is of opinion that the verdict should be set aside on any of the following grounds:

(1) that in all the circumstances of the case it is unsafe or unsatisfactory;
(2) that there has been a wrong decision on any question of law; or
(3) that there was a material irregularity in the course of the trial (Criminal Appeal Act 1968, s 13(1)).

The Court of Appeal may dismiss an appeal if it is of opinion that, notwithstanding that the point might be decided in favour of the appellant, no miscarriage of justice actually occurred (Criminal Appeal Act 1968, s 13(2)).

Where the ground for allowing the appeal is that the verdict of not guilty by reason of insanity should not stand, and the Court of Appeal considers that the proper verdict would have been that the appellant was guilty of an offence, they must substitute a verdict of guilty and sentence him accordingly; in any other case where the appeal is allowed they must substitute an acquittal (Criminal Appeal Act 1968, s 13(4)(*a*) and (*b*)).

In a case where a verdict of acquittal is substituted, it is possible for the Court of Appeal to order the compulsory admission of the appellant for assessment (Criminal Appeal Act 1968, s 14(2)). The Court is under a duty to do so where there is medical evidence from two registered medical practitioners, at least one of whom must be approved under s 12 of the Mental Health Act, that the criteria for admission under s 2 of the 1983 Act are met. The appellant is then treated as if he had been admitted under s 2 of the Mental Health Act. This power is little used.

Where an appeal is made against a special verdict, and the Court of Appeal is satisfied that there should not have been a verdict of acquittal but there should have been a finding that the accused was under disability in relation to his trial and that he did the act or made the omission charged, the Court of Appeal will be required to deal with him as if he had been found unfit to plead (see Criminal Appeal Act 1968, s 14, as substituted by the Criminal Procedure (Insanity and Unfitness to Plead) Act 1991, s 4(2) and *4.7.2* below).

4.7.2 Appeal against a finding that the accused is under disability in relation to his trial

A defendant found to be unfit to plead may appeal to the Court of Appeal against the finding (Criminal Appeal Act 1968, s 15). He is also entitled to appeal against a finding that he did the act charged or made the relevant omission (1991 Act, Sched 3, para 2). An appeal may be made on any ground involving a question of law or, with the leave of the Court of Appeal or a certificate from the trial judge, on a question of fact, or a mixed question of law and fact (Criminal Appeal Act 1968, s 15(2)).

The appeal must be allowed if the Court of Appeal is of opinion that the finding of the jury should be set aside on any of the following grounds:

(1) that in all the circumstances of the case the jury's finding is unsafe or unsatisfactory;
(2) that there has been a wrong decision on any question of law; or
(3) that there was a material irregularity in the course of the determination of the issue of unfitness to be tried (Criminal Appeal Act 1968, s 16(1)).

The Court of Appeal may dismiss an appeal if it is of opinion that, notwithstanding that the point might be decided in favour of the appellant, no miscarriage of justice actually occurred (Criminal Appeal Act 1968, s 16(1)).

Where an appeal against a finding of unfitness to plead is allowed, the appellant may be tried for the offence with which he was charged, and the court may, pending trial, remand him on bail or in custody, or make an order for his detention under Part III of the Mental Health Act 1983 (Criminal Appeal Act 1968, s 16(2),(3); 1991 Act, Sched 3, para 3(3)). In respect of appeals against findings of unfitness the 1991 Act will make few practical changes over the Criminal Appeal Act 1968. Under the 1991 Act, where an appeal is allowed against the finding that the accused did the act or made the omission charged against him, the court must quash the finding, and direct that a verdict of acquittal be recorded (but not a finding of not guilty by reason of insanity). Here the main practical change is that under the 1991 Act a trial of the facts will have to take place. Previously it was only open to the Court of Appeal to direct an acquittal where the question of unfitness had arisen after arraignment, and where sufficient of the prosecution case had already been heard to make it clear that there was insufficient evidence to convict.

Chapter 5

Judicial Remedies

5.1 The European Convention on Human Rights

The European Court of Human Rights has developed a considerable body of case law applying the provisions of Art 5 of the European Convention on Human Rights to detention on grounds of mental ill health. Article 5(1) concerns the right to liberty and security of the person against arbitrary detention or arrest (*Lawless* Case Series A: Judgments and Decisions of the European Court of Human Rights No 3, p 52). It provides that no-one shall be deprived of his liberty save on specified grounds and in accordance with a procedure prescribed by law. One of the specified grounds is the lawful detention of persons of unsound mind (Art 5(1)(*e*)).

The requirement that a decision to detain must be free from arbitrariness means that Art 5(1)(*e*) cannot be taken to permit the detention of a person simply because his views or behaviour deviate from the norms prevailing in a particular society (*Winterwerp* Case Series A No 33, p 16, para 37). There are three further minimum conditions which must be satisfied in order for there to be a 'lawful detention of a person of unsound mind'. First, except in emergency cases, the individual must be reliably shown to be of unsound mind. This has been held to entail 'the establishment of a true mental disorder before a competent authority on the basis of objective expertise'. Secondly the mental disorder must be of a kind or degree warranting compulsory confinement. The third stipulation of the European Court of Human Rights regarding lawfulness applies to the duration of psychiatric detention. It is that the validity of continued confinement depends on the persistence of such a mental disorder. This implies that it is for those carrying out and authorising prolonged detention to satisfy themselves at intervals that the criteria for detention continue to be met (*Winterwerp v The Netherlands*, above; *X v United Kingdom*, Series A Judgments and Decisions No 46; and *Van der Leer v The Netherlands*, (1990) 12 EHRR 567).

In addition to the requirement in Art 5(1) that the initial detention be lawful, Art 5(4) provides a further safeguard by requiring that everyone who is deprived of his liberty by arrest or detention shall be entitled to take proceedings by which the lawfulness of his detention shall be decided speedily by a court and his release ordered if his detention is not lawful. If the initial detention was ordered by administrative procedure the review must be available 'speedily' following the detention. If it was ordered by a court, the requirement of speedy review does not apply during the initial stages of detention, but there must be periodic opportunities for the detained person to assert before a court with the power of discharge that the conditions necessary for lawful detention no longer apply. In *X v The United Kingdom* (above, para 52) the European Court held that this means that:

> a person of unsound mind compulsorily confined in a psychiatric institution for an indefinite or lengthy period is in principle entitled, at any rate where there is no automatic review of a judicial character, to take proceedings before a court at reasonable intervals to put in issue the lawfulness . . . of his detention, whether that detention was ordered by a civil or criminal court, or by some other authority.

Article 5(4) does not guarantee a right to judicial control of such scope as to empower the court, on all aspects of the case, including questions of pure expediency, to substitute its own discretion for that of the decision-making authority, but the review should be wide enough to bear on those conditions which are essential for the lawful detention under the Convention of a person on grounds of unsoundness of mind (*Van Droegenbroeck* Series A: Judgments and Decisions No 50, p 26, para 49; *E v Norway* Series A: Judgments and Decisions No 181, para 50).

Article 5(5) provides that everyone who has been the victim of arrest or detention in contravention of Art 5 shall have an enforceable right to compensation. The European Convention is not directly enforceable in the English Courts (*Brind v Secretary of State for the Home Department* [1991] 1 All ER 720 (HL). An individual application will be accepted by the Commission of Human Rights only if the applicant has exhausted all remedies at domestic law.

Under English law the task of reviewing the lawfulness of psychiatric detention is carried out in three ways:

(1) by Mental Health Review Tribunals (MHRTs), exercising statutory jurisdiction;
(2) by the Queen's Bench Division of the High Court through both the jurisdiction to grant judicial review and *habeas corpus*, and its jurisdiction to review, and hear appeals from, the decisions of MHRTs; and
(3) the action for wrongful imprisonment.

Parts II and III of this book concern the operation of MHRTs. The remainder of this chapter deals with the review of the lawfulness of detention by the courts.

5.2 Legal protection for acts done in pursuance of the Act (s 139)

Before court proceedings can be instituted in respect of acts done pursuant to mental health legislation, English law has traditionally imposed a requirement that special leave be obtained. Article 6 of the European Convention on Human Rights declares that 'In the determination of his civil rights and obligations or of any criminal charge against him, everyone is entitled to a fair and public hearing within a reasonable time by an independent and impartial tribunal established by law'.

There were concerns that Art 6 was breached by the procedural barrier in s 141 of the Mental Health Act 1959 which required the establishment of 'substantial grounds' for believing that the defendant had acted in bad faith or without reasonable care before the High Court could give leave for civil proceedings. Section 141 was replaced by s 139 of the 1983 Act. Section 139(1) provides that:

> No person shall be liable, whether on the ground of want of jurisdiction or on any other ground, to any civil or criminal proceedings to which he would have been liable apart from this section in respect of any act purporting to be done in pursuance of this Act or any regulations or rules made under this Act ... unless the act was done in bad faith or without reasonable care.

Section 139(2) sets up a procedural hurdle in respect of acts covered by s 139(1), by requiring the leave of the High Court for civil proceedings or the consent of the Director of Public Prosecutions for criminal proceedings. However, it is less severe than s 141 of the 1959 Act in that s 139(2) does not apply to proceedings against the Secretary of State, a health authority, or against a National Health Service trust established under the NHS and Community Care Act 1991 (s 139(4); NHS and Community

Care Act 1991, Sched 9, para 24(7)). It does apply to proceedings against a local authority.

Leave under s 139 is not required for applications for judicial review since the phrase 'civil proceedings' only covers civil suits involving claims in private law proceedings (*R v Hallstrom ex parte Waldron* [1986] QB 824). Following the removal of the 'substantial grounds' requirement, a plaintiff in a private law action is entitled to leave if he can show that, on the materials available to the court at the time, the case 'requires fuller investigation' of the kind that would only happen if the action was allowed to proceed (*Winch v Jones* [1986] QB 296; *Furber v Kratter, The Times*, 21 July 1988).

5.3 Writ of *habeas corpus*

The writ of *habeas corpus* is one of right but it will not be granted as a matter of course. It may be refused if there is another equally effective remedy to question the restraint (*Re Wring* [1960] 1 WLR 138). The procedure is governed by RSC, Ord 54.

Prior to the advent of Mental Health Review Tribunals in 1959, *habeas corpus* played a more prominent role in the challenging of psychiatric detention (RJ Sharpe, *The Law of Habeas Corpus* (2nd Edn) (1989), p 157). Although the current scope of *habeas corpus* is uncertain, in theory a patient detained under the Mental Health Act can apply for a writ of *habeas corpus* to review the lawfulness of detention. The court will review the facial validity of the application and recommendations relating to admission. Note that the application for admission and/or the medical recommendations, if incorrect or defective, may be amended within 14 days from the date of admission (s 15). Thus any application for *habeas corpus* on these grounds may need to be delayed until after the 14-day period, if the defect is one that can be remedied under the Act. An example of a defect which cannot be rectified is where the two doctors giving medical recommendations for admission for treatment describe the patient as suffering from different forms of mental disorder (ss 11(6), 15(3)). It is also reasonably clear that a writ would be issued if an irregularity or want of jurisdiction in the court making an order under Part III of the Act were to affect the legality of the detention, eg, if a magistrates' court made a hospital order in respect of a person convicted of a non-imprisonable offence.

The scope of *habeas corpus* appears to be insufficiently wide to encompass a review of the substantive justification for detention.

An exception is where there is no evidence which could possibly form the basis of a finding that the criteria for detention have been met. In *R v Board of Control ex parte Rutty* ([1956] 2 QB 109 at p 119), Lord Goddard CJ said this:

> If on enquiry the court finds that there was no evidence by which the order or conviction could be sustained, they can release on *habeas corpus* or quash on *certiorari* ... But if there is evidence, whatever this court may think of it and no matter what conclusion the members of the court might have come to if they had been deciding the case which led to the conviction or order, they cannot disturb the finding, for so to do would be to act as a court of appeal in a matter in which no appeal is given.

This view may be contrasted with that of Melford Stevenson J in a more recent *habeas corpus* application (*R v Governor of Broadmoor ex parte Argles* unreported 28 June 1984) that 'The detention for treatment was lawful because the documents were properly completed, even though there may be a terrible hinterland which demonstrates that it should not have been done'. There is more recent authority which suggests that the scope of *habeas corpus* allows an examination of more than the question of whether the orders under which the patient is detained would provide a valid reason for detention. In *Perkins v Bath District Health Authority* (*The Times*, 29 August 1989) Lord Donaldson expressed the view that the scope of *habeas corpus* enables the court to consider the validity of the authority relied upon and that a combination of *habeas corpus* and judicial review would 'cover the entire field'.

5.4 Judicial review

An applicant wishing to challenge the decision of a public authority or an inferior court does so by way of an application to the Queen's Bench Division for the public law remedy of judicial review (RSC Ord 53). In this application the applicant may seek any of the prerogative orders of *certiorari*, prohibition or *mandamus*. Judicial review is of the legality of the decision rather than the merits. A decision of an inferior court or a public authority may be quashed on the grounds that the body has exceeded its jurisdiction, has broken the rules of natural justice where these apply, has erred in law on the face of the record, or has acted unreasonably (*Associated Provincial Picture Houses v Wednesbury Corporation* [1948] 1 KB 223). The court does not act as a court of appeal, nor will it interfere with the exercise of the authority's discretion unless the body has exceeded its jurisdiction or acted in a way which is *Wednesbury* unreasonable.

An injunction, a declaration or damages may be obtained in proceedings for judicial review, but such remedies may also be sought by way of action (Supreme Court Act 1981, s 31; RSC Ord 53, rr 1 and 7). However, if the aim of the proceedings is to challenge a decision of a public law nature an application for judicial review is the only permissible course. This is to avoid circumvention of the procedural requirements for judicial review that leave must be obtained and that the application must be made within three months (*O'Reilly v Mackman* [1983] 2 AC 237).

Judicial review will not be granted where there is a suitable alternative remedy, which raises the question of whether the MHRT will be regarded as a suitable alternative remedy for reviewing the lawfulness of detention. In *ex parte Waldron* ([1986] 1 QB 824, 826), an application for leave under s 139, Ackner LJ said, albeit *obiter*, that 'The tribunal cannot, in my view, be used where it is sought to challenge the underlying validity of the admission', suggesting that it is for the tribunal to review the need for continued detention but for the High Court to review the lawfulness of the initial admission.

Leave was granted to the applicant and the application for judicial review came before the High Court *sub nomine R v Hallstrom ex parte W (No 2)* and *R v Gardner ex parte L* ([1986] 2 All ER 306). McCullough J applied the principle that the Mental Health Act would not be interpreted as permitting interference with the liberty of the subject unless there were clear provisions to that effect and that therefore clear statutory authority was required before a person could be detained and treated against his will. He granted declarations to the effect that the admission of *W* under s 3 and the renewal of the authority to detain *L* under s 20 were *ultra vires*. He held that s 3 could only be used to detain people who would be treated as in-patients and could not be used as a means of attaching conditions to a person being an out-patient, and that s 20 could only be used to renew the authority to detain a patient whose mental condition was believed to require his continued detention as an in-patient.

Although there is a procedure for appeal by case stated from decisions of MHRTs it has been much more common for those aggrieved by a tribunal decision to apply for judicial review (*see* **10.9**).

5.5 Civil action

5.5.1 False imprisonment

A person who has been detained unlawfully may seek damages for false imprisonment. The tort of false imprisonment has two ingredients: the fact of imprisonment and the absence of lawful authority to justify it (*R v Deputy Governor of Parkhurst ex parte Hague* [1991] 3 WLR 340, 351). Imprisonment is defined as 'any restraint within defined bounds which is a restraint in fact' (*Meering v Graham White Aviation Co Ltd* (1919) 122 LT 44, 54).

If the procedures for detention under the Mental Health Act have been fully complied with detention will be lawful. In *Furber v Kratter* (above) a special hospital patient who had been secluded for 16 days following an attack on a nurse was given leave under s 139 to pursue her claim for unlawful imprisonment. This was based on the grounds that an imprisonment which was initially lawful could be rendered unlawful if she was kept in conditions which were seriously prejudicial to her health. The main action had not come to trial at the time of writing, but the House of Lords has since ruled that in such circumstances, the correct cause of action is negligence (*R v Deputy Governor of Parkhurst ex parte Hague* [1991] 3 WLR 340; *see 5.5.2* below).

5.5.2 Negligence

If a person making an application or a medical recommendation for compulsory admission fails to take the care that a reasonable professional would, eg, in examining or interviewing the patient, he may be liable in negligence (*Harnett v Fisher* [1927] AC 573). In *Winch v Jones*, the doctors completing the medical recommendations and the RMO were sued for negligence, the claim being settled for £27,000 (David Jessel, 'Convenience, compromise and cash' (1991) *NLJ* 266–7).

Although the detention in intolerable conditions of a person who is already in lawful custody will not render the imprisonment unlawful, when one person is lawfully in the custody of another, the custodian owes a duty of care to the detainee. If the custodian negligently allows or deliberately causes the detainee to suffer in any way in his health, he will be in breach of that duty. Moreover, if a person lawfully detained is kept in conditions which cause him for the time being physical pain or a degree of physical discomfort which could properly be described as intolerable, but which stops short of physical injury or impairment of health, damages may still be available for breach of the custodian's duty of care (*R v Deputy Governor of Parkhurst ex parte Hague* [1991] 3 WLR 340, per Lord Bridge and Lord Ackner at 355. Lord Goff too accepted that an action in negligence was available in such circumstances, but 'only in respect of the types of damage which, on accepted legal principles, give rise to such an action' (at p 356)).

Part II

Mental Health Review Tribunals

Chapter 6

Tribunal Structure and Administration

6.1 General structure

A MHRT must be established for each of the 14 regional health authorities in England and one for Wales (s 65(1)). The tribunal's duties may be performed by three or more of its members (s 65(3)). At least one of the members must be a 'legal member', one a 'medical member' and one must be neither a legal nor a medical member (Sched 2, para 4; **6.2–6.4** below). In practice it is rare for a tribunal to consist of more than three members. Responsibility for appointing the members to hear a particular case rests with the chairman of the tribunal or another tribunal member appointed by him (Sched 2, para 4; *see* **6.5** below). He normally appoints the members after receiving the responsible authority's statement. A tribunal member is precluded from serving on a particular case if he is a member or an officer of the responsible authority, if he has recently treated the patient, or has some other close acquaintance or connection with him (Mental Health Review Tribunal Rules 1983 (SI No 942), r 8(2)). A member of the tribunal will not be disqualified because he was on the panel which conducted a previous hearing involving the patient (*R v Oxford Mental Health Review Tribunal ex parte Mackman*, *The Times*, 2 June 1986).

Tribunal members receive remuneration from the Secretary of State for Health. Tribunal chairmen receive an additional retainer fee. The Secretary of State is also responsible for providing the tribunal with the tribunal clerks and officers to assist it in the performance of its duties (s 65(4); *see* **6.7** below).

The Lord Chancellor appoints chairmen and members of MHRTs (s 65(2), Sched 2; **6.2–6.5** below) and makes rules as to their proceedings (s 78).

6.2 Legal members

The legal members are appointed by the Lord Chancellor and are persons whom the Lord Chancellor considers to have suitable legal experience (Sched 2, para 1). One legal member in each tribunal region is appointed to be chairman for that region (Sched 2, para 3; *see* **6.5** below). In practice there are ten chairmen covering the 14 regions. Where a tribunal is appointed to hear a particular case the legal member is the president of that tribunal (Sched 2, para 6). The tribunal has wide discretion in the conduct of the proceedings and in practice is guided by the President (*see* **10.2**). In the case of a restricted patient the legal member must be chosen from a panel of legal members who have been approved by the Lord Chancellor to hear such cases (r 8(3); *see* **6.6** below, and **9.3**).

6.3 Medical members

The medical members are registered medical practitioners appointed by the Lord Chancellor after consultation with the Secretary of State for Health (Sched 2, para 1). In practice the medical members are psychiatrists of consultant status who are nominated by the Secretary of State on recommendation by the health authorities. The medical member has a duty to examine the patient prior to the proceedings and to form an opinion about the patient's mental condition (r 11; *see* **9.9**).

6.4 Other members

The other tribunal members are neither legal members nor medical members. They are appointed by the Lord Chancellor after consultation with the Secretary of State for Social Services and are persons having experience in administration or social services, or who are persons with other experience or qualifications which are considered suitable (Sched 2, para 1).

6.5 Chairman

As discussed in **6.2** above, the Lord Chancellor must appoint one legal member to be the chairman in each region for which the tribunal is established (Sched 2, para 3).

The chairman is responsible for appointing the tribunal members who are to hear a particular case (Sched 2, para 4). He is empowered to deal with matters which are preliminary or incidental to the hearing, and may take steps to ensure that each case is given prompt consideration (rr 5, 13; *see* **9.4** and **10.5**). A chairman may have an important influence on the conduct of proceedings in his region, eg, all chairmen have regular meetings with their tribunal members in order to discuss problems that have arisen, or to promote consistent practices throughout the region. The recent Department of Health Management Consultancy Unit Review of the MHRT Secretariat has recommended that the Department of Health enter into discussions with the Lord Chancellor's Department with a view to the appointment of a National President who would have the task of promoting a greater consistency in national policy.

6.6 Special tribunals for restricted patients

As stated in **6.2** above, the president of the tribunal in the case of a restricted patient must be chosen from a panel of legal members who have been approved by the Lord Chancellor to hear such cases (r 8(3)). The intention of this provision is to ensure that persons presiding over tribunals in cases of patients who have been convicted of serious offences have 'substantial judicial experience in the criminal courts'.

6.7 Tribunal clerks

There are five regional tribunal clerks (four in England and one in Wales) who are responsible for the administration of the tribunals. The clerks and the officers who assist them are appointed by the Secretary of State for Health. The clerks arrange on matters such as the appointment of tribunal members and advise on administrative issues. The clerk exercises some administrative powers on behalf of the tribunal. He receives the application from the patient, sends out the necessary notices (r 4), requests the responsible authority's statement and sends copies to the applicant, his representative, and any other person who is entitled to receive it (r 6). He then arranges the time and place of the hearing and notifies the parties (r 20), pays expenses and informs the applicant and other interested persons of the tribunal's decision (rr 24 and 33) (*see* generally Chapters 9 and 10). The clerk or one of his officers always attends the proceedings. The clerk is usually willing to assist with enquiries concerning the tribunal's functions. All correspondence to the tribunal should be forwarded through the clerk (for tribunal office addresses, *see* Appendix 7).

6.8 Council on Tribunals

The Council on Tribunals is established under the Tribunals and Inquiries Act 1971. Its overall function is to review the construction and working of tribunals and statutory inquiries. The Council must be consulted when procedural rules are made or amended, may investigate complaints about tribunal or inquiry procedures, and is glad to receive comments on tribunal process. While it has no power to enforce any action following its investigation its opinion is highly regarded. For example, the Council has been highly critical of the delays experienced by patients detained under ss 3, 37, and 47 between the lodging of their applications and the convening of their hearings (*Annual Reports of the Council on Tribunals* for 1985–6, (1986) paras 4.27–4.30; 1987–8 (1988) paras 4.5–4.9, 1988–9 (1989), para 2.48, 1989–90 (1990) HC 97, paras 2.70–2.72, 1990–91 (1991) HC 97, paras 3.60–3.65). For further discussion of delays, *see* **10.5**.

The Council makes an annual report which is laid before Parliament. (The Council's address and telephone number are given in Appendix 8.)

Chapter 7

Applications and References

7.1 Patients without access to Mental Health Review Tribunals

Patients detained for 72 hours or less are not entitled to apply to a MHRT. This applies to admission for assessment in cases of emergency (s 4), the doctor's or nurse's holding power (s 5), a warrant to search for and remove patients (s 135) and police powers over persons found in a public place (s 136). Patients removed to hospital for reports (s 35) or for treatment (s 36) and patients given interim hospital orders (s 38) cannot apply to a tribunal. Further, there is no provision for referring any of these cases to a tribunal.

7.2 Patients entitled to have their cases brought before Mental Health Review Tribunals

Patients detained under sections other than those in **7.1** above, or received into guardianship under the Act have the right to a review of their case by a MHRT. A patient's case may come before a tribunal in the following ways:

(1) the patient may apply to the tribunal during periods specified in the Act;
(2) in certain cases the patient's nearest relative may apply to the tribunal;
(3) the patient's case may be referred to the tribunal by the Secretary of State for Health in the case of non-restricted patients, and by the Home Secretary in the case of restricted patients. This is a general discretionary power which is exercisable at any time;
(4) if the patient's case has not been considered by the tribunal during a specified period, the hospital managers (in the case of non-restricted patients) or the Home Secretary (in the case

of restricted patients) must refer the case to the tribunal. These are automatic references.

The following tables show the periods of eligibility for applying to MHRTs and the periods for automatic references. **Table I** concerns patients admitted under Part II of the Act. **Table II** concerns patients admitted under Part III of the Act; also included in **Table 2** are the periods of eligibility for patients who were detained under legislation which predated the 1959 Act. The tables are comprehensive and thus include circumstances which may rarely occur.

7.3 Patients admitted under s 5 of the Criminal Procedure (Insanity) Act 1964, as amended by the Criminal Procedure (Insanity and Unfitness to Plead) Act 1991

Patients detained pursuant to an automatic hospital order with restrictions under s 5(1) of the Criminal Procedure (Insanity) Act 1964, have had the right to a MHRT within six months of the making of the order (s 69(2)(*a*)), and if they do not exercise that right the Home Secretary must refer their case automatically to a MHRT (s 71(5)). The Criminal Procedure (Insanity and Unfitness to Plead) Act 1991 confers sentencing discretion on the Crown Court in these cases, which means that a restriction order is no longer an automatic consequence of a special verdict or a finding of unfitness (*see 2.2.1* and *2.3.1*). However, the 1991 Act does not expressly address the entitlement to a MHRT hearing of patients who are treated by virtue of its provisions as being detained under hospital orders with or without restrictions.

Schedule 1, para 2 of the 1991 Act requires that where a court makes an admission order with restrictions under s 5(2)(*a*) of the 1964 Act (as amended) the patient shall be treated for the purposes of the 1983 Act as if he had been admitted subject to a hospital order with restrictions. The 1991 Act makes no reference to ss 69(2)(*a*) and 71(5) of the 1983 Act; these provisions are neither repealed nor amended consequentially. There is therefore considerable doubt about what the intention of the 1991 Act is regarding the rights of these patients to a tribunal within the first six months. In the absence of express provision it is suggested that no change was intended.

The rationale behind the right to apply to a MHRT within the first six months was that the hospital order with restrictions was an automatic consequence of a special verdict or a finding of unfitness, and so under the 1964 Act the judge need not have

Table I: Patients admitted under Part II of the Act

Category of admission	*Application by patient (note 1)*	*Application by nearest relative*	*Automatic reference*
Admission for assessment (28 days: s 2)	Within 14 days of admission (s 66(1)(*a*), (2)(*a*))	Within 12 months of an order under s 29 appointing an acting nearest relative (note 2) and during any subsequent 12 month period while the order is in force (s 66(1)(*h*), (2)(*g*))	
Admission for treatment (6 months followed by renewal period of 6 months and then for 12 month periods thereafter: s 3)	Within 6 months of admission (s 66(1)(*b*), (2)(*b*)) and during each subsequent renewal period, ie the 6 months immediately following and each subsequent 12 month period (ss 66(1)(*f*), (2)(*f*), 20(2))	Within 28 days of receiving notification that an order for discharge has been barred under s 25, (s 66(1)(*g*), (2)(*d*))	At the expiry of the first 6 months if no application or reference is made within that period (s 68(1)). At renewal of detention if 3 years (1 year for a child under 16 years) has elapsed since case was last considered by a tribunal (s 68(2))
	Within 28 days of receiving notification of reclassification of mental disorder (note 3) under s 16 (s 66(1)(*d*), (2)(*d*))	Within 28 days of receiving notification of reclassification of mental disorder under s 16 (s 66(1)(*d*), (2)(*d*)) Within 12 months of an order under s 29 appointing an acting nearest relative and during any subsequent 12 month period while the order is in force (s 66(1)(*h*), (2)(*g*))	

Category of admission	*Application by patient (note 1)*	*Application by nearest relative*	*Automatic reference*
Transfer from guardianship to hospital (s 19)	Within 6 months of transfer (s 66(1)(*e*), (2)(*e*)) and during the same periods as a patient admitted for treatment. Renewal periods are calculated from date of acceptance of guardianship application (s 19(2)(*d*))	Same as if patient had been admitted for treatment (s 19(2)(*d*))	At the expiry of the first 6 months from the date of transfer if no application or reference is made within that period (s 68(1)). At renewal of detention if 3 years (1 year for a person under 16 years) has elapsed since case was last considered by a tribunal (s 68(2)). Renewal periods are calculated from date of acceptance of guardianship application (s 19(2)(*d*))
Reception into guardianship (6 months followed by renewal period of 6 months and then for 12 month periods thereafter: s 7)	Within 6 months of reception into guardianship (s 66(1)(*c*), (2)(*c*)), and during each subsequent renewal period ie the 6 months immediately following and each subsequent 12 month period (ss 66(*f*), (2)(*f*), 20(2))	Within 28 days of receiving notification of reclassification of mental disorder under s 16 (s 66(1)(*d*), (2)(*d*))	
	Within 28 days of receiving notification of reclassification of mental disorder under s 16 (s 66(1)(*d*), (2)(*d*)).	Within 12 months of an order under s 29 appointing an acting nearest relative and during any subsequent 12 month period while the order is in force (s 66(1)(*h*), (2)(*g*))	

Table II: Patients admitted under Part III of the Act

Category of admission	*Application by patient (note 1)*	*Application by nearest relative*	*Automatic reference*
Hospital Order: (6 months followed by renewal period of 6 months and then for 12 month periods thereafter: s 37), Criminal Procedure (Insanity) Act 1964, s 5(2)(*a*), as substituted by s 3 and Sched 1, para 2(*a*) of the Criminal Procedure (Insanity and Unfitness to Plead) Act 1991	Between 6 and 12 months from the order and during each subsequent renewal period ie each subsequent 12 month period (ss 66(1)(*f*), (2)(*f*), 40(4), Sched 1, Part I, paras 2, 6, 9) Within 28 days of receiving notification of reclassification of mental disorder under s 16 (ss 66(1)(*d*), (2)(*d*), 40(4), Sched 1, Part I, paras 2, 3)	Between 6 and 12 months from the order and during each subsequent 12 month period (s 69(1)(*a*)) Within 28 days of receiving notification of reclassification of mental disorder under s 16 (ss 66(1)(*d*), (2)(*d*), 40(4), Sched 1, Part I, paras 2, 3)	At renewal of detention if 3 years (1 year for a child under 16 years) has elapsed since case was last considered by a tribunal (s 68(2))
Guardianship order (6 months followed by renewal periods of 6 months and then for 12 month periods thereafter: s 37), Criminal Procedure (Insanity) Act 1964, s 5(2)(*b*)(*i*), as substituted by the Criminal Procedure (Insanity and Unfitness to Plead) Act 1991	Within 6 months of the order (s 69(1)(*b*)) and during each subsequent renewal period ie the 6 months immediately following and each subsequent 12 month period (ss 66(1)(*f*), (2)(*f*), 40(4), Sched 1, Part I, paras 2, 6, 9). Within 28 days of receiving notification of reclassification of mental disorder under s 16 (ss 66(1)(*d*), (2)(*d*), 40(4), Sched 1, Part I, paras 2, 3)	Within 12 months of the order and during each subsequent 12 month period (s 69(1)(*b*)) Within 28 days of receiving notification of reclassification of mental disorder under s 16 (ss 66(1)(*d*), (2)(*d*), 40(4), Sched 1, Part I, paras 2, 3)	

Category of admission	*Application by patient (note 1)*	*Application by nearest relative*	*Automatic reference*
Hospital order with restrictions (normally without limit of time: s 41)	Between 6 and 12 months after the order and during each subsequent 12 month period (s 70)		When 3 years has elapsed since case was last considered by a tribunal (s 71(2))
Recall to hospital (s 42(3))	Between 6 and 12 months after recall to hospital and during subsequent 12 month period (ss 70, 75(1)(*b*))		Within 1 month of return to hospital (s 75(1)(*b*)), then as for hospital order with restriction
Hostpital order with or without restrictions under the Criminal Procedure (Insanity) Act 1964 (s 5(2)(*a*)), as substituted by the Criminal Procedure (Insanity and Unfitness to Plead) Act 1991, s 3 and Sched 2 para (1)(*a*) and (*b*)	Within 6 months of the order (s 69(2)(*a*)), then as for hospital order with restrictions (see **7.3** below)		At expiry of 6 months if no application is made during that period (s 71(5)), then as for hospital order with restriction
Conditional discharge (s 42(2))	Between 12 months and 2 years after conditional discharge and during each subsequent 2 year period (s 75(2)).		
Transfer from prison to hospital (ss 47(3), 48(3)) (note 4) *Cessation of restriction order* (s 41(5)) *Transfer from hospital in Northern Ireland, Channel Islands or Isle of Man* (ss 82(2), 85(2))	Within 6 months of date of order or direction (s 69(2)), then as for hospital order with or without restrictions, whichever applies.	As for hospital order with or without restrictions, whichever applies.	As for hospital order with or without restrictions, whichever applies.

Category of admission	*Application by patient (note 1)*	*Application by nearest relative*	*Automatic reference*
Transfer from hospital in Scotland (s 73(2) Mental Health (Scotland) Act 1960)			
Detention during Her Majesty's pleasure of a serviceman (s 46(3))			
Reception orders under the Lunacy Act 1890, temporary patients under Mental Treatment Act 1930, detention or guardianship under Mental Deficiency Act 1913; Sched 5	Within current period of treatment (Sched 5, para 31(2)) and during each subsequent renewal period ie each subsequent 2 year period (Sched 5, para 33, s 66(1)(*f*)).	As for admission for treatment or reception into guardianship under Part II except for patients detained under ss 6, 8(1) or 9 of Mental Deficiency Act whose nearest relative may apply during any 12 month period (Sched 5, para 34).	As for admission for treatment or reception into guardianship under Part II (Sched 5, para 34).

Notes

(1) Only one application may be made during each specified period (s 77(2)).

(2) The most common reason for appointing an acting nearest relative is that the nearest relative unreasonably objects to the making of an application for treatment. The application to the tribunal is made by the displaced relative and not the acting nearest relative (s 29(6)).

(3) Under s 16 the mental disorder from which the patient is said to be suffering may be reclassified. A report to that effect must be issued and both the patient and nearest relative informed. The application can be made by the parent *or* the nearest relative but not both (s 66(1)(*i*)).

(4) Unlike patients admitted for treatment, patients placed under a hospital order (with or without restrictions) cannot normally apply to the tribunal within the first six months of the order. The reason is that such patients have already had the appropriateness of detention considered by the sentencing court. Exception is made in cases when the decision to admit the patient was not made by a court. This occurs, when patients are transferred from prison. Such patients have a right to apply to the tribunal during the first six months of the order or direction.

addressed his mind to the appropriateness of a restriction order, and need not even have heard any expert psychiatric evidence. Under the 1964 Act there were cases where MHRTs came under an obligation to discharge patients found unfit or *McNaghten* insane because they were not mentally disordered within the meaning of the appropriate provisions of the 1983 Act (see Christopher Emmins, 'Unfitness to Plead: Some Thoughts prompted by Glenn Pearson's case' [1986] Crim LR 604; Paul Bacon, 'Unnecessary Detention: The Criminal Procedure (Insanity) Act' (1989) 86 Law Society's Gazette (19 April). It will still be possible for a person to be found *McNaghten* insane or unfit without being mentally disordered under the 1983 Act, but before a special verdict can be returned there must be evidence from two medical practitioners, at least one of whom must be duly approved (1991 Act, s 1). The intention of the 1991 Act is that in such a case the court would not impose a hospital order with restrictions where it has discretion not to do so. In a case where the sentence is fixed by law there will be no sentencing discretion. The court will be obliged to impose a hospital order with restrictions.

Patients subject to hospital or guardianship orders by virtue of the 1991 Act are to be treated for the purposes of the 1983 Act as if an order had been made under s 37(1). This means that guardianship order patients have a right to a tribunal within the first six months (s 69(1)(*b*)) and once in every period during which the guardianship order is renewed. Hospital order patients may *not* apply within the first six months (ss 66(1)(*f*), 2(*f*), 40(4), Sched 1, Part I, paras 2, 6, 9); they have the right to make an application in the second six months of detention, and thereafter once in each subsequent period of 12 months.

Patients who are made subject to a supervision and treatment order for a maximum of two years (Criminal Procedure (Insanity) Act 1964, s 5(2)(*b*)(ii) and the Criminal Procedure (Insanity and Unfitness to Plead) Act 1991, Sched 2) do not have a right to a MHRT.

7.4 The criterion of dangerousness

A tribunal considering the application by a nearest relative following the barring of a discharge order after admission for treatment (*see 3.3.2* for discussion of the discharge order by a nearest relative and the power of the responsible medical officer to bar such an order) must apply the additional discharge criterion of dangerousness. The tribunal must discharge the patient if, on release, he would not be likely to act in a manner dangerous to other persons or to himself (s 72(1)(*b*)(iii)). This means that the patient could be further detained only if there were strong reasons to suggest that he would do physical injury to himself or to other persons if discharged (*see 8.1.2* for further discussion of the dangerousness criterion). This is a more exacting standard than that which applies to other applications. Accordingly where both the patient and nearest relative have the right to apply to the tribunal the representative should advise them of the possible advantage of an application by the nearest relative to discharge the patient. The relative may then apply to the tribunal, which must apply the dangerousness criterion if when his discharge order has been barred.

It must be emphasised that the dangerousness criterion applies only to applications in respect of patients admitted for treatment and not to any other category of admission.

7.5 When to apply to the tribunal

The representative should advise the client as to the best time to apply to the tribunal. For example, an application should usually not follow too closely upon a previously unsuccessful one, and a hasty and ill-timed application which is unsuccessful may mean a delay of a year before the next right of application. On the other hand, it may be advisable for a client to apply quickly to the tribunal so that his application falls within a current eligibility period; an applicant who does not apply to the tribunal during a particular period of entitlement forfeits his right of application during that period. In advising on the timing of an application it is important to take into account the factor of delays between application and hearing (*see* **10.5**). A patient may withdraw an application without losing his entitlement to a tribunal hearing during that period; thus a patient who withdraws an application at the beginning of a statutory period may apply again to the tribunal at a later date during that period (*see* below and **9.2** for further discussion of withdrawal).

7.6 Withdrawal of an application

An applicant may withdraw his application at any stage of the proceedings provided the tribunal agrees (r 19(1); *see* **9.2** for further discussion of withdrawals). Where the tribunal authorises the withdrawal the applicant does not lose his right of application during that period and thus may re-apply to the tribunal (s 77(2)). An application which has been withdrawn is disregarded for the purposes of assessing whether the patient should automatically be referred to the tribunal. Where an application is withdrawn after the expiry of a period to which automatic reference applies, the patient's case must be referred to the tribunal as soon as possible after withdrawal (ss 68(5), 71(6)).

7.7 Automatic references

The Act places a duty on the hospital managers or the Home Secretary to refer a case to the tribunal at the end of specified intervals if no application or reference is made in respect of the case during those periods. There was no provision for automatic reference under the 1959 Act. Rather, patients had to initiate applications to the tribunal with the result that only a small proportion of eligible patients did so; some patients did not know of their rights and some were too ill or withdrawn to exercise them. Consequently some patients were detained for considerable periods without any independent assessment of the need for their detention. The 1983 Act tries to resolve this in two ways. First, hospital managers have a duty to inform patients and nearest relatives of their rights to apply to the tribunal (s 132; *see* **3.1**). Secondly, the provisions for automatic reference ensure that in cases where the patient does not apply to the tribunal of his own accord his case will nevertheless be considered by the tribunal at regular intervals.

The hospital managers are responsible for automatic reference of non-restricted patients; the Home Secretary is responsible for automatic reference of restricted patients. It may be noted from **Tables 1** and **2** that a patient detained for treatment (s 3) has a right of reference during the first six months while a patient detained under Part III of the Act has no such right. The reason is that, unlike a patient admitted for treatment, a patient detained under Part III of the Act has already, through the court, experienced an independent assessment of the appropriateness of his admission.

Patients recalled to hospital are special cases. Restricted patients who are recalled to hospital following a conditional discharge do not have the opportunity of an independent assessement of the justification for recalling them, prior to their return (see *R v Secretary of State for the Home Department ex parte K* [1990] 1 All ER 703). While they themselves cannot apply to the tribunal in the first six months after recall, their cases must be referred to the tribunal by the Home Secretary within a month of their return to hospital.

7.8 References by the Secretary of State at his discretion

Section 67(1) gives the Secretary of State for Health unfettered discretion to refer to a tribunal the case of any patient liable to detention or subject to guardianship under Part II of the Act. Section 40(4) extends this provision to patients detained under a hospital order without restrictions or subject to a guardianship order made by a court. Section 71(1) gives the same discretionary power to the Home Secretary with respect to restricted patients.

The Secretary of State may exercise his discretion to refer a case to a tribunal at any time for any reason. In practice a case may be referred to a tribunal under these provisions if the patient's condition has suddenly improved or his circumstances have changed so that his prospects of discharge are significantly enhanced. A request to the Secretary of State to refer a patient's case to the tribunal should state the reasons for giving the patient's case early consideration by the tribunal and why it would be unreasonable for the patient to wait until he next became eligible to apply to the tribunal. The Secretary of State may also refer a case to a tribunal if the patient has unwittingly forfeited a right of application in a particular period.

7.9 Automatic or discretionary reference: the patient's position

There is no provision for withdrawing an automatic or discretionary reference to a tribunal at the request of the patient. A patient who does not want his case to be considered by the tribunal need not attend the hearing. Nevertheless, the tribunal must consider his case and must reach a decision in accordance with the statutory criteria. For example, a patient who has been in hospital for many years may have no home outside the hospital and hence may not wish to be discharged. If his case is referred to the tribunal it must reach a decision and *must* discharge him if the statutory criteria are satisfied. In this instance the tribunal has a number of options. It may delay the patient's discharge to a future date (*see* **8.2**) so that arrangements for the patient's accommodation in the community are made. Alternatively, the tribunal may discharge the patient but he may remain in hospital on an informal basis until after-care arrangements in the community are completed. In the case of special hospitals, patients have been permitted to remain on an informal basis for only a short period; such hospitals are maintained specifically for detained patients who require special security and are organised accordingly.

Chapter 8

Powers

The powers of the tribunal in any case depend on the provision of the Act under which the patient is detained. This chapter deals with the powers of tribunals by reference to different categories of patient.

With patients who are *not* subject to restrictions, the tribunals have a discretion to discharge in any case. They come under a duty to discharge if the patient can satisfy them *either*:

(1) that he is *not* suffering from mental disorder; or

(2) that his detention (s 2) or his liability to detention (s 3 or s 37) for treatment is *not* warranted in the interests of his health or safety or for the protection of others.

With restriction order patients the tribunal has no discretion to discharge. They must do so if the patient satisfies them that:

(1) he is *not* suffering from mental disorder of a nature or degree which makes it appropriate for him to be liable to be detained for treatment; or

(2) that such treatment is not necessary in the interests of his health or safety or for the protection of others.

Thus in both restricted and non-restricted cases, the formal burden of proof is on the patient to satisfy the tribunal that he is *not then* suffering from mental disorder (*Perkins v Bath District Health Authority, The Times*, 29 August 1989). If it is so satisfied the tribunal comes under duty to discharge. It is for the patient to satisfy the tribunal of the absence of mental disorder of the relevant nature or degree. A patient who has failed to discharge this burden will nevertheless be entitled to discharge if he can satisfy the tribunal that his detention is not necessary in the interests of his health or safety or for the protection of others.

The case law on Art 5(4) of the Convention emphasises that prolonged detention on psychiatric grounds should rest on the continued existence of mental disorder of a nature or degree warranting detention, and it is arguable that a failure by a patient to satisfy the tribunal that he is not mentally disordered is insufficient for this purpose; the tribunal should be required to be satisfied that the patient is suffering from mental disorder. This would accord more closely with the principle stated by Lord Atkin that 'in English law every imprisonment is *prima facie* unlawful, and it is for the person directing the imprisonment to justify his act' (*Liversidge v Anderson* [1942] AC 206 at 245). The positioning of the burden of proof also leads on occasion, as Peay has observed, to convoluted formulations of decisions by tribunals, which must express themselves, in accordance with the Act, *not satisfied* that the patient is *not suffering* from mental disorder (J Peay, *Tribunals on Trial: A Study of Decision-Making Under the Mental Health Act 1983*).

The standard of proof to be applied by MHRTs has also given rise to some discussion. Jill Peay has said that, at the time of her study, the standard applied in practice was more 'akin to "beyond reasonable doubt" than to the civil standard theoretically to be applied' (J Peay, *Tribunals on Trial: A Study of Decision-Making Under the Mental Health Act 1983*, p 211). In *R v Mental Health Review Tribunal ex parte Hayes* (Court of Appeal (Civil Division) 9 May 1985, Lexis Transcript, p 16), an application for leave to seek judicial review, Ackner LJ, delivering the judgment of the Court of Appeal, referred to arguments raised on behalf of the applicant concerning the standard of proof to be applied by a MHRT as 'academic questions' which were of little concern to the court exercising its judicial review function.

8.1 Discharge of patients not subject to restrictions

8.1.1 When admitted for assessment (s 2)

The tribunal *may* direct the discharge of a patient in any case (s 72 (1)). This general discretion to discharge a patient is not fettered by specific statutory criteria.

The tribunal *must* discharge a patient if satisfied (s 72(1)(*a*)):

(1) that he is not then suffering from mental disorder of a nature or degree which warrants detention in hospital for at least a limited period for assessment or for assessment followed by treatment; or

(2) that his detention is not justified in the interests of his own health or safety or with a view to the protection of other persons.

The above criteria for discharge correspond with the criteria for admission. The tribunal *must* discharge a patient if he is not then suffering from mental illness, psychopathic disorder, arrested or incomplete development of mind (s 1(2); *see* **13.1–13.5**). The generic phrase 'any other disorder or disability of mind' could be interpreted widely. However, the disorder must be serious enough to warrant detention for assessment.

The word 'then' in criterion (1) is significant. It shows that the tribunal's duty is to assess the patient against the criteria at the time of the hearing; it does not review the justification for detention at the time of admission. The definition of medical treatment is wide and includes nursing care, habilitation or rehabilitation under medical supervision (s 145).

The ambit of the exclusion in s 1(3) was considered in two cases brought immediately following the introduction of the 1983 Act. Section 1(3) provides that a person may not be dealt with under this Act as suffering from mental disorder by reason *only* of promiscuity or other immoral conduct, sexual deviancy, or dependence on alcohol or drugs.

This question arose in *R v Mental Health Review Tribunal ex parte Clatworthy* [1985] 3 All ER 699, a case involving a restriction order patient. Mann J said (at p 701) that 'the effect of subs (3) is apparently to prevent there being a condition of psychopathic disorder where the abnormally aggressive or seriously irresponsible conduct consequent on the persistent disorder or disability of mind is conduct which is a manifestation of sexual deviancy'. The decision of the MHRT in *Clatworthy* was quashed on the grounds that inadequate reasons were given by the tribunal to enable the applicant to know why his contention that he was not suffering from psychopathic disorder had not been accepted. (See also *R v Mental Health Review Tribunal (Mersey Region) ex parte Davies* QBD 21 April 1986 (Unreported) CO/1723/85.)

In criterion (2) the grounds 'interests of his own health or safety' are alternatives to 'the protection of other persons'. Again the burden of proof is on the patient to show that detention is not necessary for one of the specified goals. The tribunal may continue to detain the patient if only one of the grounds—health *or* safety *or* the protection of others—is fulfilled. This is discussed further below in relation to admission for treatment and hospital orders. If the above criteria are not satisfied the tribunal may nevertheless discharge the patient under its general discretion to do so.

8.1.2 When admitted for treatment (s 3) or detained under a hospital order (s 37)

As with patients admitted for assessment, patients admitted for treatment and patients detained under a hospital order may be discharged by a tribunal under its general discretion which is not subject to any specific statutory criteria (s 72(1); *see 8.1.1* above). The tribunal has a duty to discharge if it is satisfied (s 72(1)(*b*)):

(1) (a) that the patient is not then suffering from mental illness, psychopathic disorder, mental impairment (b) which makes it appropriate for him to be *liable to be detained* in hospital (c) for medical treatment; or

(2) that it is not necessary for the health or safety of the patient or for the protection of other persons that he should receive such treatment; or

(3) in the case of an application by the nearest relative following the barring of a discharge order, that the patient if released would not be likely to act in a manner dangerous to himself or to other persons.

(1) *(a) not then suffering from one of the four forms of mental disorder* Under criterion (1) the tribunal must discharge a patient if satisfied that he is not suffering from one of the four specified categories of mental disorder; continued detention cannot rest upon the generic category 'any other disorder or disability of mind'. For example, a learning disabled person whose condition is no longer associated with 'abnormally aggressive or seriously irresponsible conduct' cannot be classified as mentally impaired, and would have to be discharged under this criterion.

(1) *(b) which makes it appropriate for him to be liable to be detained in a hospital* Criterion (1) for discharge is not the exact reverse of the corresponding criterion for compulsory admission. A patient may only be admitted under s 3 if the treatment which he needs for his mental disorder cannot be provided without detaining him (s 3(2)(*c*)). Yet under criterion (1), even if the patient is still suffering from mental disorder, the tribunal is obliged to discharge only if satisfied that the disorder is not 'of a nature or degree which makes it appropriate for the patient to be *liable to be detained* in hospital for medical treatment'. Therefore, a tribunal is not obliged to discharge a patient who no longer needs actual *detention* in order to have the treatment which he needs, if it takes the view that he needs to be *liable to be detained* in order to have it. This

might arise where a patient was on extended leave on condition that he continue to accept medication, and the tribunal felt that unless the patient remained liable to recall to hospital he would probably discontinue his medication.

The original draft of the Mental Health (Amendment) Bill 1982 would have introduced symmetry between the criteria for admission under s 3 and those for discharge, by providing that a patient would be entitled to discharge if not then suffering from mental disorder of a nature or degree 'which makes it appropriate for him to *be detained* in hospital for treatment' (Mental Health Amendment Bill [HL] clause 34(2)(a)). This provision did not find its way into the Mental Health (Amendment) Act 1982. There was discussion of the point in the Special Standing Committee on the Bill. Mr James Cooke, Chairman of Mental Health Review Tribunals for the South East and South West Thames Regional Hospital Board Areas, pointed out that many patients who came before tribunals under the 1959 Act were at home on leave at the time of their hearing, and had to be reassured that their home leave would not be prejudiced by a decision not to discharge them from liability to detention. He then went on to suggest that the Bill be amended as follows (Official Report Session 1981–2, Vol XI, Mental Health (Amendment) Bill Special Standing Committee, 24):

> I believe that it will be difficult to reassure patients as to their conditional liberty if a tribunal has to find that it is 'appropriate for him to be *detained in a hospital* for medical treatment'. I think it would be helpful, both to the Tribunal in applying the test, and to the unsuccessful applicant in reading the decision, if the words 'liable to be' could be inserted between the word 'be' and the word 'detained' . . .

This statement means that it is inappropriate to discharge from liability to detention a patient who is on extended leave, if he needs the spur of possible recall to hospital to require him to keep taking medication. It meant a return to the wording used in the 1959 Act. However, as far as admission under s 3 was concerned, it was made a condition that the treatment which the patient needs cannot be provided without detaining him in hospital (s 3(2)(*c*)).

A patient may well come before a MHRT seeking discharge from liability to detention, having been sent home on conditional leave after some weeks or months detention under s 3. In *R v Hallstrom ex parte W (No 2)* [1986] 2 All ER 306 it was held that s 3 could only be used to detain people whose condition required treatment as in-patients, and not as a means of attaching conditions to an out-patient. Moreover, s 20 could only be used to renew the authority to detain a person whose mental condition was believed to require his continued detention as an in-patient (*see* **5.4**).

What then of the position of a patient whose detention for treatment has been renewed contrary to *Hallstrom*, whilst he is on leave? Would he be entitled to discharge by the MHRT on the grounds that the renewal is unlawful? On a strict application of the criteria in s 72(1)(*b*)(i) the patient would not be *entitled* to discharge if the tribunal is not satisfied that he is not suffering from mental disorder of a nature or degree which made it appropriate for him to be *liable to be detained.* However, the tribunal must then go on to consider the exercise of its overriding discretion to discharge, and the applicant might argue that the tribunal is bound to follow the *Hallstrom* ruling and exercise its discretion to discharge. Before exercising this discretion, the MHRT must have regard to the likelihood that the treatment will alleviate or prevent deterioration in the patient's condition and, where the patient has mental illness or severe mental impairment, that the patient will be able to care for himself, to obtain the care he needs, or to guard himself against serious exploitation (s 72(2)(*a*),(*b*)).

Alternatively, where the tribunal has before it information which clearly establishes that the patient's detention is not lawful when viewed in the light of *Hallstrom*, it might decline jurisdiction on the grounds that, the detention being invalid, the patient is not liable to be detained. However, if this is done the patient is left in an unsatisfactory situation where his detention is treated as invalid even though it has not been formally declared invalid. A further possibility is to seek discharge through a Managers' Review (*see 3.3.3*), to raise the question of the unlawfulness of the renewal, and to seek judicial review if the managers refuse to direct discharge. If a representative becomes aware of a detention or a renewal which contravenes the *Hallstrom* ruling, the preferable course is to seek judicial review of the detention or renewal, rather than relying on an application to a tribunal which may take some time to arrange.

(1) *(c) for medical treatment* The extent to which the grounds for continued detention are narrowed by the requirement that the mental disorder must be of a nature or degree which makes medical treatment appropriate was considered in *R v Mersey Mental Health Review Tribunal ex parte Dillon* (Judgment of 19 March 1986 (CO/1381/86) QBD). The tribunal in this case declined to accept the

evidence of the RMO and a psychologist that the patient was not mentally disordered and concluded that he was suffering from psychopathic disorder. The patient had been in a Special Hospital since 1939 when he had been ordered to be detained during His Majesty's pleasure following a special verdict. He was 65 years old at the time of the application. He did not desire to be discharged from hospital and the two professionals who had given their opinions about him had reservations about what would become of him if he were discharged. The applicant sought judicial review, but did not contest the point that it was open to the tribunal to find that he was suffering from psychopathic disorder. Instead, his attack was concentrated on the question of whether his disorder was 'of a nature or degree which makes it appropriate for him to be liable to be detained in hospital for medical treatment'. The tribunal decision contained the following passage:

> The Tribunal sympathise with those responsible for the care of the applicant in that they find themselves unable to adopt any form of treatment of the applicant, other than containment in conditions of high security. Unhappily the index offence and the applicant's subsequent conduct has led the Tribunal to the conclusion that such containment is the only course open in the case of one from whom the community needs to be protected.

The applicant contended that this showed that the tribunal had misdirected itself on the question. Although the court accepted that the above passage might have given the wrong impression, it then went on to point out that 'medical treatment' for the purposes of the 1983 Act is defined so as to include care, habilitation and rehabilitation under medical supervision. Furthermore, 'There is no requirement that the medical treatment envisaged in ss 72 and 73 of the Mental Health Act 1983 should be such as might have the effect of alleviating or improving the condition of the applicant.'

This approach was also taken in *R v South East Thames Mental Health Review Tribunal ex parte Ryan* (Judgment of 19 March 1987 (CO/98/87) Div Court of the QBD, before Watkins LJ and Mann J). Here again the tribunal rejected the opinion of the patient's RMO on the basis of the views of its own medical member. The patient sought judicial review because he was not receiving medication for mental disorder at the time when his application was considered, and hence that there was insufficient evidence on which to say that the mental disorder was of a nature or degree which made it appropriate for him to be liable to be detained in hospital for medical treatment. Watkins LJ, delivering the judgment of the court, described this attack as 'ill directed' since the patient still needed to be kept in hospital for his own benefit and for that of the public. This being the case, he was receiving treatment by being kept in hospital, even though he was not in receipt of medication for his mental disorder, and the court held that the tribunal had not misdirected itself in any way. If, as these cases suggest, the fact of detention can be treatment, the words 'for medical treatment' in the formula are for practical purposes otiose, and the mental disorder need only be of a nature or degree which makes it appropriate for the applicant to be liable to be detained in hospital.

(2) *that it is not necessary in the interests of the patient's health or safety or for the protection of others that he should receive such treatment* In criterion (2) 'interests of his own health or safety' are alternatives to 'the protection of other persons'. Thus if the tribunal is not satisfied that the patient does not need in-patient care in the interests of his own health, it is not required to discharge him even if satisfied that detention is not necessary for his safety or for the protection of others.

(3) *that the patient, if released, would not be likely to act in a manner dangerous to himself or to others* Criterion (3) arises only in relation to patients admitted for treatment whose nearest relative has first tried to exercise a discharge order. Under s 23 the nearest relative may order the discharge of the patient. That order may be barred by the RMO in accordance with s 25 (*see 3.3.2*). The nearest relative may then apply to the tribunal (s 66(1)(*g*), (2)(*d*); *see also* **7.2**). The tribunal considering an application made under these provisions must discharge the patient if criterion (3) is satisfied.

There is an important distinction between dangerous behaviour in criterion (3) and behaviour which makes detention necessary in the interests of the patient's health or safety or for the protection of others under criterion (2). Dangerousness implies that the patient is likely to engage in behaviour which would result in physical injury to himself, eg, an attempt on his life, or which would involve physical harm to someone else. The terms 'health', 'safety' and 'protection' in criterion (2) encompass a wider range of actions which do not necessarily amount to dangerous behaviour, eg, causing disruption in the family, verbal abuse, or damaging property. The term 'is likely' in criterion (3) suggests that there must be a substantial and imminent risk of dangerous behaviour and not just a suspicion. This is an exacting standard which may require some evidence of dangerous behaviour in the recent past. Where criterion (3) applies, the tribunal must discharge the patient, even if detention is still justified under criteria (1) and (2). It should be noted that the criteria are alternatives, and thus the patient must be discharged if one of the criteria is satisfied. For example, a patient who the tribunal is satisfied does not need in-patient care in the interests of his health or safety or for the protection of others must be discharged even if he is clearly mentally disordered (*see also* **7.4** on the dangerousness criterion).

Where the above criteria are not satisfied the tribunal may nevertheless exercise its discretion to discharge the patient on any other grounds. In exercising this general discretion the tribunal must have regard to the following criteria (s 72(2)):

(1) the likelihood of medical treatment alleviating or preventing deterioration of the patient's condition; and

(2) in the case of patients suffering from mental illness or severe mental impairment, the likelihood that, if discharged, the patient will be able to care for himself, obtain the care he needs, or guard himself against serious exploitation.

Criterion (1) is the 'treatability' test (discussed in **1.6** and **13.6**). It will be recalled that a person suffering from psychopathic disorder or mental impairment cannot be admitted for treatment (s 3) if medical treatment is unlikely to alleviate or prevent deterioration in his condition; nor can his detention be renewed if, at the expiry of a period of detention, it is considered that medical treatment is unlikely to alleviate or prevent deterioration. Again, it must be remembered that medical treatment includes nursing, care habilitation and rehabilitation under medical supervision.

The treatability test for a person suffering from mental illness or severe mental impairment is not applicable at the point of admission but a modified treatability test applies at the time of renewal. It is perhaps inconsistent that the tribunal is not *obliged* to discharge a non-treatable patient; it must only 'have regard to' the treatability of the condition. Nevertheless, this criterion makes treatability an important factor in the tribunal's decision, especially in the case of patients suffering from psychopathic disorder or mental impairment. In the case of patients suffering from mental illness or severe mental impairment the tribunal must weigh treatability against the patient's ability to see to his own needs and guard against serious exploitation. The representative is advised to examine carefully whether an individual programme of treatment exists, whether there are clear behavioural and social criteria against which to measure the success of the programme and when the patient is expected to achieve these goals. In any case where a person with a minor disorder has remained in hospital for a long time the representative should determine whether he has responded to treatment and what further progress he is likely to make.

8.1.3 When subject to guardianship (ss 7, 37)

The tribunal has a general *discretion* to discharge a patient subject to guardianship on any grounds (s 72(4)). It has a *duty* to discharge if it is satisfied (s 72(4)):

(1) that the patient is not then suffering from mental illness, psychopathic disorder, mental impairment or severe mental impairment; or

(2) that it is not necessary in the interests of the welfare of the patient or for the protection of other persons that the person should remain under guardianship.

Under criterion (1) the tribunal must discharge the patient if he is not suffering from one of the four forms of mental disorder. Unlike patients detained in hospital there is no specification as to the nature or degree of the disorder.

In criterion (2) 'the interests of the welfare of the patient' is wider than the corresponding term 'for the health or safety of the patient' which is applicable to detained patients. The patient's welfare includes not only his physical and mental health but also his ability to handle his affairs, transactions and decisions. Thus a patient who is liable to be exploited by others may, for this reason, require guardianship under the 'interests of the welfare of the patient test', even though these may not be sufficient grounds to justify continued detention under the 'health or safety of the patient' criterion.

8.2 Delayed discharge of patients not subject to restrictions

Where a tribunal is considering the case of a detained patient it may direct that he is discharged on a future date which it must specify (s 72(3)). The tribunal must, within seven days of the hearing, communicate its decision to the patient (r 24(1); *see* **10.4**). Having made the decision to delay a discharge the tribunal cannot, prior to the specified date on which it will take effect, change the order (cf deferred conditional discharge in *8.5.2* below). The provisions for delayed discharge do not apply to patients subject to guardianship.

The 1959 Act contained no provision for delaying a discharge; where the tribunal decided to direct a patient's discharge it communicated its decision to the patient within seven days of the hearing, and the discharge took effect immediately. The result was that patients were discharged before arrangements could be made for their accommodation or care in the community. The power to delay a discharge under the 1983 Act is most frequently used in cases where there is no satisfactory accommodation for the patient outside the hospital and where support from the social services needs to be arranged. An alternative in such a case is for the tribunal to adjourn and compel the attendance of witnesses who can help to find the necessary accomodation, for example a Director of Social Services, or a representative of a housing department.

The Act does not explicitly limit the period for which an order for discharge may be delayed, but it is presumed that the delay would have to be a reasonable one and related to a valid objective such as the availability of aftercare. A tribunal could not specify a date for discharge after that on which the authority for a patient's detention expires. This follows from the fact that the tribunal derives its authority from the provisions in the Act relating to discharge. Its concern is to ensure that the patient's freedoms are not unnecessarily curtailed. It is not empowered by law, either expressly or by implication, to extend a person's detention beyond that which is specified in the Act. Clearly the provisions for delayed discharge do not override those provisions in the Act relating to the expiry of the authority for detention. The representative should use his endeavours to ensure that the earliest date is set for discharge so that the patient is in hospital no longer than is necessary.

It should be noted that a patient who is discharged may remain in hospital on an informal basis provided that the hospital authorities consent. (It has been known for a patient to remain in a special hospital on an informal basis for a short time although, for reasons discussed in **7.9**, it is not a practice which is encouraged.) However, the tribunal has no power to ensure that an informal patient remains in hospital and does not discharge himself prematurely, ie, before the arrangements for his after-care have been completed. Where the tribunal considers that premature discharge is likely and would cause a deterioration in the patient's condition it may prefer to delay his formal discharge.

In *R v Wessex Mental Health Review Tribunal ex parte Wiltshire County Council, The Times*, 29 August 1989 the tribunal decided that, although mentally disordered, a patient detained under s 2 was not suffering from mental disorder of a nature or degree which warranted his detention *for assessment*. His mental illness was long standing and the tribunal felt that no assessment had been necessary. They therefore discharged him from detention under s 2, but deferred the discharge for one week to give the authorities a chance to decide whether an application under s 3 should be made. In proceedings for judicial review of the tribunal decision, counsel for the tribunal conceded that it was not open to a tribunal to defer discharge to enable the authorities to decide whether there was some other basis of detaining the patient. Although the Court of Appeal decided the application on other grounds, and did not accept this concession, it is submitted that Counsel's concession represents the correct view of the law.

8.3 Transfer and leave of patients not subject to restrictions

Where a tribunal decides not to discharge a detained patient it may recommend that he is granted leave of absence or transferred to another hospital or into guardianship with a view to facilitating his discharge on a future date (s 72(3)(*a*)). It should be emphasised that tribunals do not have the power to direct transfer or leave of absence, but can only make recommendations to that effect. Under the 1959 Act tribunals could only discharge a non-restricted patient or reclassify the category of mental disorder; they held no advisory powers in respect of transfers or leave of absence. The 1983 Act expanded the tribunal's advisory powers so as to enable them to deal more flexibly with the patient's needs; in particular, it was recognised that many patients require a period of gradual rehabilitation in which transfer to more open conditions or periods of supervised leave may be important elements.

8.3.1 Transfer between hospitals

The power of the tribunal to recommend transfer between hospitals is probably its most important advisory power. Its primary importance is in relation to patients in special hospitals for whom transfer to a local NHS hospital or RSU is the logical next step in a programme of gradual rehabilitation. While a tribunal's recommendation of transfer can have no practical effect unless the patient's RMO agrees that the patient is ready to be transferred and a consultant in a local hospital is prepared to accept him, it can in itself be a factor to be taken into account by the RMO and the consultant in making their decisions. The representative is referred to chapter 15 for a detailed discussion of the issues relating to transfers from special to local hospitals.

8.3.2 Transfer into guardianship

Under s 72(3)(*a*) the tribunal may recommend that a patient who is detained in hospital is transferred into guardianship. Transfer into guardianship may be a useful transitional stage prior to discharge for patients in special hospitals, as well as those in local hospitals who are not well enough to be discharged but who no longer require detention in hospital. As with transfer between hospitals a tribunal's primary role in making a recommendation for transfer into guardianship is to persuade the patient's RMO that such transfer is appropriate and to persuade a local social services authority to accept responsibility for the patient's care.

8.3.3 Leave of absence

Under s 72(3) the tribunal may recommend that a patient is granted a period of leave of absence from hospital; the authority to grant leave lies with the patient's RMO (s 17), and he may impose conditions (s 17(1)) such as a requirement to live at a specified address or to attend an out-patient clinic for treatment.

8.3.4 Further consideration of a case

For discussion of the tribunal's duty to consider a case further in the event that its recommendation has not been complied with, *see 10.4.1.*

8.4 Reclassification of patients not subject to restrictions

Where a tribunal does not discharge a patient but is satisfied that the patient is suffering from a form of disorder different from the one specified in the detention papers it may direct that the form of mental disorder be amended accordingly (s 72(5)).

It will be recalled that the criteria for renewal of detention and for discharge by the tribunal differ according to whether the disorder is a major disorder (mental illness or severe mental impairment or a minor disorder) (*see 8.1.2* above and *1.6.1*). Thus reclassification can have important consequences as far as the patient's future detention is concerned. For example, if a patient is reclassified as having a minor rather than a major disorder, the authority for his detention cannot be renewed unless there is likely to be some benefit from treatment (s 20(4)). See however, the discussion of the meaning of medical treatment in *8.1.2*(1)(*c*).

Evidence that the mental disorder should be reclassified may come from the medical member of the tribunal or from an independent psychiatrist commissioned by, or on behalf of, the patient. (In practice it is unlikely that such evidence would come from a RMO, because the RMO has the power to reclassify without reference to the tribunal.) It should be remembered that reclassification into the category of psychopathic disorder may have undesirable consequences for the patient, since many non-forensic units are very reluctant to accept patients with this classification.

8.5 Patients subject to a restriction order

The 1983 Act significantly extends the powers of MHRTs in respect of patients subject to a restriction order. Under the 1959 Act they could only advise the Home Secretary as to the exercise of powers by him. The final decision rested with the Home Secretary who could accept or reject the tribunal's advice it without giving reasons. In *X v United Kingdom* (Series A: Judgments and Decisions of the European Court of Human Rights No 46) it was held that under Art 5(4) of the European Convention a detained patient has the right of periodic access to a judicial body to determine the justification for continued detention. A MHRT with only advisory powers did not constitute a judicial body. The 1983 Act takes the consequences of this judgment by giving tribunals the power to discharge a patient subject to a restriction order. The power runs concurrently with that of the Home Secretary who retains the power to discharge a patient absolutely or subject to conditions, to recall the patient and to remove a restriction order (*see* **4.4**).

8.5.1 Absolute discharge

The tribunal's general discretion to discharge a patient on any grounds does not apply in relation to restricted patients (*see* **8.1** above). The tribunal must assess the patient against the relevant statutory criteria and can only discharge the patient if those criteria are met. The tribunal must give a direction for *absolute* discharge if it is satisfied (s 73(1)):

(1) that the patient is not then suffering from mental illness, mental impairment or severe mental impairment or from any of those forms of disorder which makes it appropriate for him to be liable to be detained in hospital for medical treatment; or

(2) that it is not necessary for the health or safety of the patient or for the protection of others that he should receive such treatment; and
(3) that it is not appropriate that the patient remain liable to be recalled to hospital for further treatment.

The patient must establish his entitlement to discharge under either criterion (1) or (2), which are the criteria listed in s 72(1)(*b*)(i) or (ii) and apply to patients who are admitted for treatment or who are detained under a hospital order. The reader is referred to *8.1.2* above for detailed discussion of these criteria. Criterion (3) is discussed below in relation to conditional discharge. The tribunal must grant an absolute discharge if criteria (1) and (3) are satisfied or if (2) and (3) are satisfied or if all the criteria are satisfied. *It cannot discharge on any other grounds.* The effect of an absolute discharge is that both the hospital order and the restriction order are discharged (s 73(3)).

The question of the circumstances in which a restriction order patient is entitled to absolute discharge was raised in *R v Merseyside Mental Health Review Tribunal ex parte K* [1990] 1 All ER 694. K was conditionally discharged from hospital in 1985 by a tribunal which found that there was no evidence that he was suffering from mental disorder, but felt that it was appropriate that he remain liable to recall to hospital. Following his conditional discharge he committed a number of offences, for which he was sentenced to six years' imprisonment. In 1986 he applied to a MHRT for absolute discharge, fearing that on the expiry of his sentence he would be recalled to hospital by the Home Secretary. The tribunal heard his case and expressed itself 'satisfied that the patient was not suffering from any mental disorder', but that it was appropriate for him to remain liable to recall for further treatment. K sought judicial review of the tribunal decision on the grounds that as soon as the tribunal found as a matter of fact that he was no longer suffering from mental disorder, he was entitled to absolute discharge: he should not be subject to the Mental Health Act. Section 1(1) says that the Act 'shall have effect with regard to the reception, care and treatment of mentally disordered patients', and a patient is defined in s 145(1) as 'a person suffering or appearing to suffer from mental disorder.' A conditional discharge must presuppose possible recall to hospital for further treatment, but in the light of the findings of the two tribunals there was nothing to treat.

The Court of Appeal held (per Butler-Sloss LJ at p 699f) that 'Section 73 gives to the tribunal power to impose a conditional discharge and retain residual control over patients not then suffering from mental disorder or not to a degree requiring continued detention in hospital'. One of the key issues in the case was the interaction between ss 72 and 73. Under s 72(1) the tribunal must direct the discharge of a patient who is not then suffering from mental disorder of a nature or degree which makes it appropriate for him to be *liable to be detained* in hospital for treatment. But in the case of a restricted patient, s 73 applies. The tribunal cannot absolutely discharge a restricted patient unless it is satisfied that it is not appropriate for him to remain *liable to recall* to hospital for further treatment. Thus, even if a tribunal finds that a patient is not mentally disordered, it must direct conditional discharge unless satisfied that it is not appropriate for the patient to remain liable to recall. However, in this context, *liable to detention* and *liable to recall* amount in practice to broadly the same thing. Unrestricted patients on conditional leave are liable to detention, because they may be recalled by the RMO; conditionally discharged restricted patients are liable to recall by Home Secretary's warrant.

It is difficult to see how a tribunal can say that the patient's mental condition is not such that it is appropriate for him to be liable to be detained, but that it is appropriate for him to remain liable to recall. The problem arises, it is submitted, because of the change in the wording of the Mental Health (Amendment) Bill in the Special Standing Committee described at *8.1.2*(1) above. Under the original wording a tribunal would have been obliged to direct discharge if the patient was not suffering from mental disorder of a nature or degree which warranted detention in hospital, and would then have had to go on to decide whether it is appropriate for the patient to remain liable to recall. These are two logically distinct steps. Under the first it is being decided whether he is mentally disordered to an extent requiring detention; under the second the tribunal must ask whether, even though he does not need to be detained, he needs to remain liable to recall. In the Court of Appeal in *ex parte K*, Butler-Sloss LJ said this:

> In order to succeed, the patient must demonstrate that different consequences flow from a finding under the first part of paragraph (b)(i) than from a finding under the second part, and that a tribunal, having found as a fact that he was not suffering from mental disorder, was precluded from making any order other than absolute discharge . . . For my part, I do not believe this argument to be correct.

Butler-Sloss LJ further observed that the power to order conditional discharge is designed to support the patient and protect the public, and that the tribunal's exercise of this discretionary power should not be lightly set aside. It is questionable whether this decision complies with Art 5(1)(e) and 5(4), of the European Convention on Human Rights, which provide that where detention takes place on psychiatric grounds there must be objective evidence of unsoundness of mind of a nature or degree warranting detention, and that such detention depends for its continuing validity on the persistence of such a degree of mental disorder.

K's concern in bringing these proceedings was that the Home Office would be content to let him remain in prison during his sentence, but that a recall warrant would be issued returning him to detention in hospital once his sentence expired. This indeed happened. During the month before K's release date from prison the Home Secretary issued a warrant under s 42(3) of the 1983 Act recalling him to Broadmoor on his earliest release date from prison. K sought unsuccessfully to challenge this recall in proceedings for judicial review (*R v Secretary of State for the Home Department ex parte K* [1990] 1 All ER 703; see **4.4**). The delay of transfer to hospital until close to a prisoner's release date is discouraged by the Code of Practice, para 3.13, which says that 'A transfer in such circumstances may well be seen by the prisoner as being primarily intended to extend his detention and result in an unco-operative attitude towards treatment.'

In contrast to non-restricted patients there is no provision requiring a tribunal to consider the treatability of a restricted patient, irrespective of the classification of mental disorder. It is curious that this should be so as the court, in making the hospital order with restrictions, must apply the treatability test to minor disorders.

8.5.2 Conditional discharge

Where the tribunal considers that either criterion (1) or criterion (2) or both are satisfied but that criterion (3) is not satisfied, it must direct the conditional discharge of the patient (s 73(2)). The patient must abide by any conditions laid down by the tribunal or subsequently imposed by the Home Secretary. A patient who is conditionally discharged may be recalled to hospital by the Home Secretary (s 73(4)). The Home Secretary may also vary any condition which has been imposed either by the tribunal or by himself (s 73(5)).

It should be noted that the tribunal is not obliged to lay down any specific conditions when it makes its order for conditional discharge. However, in practice it is unlikely that a patient will be conditionally discharged without conditions being imposed either by the tribunal or by the Home Secretary. The rationale of the power of recall rests on the opportunity to detect any deterioration in the patient's condition and to intervene before any further offence is committed. This requires reasonably frequent oversight of the patient's condition and circumstances; thus psychiatric and/or social supervision is normally a condition of discharge. Other conditions frequently imposed are a requirement to live at a specific address, to attend a specific workplace, to report at intervals to a probation officer or to accept social supervision by a social worker in the community. The social worker or probation officer normally undertakes to report any significant changes to the Home Secretary, eg, prospect of marriage or a change of job. The Home Secretary may recall a patient on any grounds (ss 73(4), 42(3)). Failure to abide by a condition of discharge may precipitate recall to hospital if it is considered symptomatic of a deterioration in the patient's condition or circumstances, or if adhering to the condition is essential for the patient's rehabilitation or the monitoring of his progress or early warning of possible danger to the public. Where, after a period of monitoring, the patient has made reasonable progress and appears to lead a stable life outside the hospital, some or all of the conditions may not be enforced. This is normally a gradual process, accompanied by less frequent psychiatric or other supervision.

In *Secretary of State for the Home Department v Mental Health Review Tribunal for Wales* [1986] 1 WLR 1160, [1986] 3 All ER 233, it was held that a tribunal must be satisfied that the patient should be released from the hospital before directing conditional discharge. The tribunal had directed that the patient, who was severely mentally impaired, be conditionally discharged, but that it be a condition of his discharge that he continue to reside in the hospital which had been his home for more than 21 years. The direction had been made on the grounds that the patient needed supervision, guidance on personal hygiene and social rehabilitation, and the tribunal had decided that this was not treatment within s 145(1). Mann J held a direction of conditional discharge was inconsistent with a condition of continued residence in hospital, and was therefore unlawful. The tribunal's finding that the patient needed supervision and training was, in fact, a finding that he needed medical treatment within s 145(1), and therefore the tribunal had been wrong in deciding that the criteria placing it under a duty to direct conditional discharge had been met.

The tribunal may defer a direction for conditional discharge until arrangements for the patient's care are made to its satisfaction (s 73(7)). The power to defer a conditional discharge differs significantly from the tribunal's power to delay a discharge in the case of a non-restricted patient (*see* **8.2** above). Where the tribunal delays the discharge of an unrestricted patient it makes an order for discharge which is to take effect at a specified date in the future; discharge must be effected on or by that date, irrespective of whether arrangements for the patient's care have been completed. On the other hand where a tribunal considering the case of a patient subject to a restriction order defers a direction for his conditional discharge, it postpones the coming into effect of the discharge direction until arrangements are made to its satisfaction.

Where the tribunal has made a deferred direction for conditional discharge, it may direct that the decision take effect without a further hearing (r 25(1); *see 10.4.2* for further discussion).

In *Secretary of State for the Home Department v Mental Health Review Tribunal for the Mersey Regional Health Authority* [1986] 1 WLR 1160, [1986] 3 All ER 233, it was held that the tribunal cannot defer a conditional discharge until arrangements are made for admission to another hospital. The patient was detained subject to a restriction order in a special hospital. The tribunal in his case found that his behaviour had improved substantially over recent months, that he was no longer on any medication, that detention was no longer necessary in the interests of his own health or safety or for the protection of other persons, and that it was appropriate for him to remain liable to recall. However, the tribunal also found that the patient would be unable to cope upon discharge from a special hospital direct into the community and a period in 'half-way house' was essential in the patient's interests and in the interests of the community. In order to facilitate this step, the tribunal directed the patient's conditional discharge, but deferred the direction, in a purported exercise of their powers under s 73(7), until arrangements had been made for the admission of the patient to a less secure hospital. This was done with a view to his subsequent discharge to a local hostel or to his home.

Mann J noted that s 73(7) allowed a direction for conditional discharge to be deferred 'until such arrangements as appear to the tribunal to be necessary for that purpose have been made to their satisfaction.' Although, on the face of it, this provision confers wide discretion on the tribunal, Mann J said this ([1986] 3 All ER 233 at p 238c):

The purpose in question is that of discharge, albeit conditionally. In this case, the arrangement was one which when made ensured continued detention, but brought deferment of discharge to an end. In my judgment, the stipulation of such an arrangement is not within the powers of the Act in so far as they apply to restricted patients and is accordingly unlawful. I observe in passing that, in regard to patients who are not restricted patients there is, in s 72(3), provision for the achievement of an interim regime.

The tribunal had been trying to use its power to direct conditional discharge as a way of directing a transfer to a less secure hospital, a power which does not exist for restricted patients, even though it is established good practice for a special hospital patient to be transferred to a local hospital before being discharged so that security can be relaxed gradually and the patient's reaction can be monitored. Although Mann J expressed sympathy with what the tribunal was trying to achieve, he nevertheless declared it to be an unlawful use of the power to defer conditional discharge.

The powers of a tribunal to direct deferred conditional discharge under s 73(7) were also at issue in *Campbell v Secretary of State for the Home Department* [1988] 1 AC 120, where it was held that a decision to defer conditional discharge was a final decision which could not be re-opened. An application for judicial review was brought by the Home Secretary on the grounds that his procedural rights had been infringed in respect of the hearing of a restricted patient's case. The patient applied to a MHRT which, in February 1985, directed that he be conditionally discharged, but deferred the conditional discharge until June. The terms of the decision were that the applicant could have the expectation of being conditionally discharged on 28 June if, by that date, appropriate arrangements had been made to meet the conditions of the discharge, these being that suitable hostel accommodation be found with an active rehabilitation programme, that the patient be supervised by a probation officer, and that the patient attend an out-patient clinic supervised by a psychiatrist yet to be nominated. The decision was purportedly made under s 73(7). The reasons given for the decision were that the tribunal was 'satisfied that the patient continued to suffer from psychopathic disorder but not of a nature or degree which makes it appropriate for him to be liable to be detained in hospital for medical treatment but were satisfied that the patient should remain liable to recall.'

The patient's RMO had opposed discharge. Discharge was supported by the independent psychiatrist engaged by the patient to provide a report. The Home Secretary sought judicial review of the decision on three grounds. The first was that, prior to the hearing, the Secretary of State was not provided with the independent psychiatric report contrary to r 12. Secondly, that the Secretary of State had not been given 14 days' notice of the hearing as required by r 20. Finally, that in consequence of the failure to comply with the rules, the Secretary of State had not been given the opportunity to submit supplementary observations which might have affected the tribunal's decision, and the Secretary of State was unable to seek the leave of the tribunal to make oral representations. At first instance Woolf J took the view that any defect in the proceedings could be cured by a rehearing without quashing the original decision and hence depriving the applicant of a 'provisional decision' in his favour. This decision was based on the view that, since the tribunal decision was provisional not final, r 28 applied. Rule 28 provides that:

> Any irregularity resulting from failure to comply with these rules before the tribunal has determined an application shall not of itself render the proceedings void, but the tribunal may, and shall, if it considers that any person may have been prejudiced, take such steps as it thinks fit before determining the application to cure the irregularity, whether by amendment of any document, the giving of any notice, the taking of any step or otherwise.

On appeal, the Court of Appeal and the House of Lords both held that the tribunal decision to direct deferred conditional discharge was a final determination of the case which could not be cured by a rehearing by the same tribunal panel. The tribunal has no power to go back on the decision, only to decide whether appropriate arrangements have been made. The tribunal's purpose in directing deferment to a fixed date was to set a time limit on the making of the necessary arrangements. This was also declared to be unlawful. Lord Bridge said this (p 128):

> There is no authority for this in the Act or in the rules and in the nature of the case it is impossible for a tribunal to predict ... how long it will take to make the necessary arrangements. The decision should simply indicate that the direction is deferred until the necessary arrangements have been made to the satisfaction of the tribunal and specify what arrangements are required, which can normally be done, no doubt, simply by reference to the conditions to be imposed. Whoever is responsible for making the arrangements should then proceed with all reasonable expedition to do so and should bring the matter to the tribunal's attention as soon as practicable after it is thought that satisfactory arrangements

have been made. Pursuant to rule 25, the tribunal may then decide that the arrangements are to their satisfaction without a further hearing.

Once the tribunal has made a deferred direction for conditional discharge, it cannot reconsider whether that was the right decision. However, Lord Bridge suggested that in a case where discharge no longer seemed appropriate, the tribunal has a discretion to decide whether the arrangements are satisfactory, and could avoid coming to any decision on their adequacy as a way of avoiding implementing their original decision. If the patient has not been discharged before his case next comes before a tribunal for its consideration following an application or a reference, the tribunal must deal with the fresh application or reference; no discharge can be made on the basis of the earlier deferred direction (s 73(7)).

8.5.3 Reclassification

Where a tribunal does not discharge a patient but is satisfied that the patient is suffering from a form of mental disorder different from the one specified on the forms relating to his detention, it may direct that the form of mental disorder is amended (s 72(5),(6)).

The application of s 72(5) (power of reclassification in respect of non-restricted patients; *see* **8.4** above) to restricted patients was probably unintentional. While reclassification may have important consequences for the subsequent detention of a non-restricted patient, it has no consequences for the restricted patient, and the fact that neither the RMO nor the Secretary of State has the power to reclassify a restricted patient supports the argument that granting that power to tribunals was unintentional. Hence it is unlikely that tribunals will wish to use it.

8.5.4 Transfer, leave and the removal of restrictions

Section 72(3), which authorises a tribunal to recommend that a non-restricted patient should be transferred to another hospital, into guardianship or given leave of absence (*see* **8.3**) does not apply to patients subject to a restriction order, see *Grant v Mental Health Review Tribunal for the Trent Region* and *R v Mental Health Review Tribunal ex parte O'Hara, The Times*, 28 April 1986. Following the ruling in these cases, the Home Office issued a statement indicating that they would be happy to continue to receive recommendations from tribunals in restricted cases. However, in such a case the tribunal has no statutory power to consider the case further in the event of the recommendation not being acted upon.

Note that the power of the hospital managers to transfer a patient, and the power of the RMO to grant a period of leave of absence cannot be exercised without the Home Secretary's consent in the case of restricted patients (s 41(3)(c)). Thus, where the hospital managers or the RMO accept a tribunal's recommendation for transfer or leave of absence, the recommendation must be forwarded to the Home Secretary for approval before it can be implemented. It is rare for the Home Secretary to withhold approval for a recommendation which has the RMO's or the hospital managers' consent. Where a patient has been granted leave of absence, the Home Secretary can recall him at any time; the RMO's power of recall ceases after six months from the first day of the leave of absence, unless the patient has been returned to the hospital in the meantime (ss 17, 40(4), 41(3)(*c*), Sched 1, Part II, paras 2, 3). For a discussion of a tribunal's recommendation for transfer, see chapter 15.

Where the Home Secretary removes a restriction order the patient remains liable to detention in accordance with the hospital order alone.

8.6 Patients subject to a restriction direction

8.6.1 Absolute and conditional discharge

Where a patient has been transferred from prison to a hospital under a restriction direction (*see* **2.5**) the tribunal is not empowered to order his discharge. This is because, technically, the patient is still subject to his sentence and thus any decision regarding his discharge must be taken by the Home Secretary. The tribunal's role is limited to notifying the Home Secretary whether the patient would be entitled to be absolutely discharged had he been subject to a restriction order (s 74(1)). Thus the tribunal must consider the same statutory criteria that apply to a patient subject to a restriction order (*see 8.5.1* above). If the Home Secretary is notified that the patient would be entitled to be absolutely discharged he may, within 90 days, consent to the discharge and the tribunal must accordingly discharge the patient (s 74(2)). If, at the end of the 90-day period, the Home Secretary has not given his consent, the hospital managers must transfer the patient back to prison or to the other institution from whence he came; the patient would then serve the remainder of his sentence or be dealt with as if he had not been transferred to hospital (s 74(3)). This is a logical result, for, if the person is entitled to an absolute discharge, there is no case for continuing to detain him in a hospital. The issue becomes whether the person is dangerous and requires further detention in prison to complete his sentence or whether he can be released. This is a matter for the Home Secretary.

Where the tribunal notifies the Home Secretary that the patient would be entitled to be conditionally discharged it may add a recommendation that the patient should remain in hospital if his discharge is not approved (s 74(1)(*b*)). As with absolute discharge, if, within 90 days, the Home Secretary gives his consent, the tribunal must conditionally discharge the patient (s 74(2); it may defer the direction for conditional discharge in the same way as for patients subject to a restriction order (ss 73(7), 74(6); *see 8.5.2* above)). If the Home Secretary does not give his consent and the tribunal has not recommended that the patient should remain in hospital, then the hospital managers must return him to the prison or other institution from which he came (s 74(3)). If the tribunal has recommended that the patient should remain in hospital if not discharged, then he cannot be returned to prison. This is also a logical result. For the patient who is entitled to conditional discharge but is not so discharged there is a choice to be made: whether he would benefit from further hospital care as opposed to prison confinement. The MHRT assists the Home Secretary in this choice by making the appropriate recommendations. Where the representative has instructed an independent psychiatrist he should pay specific attention to this issue.

As in the case of other persons under a restriction direction, the tribunal must assess the statutory criteria which apply to patients subject to a restriction order and must inform the Home Secretary whether the patient would be entitled to absolute or conditional discharge; if entitled to conditional discharge, the tribunal may add a recommendation that the patient should remain in hospital if not discharged. Where the Home Secretary is informed that the patient is entitled to absolute or conditional discharge, and no further recommendation is made, the Home Secretary must issue a warrant remitting the patient to his original place of detention (s 74(4)). Representatives should explain to patients the risk that they will be returned to prison, and seek clear instructions. Some patients want to return to prison. Persons transferred to hospital under s 48 (this includes persons remanded in custody, detained under the Immigration Act 1971 and civil prisoners) are an exception to the above. In such cases neither the tribunal nor the Home Secretary has the power to discharge the patient.

8.6.2 Reclassification

As in the case of patients subject to a restriction order, the tribunal may reclassify the patient as suffering from a different form of mental disorder from that specified on the detention papers (s 72(5)). The application of this section to restricted patients was probably unintentional and tribunals are unlikely to use this power. This is explained further in *8.5.3* above.

8.6.3 Advising the Home Secretary

The tribunal has a role in advising the Home Secretary on patients subject to a restriction direction similar to that in relation to patients subject to a restriction order; the representative is referred to *8.5.4*.

When an offender is transferred to a hospital with a restriction direction the Home Secretary has a general discretion to transfer him back to prison at any time during the period of his sentence (taking into account periods of remission). There is a provision in s 50(1) of the Act for the RMO, any other registered medical practitioner or a MHRT to inform the Home Secretary if the person no longer requires treatment or if no effective treatment can be given to him in the hospital. After receiving such advice the Home Secretary can direct that the patient be sent back to prison or can discharge him on licence or under supervision. There is similar provision for persons on remand, civil prisoners and others detained under s 48, except that such persons can only be sent back to the prison or other institution in which they were originally detained (s 51(3)). The representative should be aware of this advisory function of the MHRT.

8.7 Conditionally discharged patients

The Act gives the right to conditionally discharged patients to apply to tribunals; such patients did not have a right to a tribunal hearing under the 1959 Act. It will be remembered that patients who have been conditionally discharged are normally living in the community under some degree of supervision by a social worker or probation officer; they may be required to live at a specified address and accept some medical treatment. In some cases the conditions may no longer be enforced (*see* 8.5.2 above). The tribunal has the following powers.

8.7.1 Change of conditions

The tribunal may vary any condition by which the patient must abide or impose a new condition (s 75(3)(a)). Thus the tribunal may change a condition in accordance with a change in the patient's circumstances or remove a condition if it is no longer necessary. It is theoretically possible for the tribunal to impose conditions more onerous than those applying so far. However, the tribunal's general statutory role is to review the justification for detaining the patient or for otherwise restricting his liberty. Only in the most exceptional circumstances will the tribunal be likely to conclude that its duty is to impose upon the patient conditions more restrictive than those already imposed by the Secretary of State or by a previous tribunal.

8.7.2 Cessation of restriction order or direction

The tribunal may direct that the restriction order or direction is lifted (s 73(5)(b)). The patient will then cease to be liable to be detained under the hospital order or transfer direction (s 75(3)) and will not be subject to recall to hospital.

8.7.3 Reclassification

As with other restricted patients the tribunal has the power to reclassify the form of disorder from which the patient is suffering (s 72(5)). This power is unlikely to be used for reasons discussed previously in *8.5.3* above.

8.8 Removal of patients without a right of abode in the UK

The Home Secretary is empowered by s 86 to authorise the removal to another country of patients who are neither British nor Commonwealth citizens and who have no right of abode in the UK. The patient must be suffering from mental illness, be receiving treatment as an in-patient, and be detained under an application for admission for treatment, a hospital order, or an order or direction having the same effect. The Home Secretary must be of the opinion that proper arrangements have been made for the patient's removal to the other country and for his care and treatment there, and that it is in the interest of the patient to remove him to that country. The approval of a MHRT is required before this power may be exercised, and the Tribunal would wish to be satisfied that the criteria outlined have been met (*R v Secretary of State for the Home Department ex parte Talmasani* [1987] 1 MM AR 32 (CA) and *R v Same ex parte Alghali* [1986] 1 MM AR 376.

Chapter 9

Pre-hearing Procedures

9.1 Applying to the tribunal

An application must be made in writing by the applicant or by a person authorised by him for this purpose (r 3(1)); it may also be made by the applicant's representative (r 10(4); *see* **9.6** below). It is not necessary for the applicant to complete a specific form although such a form is available from the tribunal office on request. Any written request which may reasonably be interpreted as a request for consideration by a MHRT constitutes a valid application. A model application is included in Appendix 4.

Wherever possible an application should contain the following information (r 3(2)):

(1) the patient's name;
(2) the patient's address including the address of the hospital where he is detained. If the patient is subject to the guardianship of someone other than a local authority, the address of the guardian should be given. In the case of a conditionally discharged patient or one who has been granted leave of absence from hospital the address of the hospital where he was last detained and his current address should be given;
(3) where the nearest relative (see Appendix 6) is the applicant, his name, address and his relationship to the patient;
(4) the section of the Act under which the patient is detained;
(5) the name and address of the applicant's representative or, if he has not yet authorised one, whether he intends to do so or whether he wishes to conduct his own case.

Failure to provide part or all of the information does not invalidate the application. Where it is not included it must be provided as far as possible by the responsible authority or, in the case of a restricted patient, the Home Secretary, at the tribunal's request (r 3(3)).

The applicant does not need to give reasons justifying his application but he may do so if he wishes. Alternatively, the applicant may submit such reasons to the tribunal in accordance with r 12(1) which also allows him to comment on the documents released to him by the tribunal (see *9.8.1* below).

The applicant must send his application to the relevant tribunal office (any document directed to the tribunal or to the chairman should be sent to the tribunal office (r 27(*a*)). In the case of a detained patient the relevant tribunal is the tribunal responsible for the area in which the hospital is situated; in the case of a patient subject to guardianship, it is the tribunal responsible for the area in which the patient resides (s 77(3),(4)). (For the addresses of the tribunal offices see Appendix 7.)

9.2 Withdrawing an application

Rule 19(1) provides that a patient may withdraw his application at any stage of the proceedings, provided the request is made in writing and the tribunal agrees to the withdrawal. The chairman may agree to withdrawal on behalf of the tribunal (r 5). In practice, if a tribunal has been appointed, the decision to consent to withdrawal is left to the panel via the President. Withdrawals of s 2 applications are not accepted. The requirement that the tribunal consent to withdrawal reflects the important supervisory role of the tribunal in ensuring that patients' rights are not infringed. The tribunal will normally give its consent unless it considers that the request for withdrawal is the result of pressure on the applicant, or if it considers that an application is clearly in the patient's best interests.

Where an application is withdrawn, it is as if no application has been made; thus the applicant may apply again to the tribunal during the same period of entitlement (s 77(2)). Similarly, a withdrawn application is disregarded for the purposes of automatic references (ss 68(5), 71(6); *see* **7.5** for further discussion).

If a patient ceases to be liable to be detained or subject to guardianship in England and Wales, any application relating to the patient is deemed to be withdrawn (r 19(2)). Where an application is withdrawn or deemed to be withdrawn, the tribunal must inform the parties (r 19(3)).

The Department of Health Management Consultancy Unit

(*Review of the Mental Health Tribunal Secretariat*, January 1991, paras 3.32–3) observed that between April 1989 and March 1990 in the Nottingham and Liverpool office areas, somewhere between 30 and 40 per cent of all unrestricted applications failed to reach a hearing because either the patient withdrew or the RMO reclassified the patient as informal. In the London area, where it was reported that patients were visited by the legal member if they withdrew, some 50 per cent of patient inspired withdrawals were re-instated following the visit. This serves to re-emphasise the importance of some mechanism to ensure that patients are not pressured to withdraw. It may also be important to ensure that a patient who has been discharged from detention, but remains as an informal patient is genuinely willing to stay in hospital. Representatives should visit to ensure that withdrawal is really what the patient wants.

9.3 Appointment of the tribunal

The chairman of the tribunal must appoint the members of the tribunal to hear a particular case (r 8(1); *see also* **6.5**). An exception arises where the application belongs to a class or group of proceedings for which members have already been appointed (r 8(1)). This occurs in cases where the tribunal has previously been constituted; eg, the hearing of a postponed application, further consideration by a tribunal in cases where its recommendations have not been implemented, a further decision by a tribunal following a provisional decision and cases where the tribunal re-convenes following an adjournment. In such cases the tribunal will consist of those members who were originally appointed to hear the case.

In the case of restricted patients the persons qualified to serve as president of the tribunal are persons approved by the Lord Chancellor as having special experience of criminal cases; this includes circuit judges and recorders (r 8(3) and **6.6**).

A person cannot serve as a member of a tribunal if he has a personal connection with the patient or has recently given him medical treatment, or if he is a member or officer of the responsible authority, or any health authority which has a right to discharge the patient (r 8(2)(*a*),(*b*),(*c*)).

In *R v Oxford Mental Health Review Tribunal ex parte Mackman, The Times*, 2 June 1986 it was held that it was acceptable for the legal member of the tribunal to preside over more than one hearing involving the same patient; this ruling applies to the other members of the tribunal. The patient had argued that, as the legal member had heard a previous application from him, he was barred from doing so again.

The tribunal members who are to hear a particular case are normally appointed following receipt by the tribunal of the responsible authority's statement. Nevertheless the rules do not specify a particular time when the members must be appointed and thus they may be appointed immediately following receipt of the patient's application. Where the tribunal has not yet been appointed, certain powers may be exercised by the chairman (r 5; *see* **9.4** below).

9.4 Preliminary and incidental powers of the chairman

The chairman is empowered to exercise the following powers of the tribunal at any time prior to the hearing (r 5):

(1) to receive documents and to disclose them to the parties and representatives (rr 6, 10, 12);
(2) to give notice of the proceedings and the hearing to persons who are entitled to receive it (rr 7, 20);
(3) to make decisions regarding the postponement of a hearing (r 9) and withdrawal of an application (r 19);
(4) to call for further information and reports (r 15), subpoena a witness and take evidence on oath (r 14(1));
(5) to transfer the proceedings to another tribunal (r 17);
(6) to extend and abridge the time specified for performing a function under the Rules (r 26);
(7) to deal with any irregularities that arise (r 28).

This provision has two major purposes: first, it allows matters to be dealt with prior to the appointment of the tribunal and secondly, it eliminates the need for all the tribunal members to meet in order to perform any of the above functions.

Note that there is nothing in the rules which prevents the tribunal from meeting prior to the hearing in order to decide a preliminary issue such as the disclosure of documents or any other matter arising in relation to the application. Such pre-hearing reviews might, for example, be conducted in order to decide whether a request for a public hearing should be granted. The rights of the parties in relation to a pre-hearing review are not explicitly covered by the Rules. However, it is to be expected that all parties would have the opportunity of presenting evidence and views which are relevant to the preliminary matter to be decided. (Note that in the case of *R v Oxford MHRT, ex parte Royston*, unreported QBD 14 July 1983, it was ordered, by consent, that the tribunal must have regard to the Rules in determining the rights of the parties to attend at a preliminary review.)

9.5 Notice

There are three forms of notice that the tribunal is required to give.

9.5.1 Notice of the application (r 4)

On receiving an application the tribunal must give notice to the responsible authority, the patient (if he is not the applicant) and, in the case of a restricted patient, the Home Secretary (r 4(1)). Notice given under this provision serves two main purposes: first, it informs the recipients that an application in respect of the patient has been received and secondly, it requires the responsible authority and the Home Secretary to provide statements to the tribunal in accordance with r 6 (*see* **9.7** below).

9.5.2 Notice of the proceedings (r 7)

On receiving the statements from the responsible authority and the Home Secretary the tribunal must give notice of the proceedings to the following persons:

(1) where the patient is in a mental nursing home, the registration authority of the home, and any health authority which has the right to discharge him;
(2) where the patient is subject to the guardianship of someone other than the local authority, to that guardian;
(3) where the patient's affairs are under the Court of Protection, to that Court;
(4) the patient's nearest relative, unless he is the applicant;
(5) any other person who in the tribunal's opinion should have an opportunity of being heard.

The tribunal decides the persons to whom notice should be given under (5) above from the information provided in the statements of the responsible authority and the Home Secretary. This may not include close friends or other relatives of the patient if they have not been mentioned in the statements; the representative may draw to the tribunal's attention the names of such persons.

9.5.3 Notice of the hearing (r 20)

The tribunal must give at least 14 days' notice of the date, time and place of the hearing to all parties, their representatives and, in the case of a restricted patient, the Home Secretary; the period of notice may only be reduced if all the parties consent (rr 10(4), 20). If the Home Secretary has not been given notice, or adequate documentation and is consequently not represented, the proceedings will be invalidated; see *Campbell v Secretary of State for the Home Department* [1988] 1 AC 120, [1987] 3 WLR 522, [1987] 3 All ER 8 (HL) where the Home Secretary had not been informed in advance of the date of the tribunal hearing and had received the independent psychiatric report only on the very day of the hearing.

The following persons are parties to the proceedings: the applicant, the patient, the responsible authority, any person who has received notice of the proceedings in accordance with r 7 above and any person who is added as a party by direction of the tribunal (r 2). In practice, the tribunal is often willing to fix a date for the hearing which is convenient for the representative provided that this does not unreasonably delay the hearing of the application. The representative should inform the tribunal how long he considers the preparations in the case will take and what dates are inconvenient for him. It must always be borne in mind that the patient's interests are paramount, and his detention should not be prolonged to suit the convenience of the representative, the responsible authority, the tribunal or anyone else. The case should be determined as quickly as is consistent with the time necessary for a thorough review (*see* **10.5**, for further discussion).

9.6 Representation

Any party to the proceedings may be represented before the tribunal (r 10(1)); this means that the applicant, the patient (where he is not the applicant), the responsible authority and any other person who has received notice of the proceedings in accordance with the above is entitled to be represented. (Normally it is only the applicant or, in reference cases, the patient who is represented.) Note that assistance by way of representation (ABWOR) is available to the applicant and to the patient. Thus any other party who sought legal representation would need to meet the costs of representation himself; he may, however, be assisted under the green form provisions with extensions where necessary (*see* **12.3**). Unless otherwise stated references in this text to the representative are to a representative of the applicant or, in reference cases, the patient.

A representative may be any person except a patient liable to detention or a person subject to guardianship under the Act or any person who is receiving treatment for mental disorder at the same hospital or home as the patient (r 10(1)). The predominance of legal representation is largely due to the availability of financial assistance under the green form and ABWOR provisions. A representative must inform the tribunal of his authorisation as representative and of his postal address (r 10(2)); this is in addition to any information concerning his representation that the applicant may have given to the tribunal in his application (*see* **9.1** above). Failure by the representative to inform the tribunal would not prevent the representative from acting for someone but may cause administrative problems and delay the proceedings. Thus the representative is advised to inform the tribunal of his authorisation and his address as soon as he agrees to represent the client.

Where a patient does not want to conduct his own case and does not authorise a representative to act for him the tribunal may appoint someone to act for him as his representative (r 10(3)). The patient will normally state in his application to the tribunal whether he intends to be represented or to conduct his case himself (r 3(2); **9.1** above). A patient who initially intended to conduct his own case may, at any stage of the proceedings, change his mind and state his desire to be represented. In order to appoint someone to represent the patient it may be necessary for the tribunal to adjourn the proceedings (r 16; *see* **10.3**). A tribunal may appoint any representative whom it considers to be appropriate and may use The Law Society's panel of representatives for automatic references (*see* **11.3**) for this purpose. Two important points should be noted. First, the patient is not bound to accept the tribunal's appointee; thus, he may appoint someone of his own choosing or may decide to conduct his own case. Secondly, the tribunal is not under a *duty* to appoint a representative although it is empowered to do so. Where a patient has expressed clearly his desire to be represented and the tribunal does not appoint someone to represent him a claim under Art 5(4) of the European Convention on Human Rights may arise. The European Court has repeatedly emphasised the need for effective legal representation as part of the special procedural guarantees required in mental health cases (*Winterwerp's* case, judgment given 24 October 1979, paras 60–61, 101–102).

The tribunal must send the representative all notices and documents that the person he is representing is entitled to receive (r 10(4)). In addition any legal representative and certain other authorised representatives are entitled to receive any documents which the tribunal has decided not to disclose to the applicant or to the patient (r 12(3)); the representative is referred to **9.8** below for a detailed consideration of disclosure of information. Where a tribunal sends documents to a representative, the person he represents will be considered to have received those documents (r 10(5)). Thus the tribunal is not required to send another copy of the document to the person who is represented, and it is for the representative to inform the person he represents of their content. Note that this provision appears to apply only to documents sent to the representative and not to copies of notices; it follows that the tribunal must send copies of all notices to both the representative and the person he represents.

Rule 10(4) further authorises the representative to take all steps and do all things that the person he represents is entitled or required to do under the Rules.

In addition to a representative, the patient or any other party may be accompanied by any other person(s) unless the tribunal directs otherwise (r 10(6)). Such persons may wish to address the tribunal or simply to give the patient advice and support. This provision could cover the attendance of a 'Mackenzie man', ie, a person who does not represent the patient but assists him in presenting his case to the tribunal himself.

9.7 Information for the tribunal

The tribunal will have before it the following written information.

9.7.1 Statement by the responsible authority

The responsible authority is required to provide the tribunal with a statement in accordance with the following provisions in all cases apart from assessment applications (*see 11.1.3*) and applications in respect of conditionally discharged patients (*see 9.7.3* below). The responsible authority must send its statement to the tribunal within three weeks of receiving notice of the application; in the case of a restricted patient a copy of the statement must also be sent to the Home Secretary (r 6(1)).

The statement must contain the following information (r 6(1)).

(1) In so far as it is known to the responsible authority (Sched

1, Part A): the patient's name, age, date of admission to hospital or reception into guardianship and details of the original authority for detention or guardianship and subsequent renewals, legal category of mental disorder, name of the RMO and any other doctor in whose care the patient has recently been (eg, the patient's GP) and the periods spent under their care, dates of all previous tribunal hearings together with the decisions reached and the reasons for them (this does not include the advice given to the Home Secretary by tribunals in the cases of restricted patients in accordance with the 1959 Act), details of any receivership or Court of Protection proceedings, name and address of the person's nearest relative or any other person exercising that function and of any person who has a close interest in the patient and details of any leave of absence granted to the patient during the previous two years.

(2) An up-to-date medical report prepared for the tribunal. The report must include a relevant medical history and a full report on the patient's mental condition (Sched 1, Part B). Note that the report must be prepared specifically for the tribunal; generally, a tribunal should not accept a report which has been prepared for some other purpose unless it contains all the above information and was written after the patient's application to the tribunal was made. For example, a report from the patient's RMO to a local hospital consultant concerning the patient's suitability for transfer may be a suitable report for the tribunal provided it contains both a relevant medical history and a complete report on the patient's mental condition and it has been very recently compiled.

Normally the responsible authority asks the patient's RMO to provide the up-to-date medical report to the tribunal, and he writes a report specifically for this purpose. The content of medical reports is variable; for example, where a patient has previously applied to the tribunal the RMO may simply write an addendum to the medical report which was submitted to the tribunal in respect of the previous application. While it may be reasonable to refer to a previous account of the patient's medical history, details of the patient's medical treatment and progress since the previous report should be fully recorded and a full report on the patient's current mental condition made. It is not sufficient to record that the patient's condition is unchanged. The representative should draw to the tribunal's attention any failure by the RMO to provide a complete, thorough and relevant medical report. He may do this in pursuance of r 12(1) (*see 9.8.1* below). In **13.7** and **13.8** the representative is advised as to how he should examine the RMO's report and as to the means by which he may obtain further information on the patient's condition. The representative is also referred to **9.10** below, for powers of the tribunal to obtain further information.

It may be observed that the responsible authority is not required to comment on the patient's suitability for discharge or transfer in the medical report, and it is therefore possible for a medical report to consist solely of an objective account of the patient's medical history and mental condition.

(3) The following reports in so far as it is reasonably practicable to provide them (Sched 1, Part B):

(a) An up-to-date social circumstances report prepared for the tribunal including reports on the patient's home and family circumstances, attitude of his nearest relative, employment and occupation prospects, housing facilities if he were to be discharged, financial circumstances, community support and relevant medical facilities. Note that the responsible authority has an unqualified duty to provide a medical report but must only provide a social circumstances report in so far as it is reasonably practicable to do so. Circumstances in which it may be argued that it is not reasonably practicable to provide a full social circumstances report include cases where the patient has lost contact with family and friends; in this case it might be impracticable to report on the patient's home circumstances but a report on facilities available through the statutory authorities or voluntary bodies should be provided. A photocopied list of hostel facilities in the area will not be sufficient.

Note that the qualification 'in so far as it is reasonably practicable to provide them' did not apply to the duty to provide social circumstances information under the 1960 Rules nor was it included in the original draft of the 1983 Rules. Given the importance of such information the added qualification is regrettable, but it should not permit the responsible authority to produce an inadequate social circumstances report based on its own assessment of the patient's prospects of discharge; that is a decision for the tribunal to make. The representative should expect a full social circumstances report to be provided to the tribunal in most cases. The importance of social circumstances information and steps that may be taken to obtain further information are discussed in chapter 14.

It should be noted that where the nearest relative has made the application for the patient's admission for treatment, the hospital managers have a duty under s 14 of the Act to obtain from the responsible social services authority a report on the patient's social circumstances (*see 1.5.1*). This report should normally be made available by the hospital managers to the tribunal and may provide helpful information about the patient's home and social circumstances prior to admission, but since it does not directly address the issue of discharge, it cannot be regarded as a substitute for an up-to-date social circumstances report prepared specifically for the purposes of the tribunal.

(b) The responsible authority's views on the patient's suitability for discharge. As discussed above the RMO normally gives his opinion as to the patient's suitability for discharge or transfer in his medical report. It is very rare for the responsible authority to reach a different decision from the RMO on this issue.

(c) Any other information or observations on the application which the responsible authority wishes to make. It may submit reports from psychologists or other care professionals to the tribunal.

9.7.2 The Home Secretary's statement

In the case of restricted patients other than those who have been conditionally discharged, the Home Secretary must, within three weeks of receiving the responsible authority's statement, provide the tribunal with a further statement containing any further information which is relevant to the application (r 6(2)). The nature of this information is not specified in the Rules but may include medical reports from previous tribunal applications, medical and other reports to the sentencing court and recent reports from psychologists or other health professionals; reports of the Aarvold Board are considered to be confidential to the Home Secretary but the statement will draw attention to the Board's conclusions or main concerns (*see* **4.5**).

As the Home Secretary has a concurrent jurisdiction to discharge the patient, he may wish to give his opinion to the tribunal, and since his opinion as to the patient's suitability for discharge will be influential, it is essential that the representative obtains all the information and opinions given (formally or informally) to the tribunal by the Home Office; disclosure of such information to the representative is discussed in *9.8.2*.

9.7.3 Statement relating to conditionally discharged patients

In the case of an application by a conditionally discharged patient it is the Home Secretary and not the responsible authority who must provide the tribunal with the requisite information. This is because the patient is no longer subject to detention and hence not under the direct care of the responsible authority; any reports which have been made on the patient are available to the Home Secretary, who must, within six weeks of receiving notice of the application, provide the tribunal with a statement containing:

(1) the following information, in so far as it is known to the Home Secretary (r 6(3)(*a*), Sched 1, Part C): the patient's name, age, history of authority for detention and date of conditional discharge, details of offence, legal category of mental disorder, name and address of any doctor, social worker or probation officer who has been responsible for the patient's care and supervision in the community and the period which the patient has spent under the care of that person;
(2) the following reports in so far as it is reasonably practicable to provide them (r 6(3)(*b*), Sched 1, Part D):
    (a) if there is a doctor responsible for the patient's care, an up-to-date medical report;
    (b) if there is a social worker or probation officer responsible for the patient's care, an up-to-date report on his progress since discharge;
    (c) a report on the patient's home circumstances;
    (d) the Home Secretary's views on the patient's suitability for absolute discharge;
    (e) any other observations on the application.

Note that the Home Secretary must only provide the reports if it is reasonably practicable to do so. Since a tribunal's decision as to whether the patient should be absolutely discharged or whether the conditions of his discharge should be altered (*see* **7.7**) rests on the patient's progress since discharge, how he has coped in the community and the nature and extent of the medical and social support he has needed, the representative must ensure that the tribunal has this information before reaching a decision. When it is not provided in the Home Secretary's statement the representative should draw this fact to the tribunal's attention. The tribunal may adjourn the proceedings so that the Home Secretary can obtain the necessary reports or it may direct that the information is obtained in other ways which are discussed in **9.10** below. In view of the possible delays involved if there is an adjournment, it will often be prefereble to seek to have the absence of information dealt with as a preliminary issue, prior to the hearing (*see* **9.4**).

9.7.4 Case and nursing notes

The tribunal often has the case and nursing notes relating to the patient at the hearing; these are normally supplied to it by the hospital before the hearing begins, and usually contain reports by the patient's RMO, routine reports by the nursing staff, letters to other professionals such as the patient's GP, or to relatives, and reports by other health professionals such as social workers and psychologists.

The tribunal is not as such explicitly entitled under the Rules to obtain these notes although the medical member is, and he may take copies of them for the purposes of the application (r 11; *see* **9.9** below). The tribunal may, if necessary, subpoena the notes if the hospital refuses to provide them (r 14(1); *see 9.10.1* below). The question arises whether case and nursing notes are relevant information which must be disclosed to the parties. The opinion of the medical member seems to be part of the tribunal's deliberative process, and therefore not subject to the rule requiring disclosure. If an independent psychiatrist is appointed, he will have access to the case and nursing notes (*see* **9.9** and **13.7**).

9.7.5 Independent psychiatric report

The applicant may engage a psychiatrist to provide an independent report on his medical condition (*see 13.8.3*). An independent psychiatrist owes a duty of confidence to the patient (*W v Egdell* [1989] 2 WLR 689, [1989] 1 All ER 1089 (Ch D); [1990] 1 All ER 835 (CA)). However, this confidential duty is subject to the exception described by Sir Stephen Brown P. in *W v Egdell* (CA):

A consultant psychiatrist who becomes aware, even in the course of a confidential relationship, of information which leads him, in the exercise of what the court considers a sound professional judgment, to fear that such decisions may be made on the basis of inadequate information and with a real risk of consequent danger to the public, is entitled to take such steps as are reasonable in all the circumstances to communicate the grounds of his concern to the responsible authorities.

The doctor may disclose the information to the responsible authorities even where the patient has withdrawn his application (*see* **9.2** above). Independent psychiatric reports and the availability of finance under the Assistance by way of Representation scheme (ABWOR) are discussed further in *12.4.3* and *13.8.3*.

9.8 Disclosure of information

9.8.1 To the applicant

(In this head 'the applicant' includes the patient, even when he is not the applicant.)

Rule 6(4) authorises the responsible authority and the Home Secretary to set aside any part of their respective statements which they consider should not be disclosed to the applicant on the grounds that its disclosure 'would adversely affect the health or welfare of the patient or others'. Those parts of the statement should be made in a separate document which must contain the reasons for believing that disclosure would have that effect. It may be argued that it is seldom in a person's interests not to know information about himself which directly affects him, but sometimes there will be information which may reasonably be set aside under this provision, for example, a relative may oppose the patient's discharge but for valid reasons may not wish the patient to know. Facts about the patient's background and opinions about his treatment and prognosis should not normally be withheld unless there are clear and specific reasons for doing so; nor would it be proper for an entire report to be set aside under this provision. The reasons given by the responsible authority or the Home Secretary for non-disclosure should be specific; it is not sufficient to restate the statutory terms (eg, 'disclosure would adversely affect the patient's health') or to give non-specific reasons (such as 'disclosure would damage the doctor-patient relationship'). The tribunal must send the applicant a copy of the authority's statement excluding information which has been set aside under this provision (r 6(5)).

However the final decision as to whether documents should be disclosed to the applicant lies with the tribunal. Under r 12(1),(2) the tribunal must send a copy of every document it receives to the applicant; this includes not only the statements by the responsible authority and Home Secretary but also any other letter, statement or report which it has received but which is not part of the statements. Where information had previously been withheld from the applicant the tribunal must reconsider the issue and must release the withheld documents unless, in its view, disclosure would adversely affect the health or welfare of the patient or others. Thus the Rules require the tribunal to reach an *independent* decision as to the need to withhold information; it should not merely rubber stamp the opinion of the responsible authority or the Home Secretary. It is suggested that all information should be disclosed to the applicant unless there are clear and specific reasons for not doing so.

In practice the tribunal will not normally give consideration to the disclosure of information until the hearing itself, unless it is requested to do so beforehand by the applicant or his representative. If the applicant is not represented and information is not disclosed to him it will be extremely difficult for him to answer the case against him. In such a case there would be a question as to whether there was a breach of the tribunal's duty under domestic law to act judicially and further, whether there was a breach of Art 5 of the European Convention. If the applicant is represented then in most cases the representative will receive all the documents available to the tribunal but he cannot disclose to any person (including the applicant) any sections withheld by the tribunal. This may seriously inhibit a proper preparation of the case (*see 9.8.2* below for further information). Note that if the tribunal decides that information should not be disclosed to the applicant it must record its decision in writing but is not required to give reasons for it (r 12(2)).

Under r 12(1) the applicant may submit comments to the tribunal on any documents released to him; r 10(4) extends this provision to the representative (*see* **9.6.** above). This is a potentially useful provision which is little used. Research has indicated that the tribunal's decision is significantly influenced by the written information available to it before the hearing. The representative may bring to the tribunal's attention any issue relating to the disclosure of information, inaccuracies in the documents and key issues which have not been addressed, any further medical or after-care information which the tribunal should consider but which is not contained in the tribunal's documents, and factors which support the patient's case for discharge or transfer (see also chapters 13 and 14).

9.8.2 To the representative

The tribunal must disclose *in full* every document to the applicant's representative provided the representative is (r 12(1), (3)):

(1) a barrister or solicitor; or
(2) a doctor; or
(3) a person whom the tribunal considers to be suitable by virtue of his experience or professional qualification.

Representatives in category (3) might include Members of the Panel of MHRT representatives, recognised by the Law Society (*see* **11.3** below), social workers, psychologists and other health professionals, law centre and Citizens Advice Bureaux workers, members of community health councils or appropriate voluntary organisations such as the National Association for Mental Health (MIND) or the Royal Society for Mentally Handicapped Children and Adults (MENCAP) and persons with experience of representation before these or other tribunals. Hereinafter, representatives authorised in accordance with the above provisions are referred to as *authorised representatives;* this should not be confused with the same term which is used in the Rules to refer to *any* representative whom a person has authorised to act for him.

Where information which has been withheld from the applicant is released to the representative, he must not disclose it either directly or indirectly to the applicant or to any other person without the tribunal's permission (r 12(3)). Thus the representative cannot show the withheld information to the applicant or raise the contents with him in discussion. Not only may this damage the normal lawyer–client relationship but it may impede effective presentation of the case. The applicant may be aware that his representative is withholding information from him; this may increase his sense of injustice and diminish his confidence in his representative. Unless the applicant or any other person, without prompting from the authorised representative, makes statements concerning the matters contained in the withheld information the representative will be unable to check the accuracy of that information. The representative should scrutinise carefully the reasons given by the responsible authority or Home Secretary for non-disclosure. If important information cannot be disclosed to the applicant the representative should put the case for full disclosure to the tribunal; he should do so well before the hearing. Note that although the representative cannot disclose the information directly or indirectly, there is no reason why he cannot ascertain by non-leading discussion whether the information is already within the knowledge of the patient and to hear the patient's views on the matter.

Note that r 12(3) applies also to disclosure to *any other person*; this could include an independent psychiatrist or social worker. Thus, information which has been withheld from the applicant could not be disclosed to the independent expert without the tribunal's permission. It can be argued that an independent expert cannot reach an informed opinion without knowing all the relevant information; moreover, such persons may, in view of their professional ethics, be trusted not to divulge the withheld information to the applicant. It is expected that tribunals will usually permit disclosure to an independent expert. Material in an independent expert's report which contains or refers to information which has been withheld from the applicant should be presented to the representative in a separate section, otherwise the report may not be seen at all by the applicant. Usually, the remainder of the report may be disclosed to the applicant.

9.8.3 To the Secretary of State in a restricted case

In a case involving a restricted patient the Home Secretary is entitled to a copy of all relevant documents received by the tribunal (r 12(1)). Breach of this requirement will invalidate the proceedings; see *Campbell v Secretary of State for the Home Department* [1988] 1 AC 120.

9.9 Medical examination of the patient

The medical member of the panel is under a duty, prior to the hearing, to examine the patient and take any other steps which he considers necessary to form an opinion of the patient's mental condition; these may include examining the patient's medical records (r 11). In practice, the medical member examines the patient a few days before the hearing and presents his opinion to the other two members when they convene. Common practice appears to be for the President to ask the medical member before the hearing to give a description. This enables all the tribunal members to ensure that the information presented by the doctor is aired at the hearing. The medical member's opinion is considered as part of the deliberative process of the tribunal. This places him in a position where he is both a member of the decision-making panel, and expert witness. The problems to which this dual role can give rise were described in 1983 by the Council on Tribunals, which expressed its concern that the medical member is (*The Annual Report of the Council on Tribunals 1982–3*, (1983) HMSO para 3.22):

> effectively a witness and a member of the tribunal deciding the validity of his own evidence, and that the applicant should have an opportunity of knowing what evidence he has given and commenting on it. Under the present system a medical member examines an applicant before the hearing and then (generally in the course of the hearing) raises any material factors which in his view should be open for comment; he then advises the tribunal in private. While this is not ideal, it is probably the best that can be devised.

In *R v Mental Health Review Tribunal ex parte Clatworthy* [1985] 3 All ER 699, the tribunal preferred the view of its own medical member to the evidence of the RMO and the psychiatrist commissioned by the patient to give an independent report, who had both agreed that the patient was not suffering from psychopathic disorder within the meaning of the Act. Mann J said this (p 704):

> Where a tribunal desires to proceed on the basis of some point which has not been put before it and which on the face of the matter is not in dispute, it is in my view in the highest degree desirable that the person whose case is being considered by the tribunal should be alerted to the possibility ... Were it to be the case ... that this tribunal proceeded on some basis unknown to others but known to themselves, then I would have regarded that decision as flawed by reference to [the principle of natural justice which requires that a party should know the case against him].

The tribunal is entitled to rely upon the opinion of its own medical member in such a case only if the applicant or his representative is made aware of those views. If material evidence is contained in the medical member's report which is not apparent in any document made available to the parties, the report or its substance should be disclosed; see also *R v Mental Health Review Tribunal (Mersey Region) ex parte Davies* QBD 21 April 1986 (Unreported) CO/1723/85.

Note that under r 11 the medical member may also make notes from the medical records and take copies of them. Where the notes or copies of the records are submitted to the tribunal, the authorised representative is entitled under r 12(3) to receive copies of them.

They must also be disclosed to the applicant unless withheld by the tribunal under r 12(2).

9.10 Obtaining information

9.10.1 Evidence and subpoena

The tribunal may obtain information by taking evidence on oath, but this is rarely done; it may also subpoena any witness to appear before it or to produce documents. However, it cannot compel a person to give any evidence or produce any document which he could not be compelled to give or produce in a court (r 14(1)). Tribunals very seldom use these powers, but there may be circumstances where information cannot be obtained in any other way. For example, if the responsible authority fails to provide a complete statement the tribunal will normally try to obtain the missing information from the RMO at the hearing. Where there is reason to believe that the missing information will *significantly* affect the tribunal's decision, the representative may wish to assess it prior to the proceedings; he may then ask the tribunal to subpoena the information from the responsible authority. The representative of a restricted patient may wish to see documents concerning the patient which have been submitted to the Home Secretary but which have not been included in his statement, eg, the psychiatric reports supplied to the sentencing court, a psychologist's report, or the conclusions of the Aarvold Board (*see* **4.5**). Where the Home Secretary is unwilling to disclose this information it may be necessary for the tribunal to subpoena it. Nursing staff and other health professionals have considerable contact with the patient and may be able to report on his behaviour on the wards or on the details of a disputed incident; they may, however, be unwilling to appear before the tribunal. Where the representative believes that such an account or opinion materially affects the applicant's case he may ask the tribunal to subpoena the person concerned to appear before it (see further **10.8** below).

Tribunals have used supoenas to compel attendance of a Director of Social Services where no social worker had attended to give a social circumstances report.

The tribunal may consider as evidence any document or information even if it would be considered inadmissible in a court of law (r 14(2)). Thus it may consider hearsay evidence, opinions from non-professional witnesses and accounts of incidents from other patients. It will, of course, give appropriate weight to evidence according to its nature and source.

9.10.2 Further information

Under r 15(1) the tribunal has a wide discretion to call for any further reports or information and it may give directions as to how that information should be obtained and by whom. The tribunal may exercise this power before or during the hearing. If possible, the representative should make any request for additional information in advance of the hearing in order to reduce delays. For example, where a social circumstances report has not been included in the responsible authority's statement but a report on home circumstances or hostel facilities appears to be crucial to the case, the tribunal may ask the responsible authority or direct the relevant social services authority to provide it. The rules of disclosure of information discussed in **9.8** above apply to any further information obtained under this rule (r 15(2)). Alternatively, the tribunal may direct that the information be presented orally at the hearing.

9.10.3 Adjournment

The tribunal may adjourn a hearing at any time in order to obtain further information (r 16(1)); the power of adjournment is considered in **10.3**.

9.11 Postponement and the hearing of two or more applications at once

Where an application or reference is made in respect of a patient whose case has recently been considered by the tribunal, the tribunal may postpone the hearing, but the case must be considered within six months of the previous application or before the current period of detention ends, whichever is earlier (r 9(1)). It follows that where the patient's case had previously been determined upon a *reference* to the tribunal the six-month period does not apply, and the tribunal must consider the new application before the current period of detention ends.

The purpose of postponement is to allow a reasonable interval between hearings. The hearing can be postponed only if the tribunal is satisfied, after making appropriate inquiries of the applicant and (where he is not the applicant) the patient, that the patient's interests would be thus served (r 9(2)). If a patient's circumstances have significantly improved since his case was last considered by the tribunal or suitable accommodation has become available for him in the community, it could be argued that postponement would not be in his interests.

Where a tribunal postpones a hearing it must state its reasons in writing; it must also state the period for which the application is postponed. A copy of this statement must be sent to all parties and, in the case of a restricted patient, to the Home Secretary (r 9(4)). The tribunal must then give at least seven days' notice before the end of the period of postponement that the hearing is to proceed; such notice must be given to the responsible authority, the patient (where he is not the applicant) and, in the case of a restricted patient, the Home Secretary (r 9(5),(4)). Following receipt of this notice the responsible authority and the Home Secretary must provide the tribunal with the necessary reports in accordance with r 6 (*see* **9.7** above).

If a new application or a reference is made in respect of a patient while a postponed application is pending, the tribunal may consider it at the same time as the postponed one (r 9(6)). Similarly, where two or more applications in respect of a patient have been made (eg, where both the patient and his nearest relative have applied) the tribunal may consider them at the same time (r 18).

9.12 Circumstances where applications cannot be postponed (r 9(3))

(1) An application made following reclassification of the patient's mental disorder (s 66(1)(*d*);

(2) an application made following the first renewal of the authority for the patient's detention (s 66(1)(*f*)). The application may be postponed, however, if a previous application or reference was made in the three months prior to renewal;

(3) an application made by a nearest relative following the barring of his discharge order (s 66(1)(*g*));

(4) where the previous determination of the case by the tribunal was made before a break or change in the authority for the patient's detention or guardianship. A break or change in the authority for detention is deemed to have occurred, *inter alia*, on his admission to hospital for treatment (s 3) or under a hospital order without restrictions (s 37); on his reception into guardianship (ss 7, 37); or on the cessation of a restriction

order or direction (s 41(5); r 9(7)). For example, an application made by a patient admitted for treatment (s 3) could not be postponed if the previous determination was in relation to an application in respect to an admission for assessment (s 2).

Chapter 10

Hearing Procedures

10.1 Public and private hearings

Unless the patient requests otherwise, the tribunal sits in private. It must sit in public if the patient requests it and if it is satisfied that a public hearing would not be contrary to the patient's interests (r 21(1)). There is no provision specifying when a request for a public hearing should be submitted to the tribunal, so it may be made at any time before, or even during, the proceedings. The tribunal may wish to know the RMO's opinion as to whether a public hearing would be contrary to the patient's interests, and in the past some tribunals have conducted a pre-hearing inquiry to determine this. Therefore, to avoid the need for an adjournment it is advisable to submit a request for a public hearing at the earliest possible date. It should be noted that only the patient and not a nearest relative applicant is entitled to request a public hearing. Where a tribunal refuses a request for the public hearing it must record its reasons in writing and must inform the patient of them (r 21(2)). The reasons should be substantive and should not merely restate the statutory language. Note that the tribunal may decide that a hearing begun in public may continue in private; again, the tribunal must record its reasons and inform the patient of them (r 21(2)).

The representative should discuss with the patient the advantages and disadvantages of a public hearing. While a public hearing may mean that the tribunal is publicly accountable and the patient may feel more confidence in its procedures and its decision, against this must be weighed the fact that the information is of a highly personal nature, and may therefore be better discussed in private.

Technically, the difference between a public and a private hearing depends on how the tribunal exercises its discretion to admit and exclude people from the hearing. Under r 21(3) the tribunal may admit any person to a private hearing and may specify terms and conditions upon which that person is admitted. Rule 21(4) authorises the tribunal to exclude any person from *any* hearing, public or private. Normally, where a request for a public hearing is granted, it is presumed that any person and, in particular, members of the press will be allowed in to the hearing. The one person who cannot be excluded from *any* part of the proceedings, apart from a member of the Council on Tribunals, is the applicant's authorised representative (r 21(4)); the term 'authorised representative' in this context is defined in *9.8.2*.

Apart from these persons, the tribunal may exclude any other person or class of person from any part, or parts, of the hearing. Where the tribunal excludes the applicant or the patient or their representatives (it could only do so in the case of a representative who was not authorised (*see 9.8.2*)) or the responsible authority's representative (normally the RMO), it must inform them of its reasons and record them in writing (r 21(4)). Anyone else may be excluded without reasons being given.

It should be emphasised that in relation to both public and private hearings information about the proceedings and any persons concerned in them cannot be made public without the express permission of the tribunal (r 21(5)). This provision was the object of the ruling of the House of Lords in *Pickering v Liverpool Daily Post and Echo Newspapers plc and others* [1991] 1 All ER 622, where it was held that disclosure in breach of the rule did not give rise to an action for breach of statutory duty. For a discussion of this case and the rights of patients to protection against disclosures in the press of the information concerning proceedings before MHRTs *see* **10.8** below.

10.2 Conduct of the proceedings

The tribunal has a general discretion to conduct the proceedings in the manner that it considers suitable, bearing in mind the health and interests of the patient (r 22(1)). Rule 22 requires the tribunal to seek to avoid formality in its proceedings, the aim being to encourage the parties to discuss the case openly with a minimum of confrontation, but the procedures may be informal only to the extent that the following statutory rules permit. First, the tribunal president must explain at the beginning of the hearing the procedure to be followed by the tribunal (r 22(3)). At this point the representative may put to the tribunal his requests regarding the procedure, such as the presence throughout the proceedings of any particular person or the calling of a particular witness. Some tribunals invite the representative to give his views regarding the order of evidence, and the representative can always ask for such a discussion.

Secondly, although r 22(2) states only that the tribunal must interview the patient if he so requests and without the presence of any other person again if requested. In practice the tribunal always interviews the patient before reaching a decision irrespective of a specific request, unless the patient positively objects. This 'right' of private interview is separate from the right to give evidence under r 22(4). The tribunal should offer the patient the opportunity of such an interview, which is usually given after the other evidence has been heard. The representative will, of course, remain present. Where a case is referred automatically to the tribunal the patient may refuse to participate in the proceedings (*see* **7.9**).

Thirdly, unless they are excluded from the proceedings, the applicant, the patient (where he is not the applicant) and the responsible authority have the following rights (r 22(4)):

(1) to give evidence to the tribunal;
(2) to hear each other's evidence and to put questions to each other;
(3) to call witnesses and to question any witness or other person appearing before the tribunal.

If the applicant or patient is excluded from the hearing, his authorised representative is entitled to remain throughout the hearing (r 21(4)); *see* **10.1** above) and has the same rights with respect to the hearing as the person he represents (r 10(4); *see* **9.6**). Any other party or, with the tribunal's permission, any other person may appear at the hearing and take such part in the proceedings as the tribunal thinks proper (r 22(4)). However, they do not have specific rights with regard to giving and hearing evidence and calling and questioning witnesses as do the applicant, the patient, and the responsible authority.

Finally, after all the evidence has been given, the applicant and, where he is not the applicant, the patient have the opportunity to address the tribunal (r 22(5)). This allows the applicant or patient or his representative (r 10(4)) to sum up the case and to add any final points.

In addition to the tribunal's general discretion in conducting the proceedings it has a special discretion to give such directions as it thinks fit to ensure 'the speedy and just determination of the application' (r 13). It is debatable whether this provision allows the tribunal to take any further actions beyond those which it is already empowered to take under the Rules. This provision is discussed further in **10.5** below.

10.3 Adjournment

The tribunal may adjourn a hearing at any time and may do so in order to obtain further information or for such other reason as it thinks appropriate (r 16(1)), and will normally grant a request for adjournment by a representative if there are reasonable grounds for it. It may adjourn to permit the representative to consider information which had not been disclosed to him prior to the hearing; to obtain an independent opinion on the patient; for further reports from the responsible authority, the Home Secretary, a social services authority or other person or authority; to allow an important witness to attend the proceedings; to allow an unrepresented patient to instruct a representative of his own or of the tribunal's choosing; or to await the outcome of psychological or other tests.

In *R v Mental Health Review Tribunal ex parte Cleeland*, the Court had to determine whether a tribunal's refusal to adjourn the proceedings prevented the applicant from submitting evidence which would have materially affected the tribunal's decision. The applicant, who had been transferred from prison to a special hospital sought to call two prison doctors who would say that he was not suffering from mental illness. The doctors could not be located in time for the hearing and the tribunal refused to adjourn for this purpose. Popplewell J held that it was appropriate for the tribunal to refuse adjournment because even if the evidence sought had been available it would not have changed the tribunal's decision. The tribunal had accepted the applicant's contention that the doctors, if called, would have testified that they had examined the patient and had not found evidence of mental illness. Even if this evidence had been presented, the tribunal would not have discharged the patient.

The tribunal may grant an adjournment to obtain further information about the present mental health of the patient. Although the second limb of r 16 allows an adjournment for such other purposes as the tribunal may think necessary, it has no power to adjourn to give the patient an opportunity to improve or to see whether an improvement already made is sustained, (see *R v*

Nottingham Mental Health Review Tribunal ex parte Secretary of State for the Home Department, and *R v Northern Mental Health Review Tribunal ex parte Secretary of State for the Home Department*, (CA), *The Times*, 12 October 1988). The Court of Appeal held that the purpose of the power to adjourn was primarily for the purpose of obtaining information about the patient's current condition. Where the tribunal is satisfied that the criteria for discharge are not satisfied at the time of the hearing, it has no power to adjourn to give the patient an opportunity to improve. The Court held that it is the function of the Home Secretary and not the tribunal to monitor the condition of a restricted patient.

Before adjourning, the tribunal may give directions to ensure that the case is given prompt consideration (r 16(2)). Thus it may set a date for resuming the hearing, and it may direct that certain reports should be provided to it by a particular date. The hearing must be resumed if the applicant, the patient, where he is not the applicant, or the responsible authority requests it and the tribunal is satisfied that it is in the patient's interests to resume (r 16(3)). Upon receiving notice of the resumed proceedings or earlier if possible, the representative should ask the tribunal to disclose to him any documents which are relevant to the application but which have not been disclosed to him. Further, it may be argued that the rules relating to the disclosure of information (r 12) and procedures at the hearing (r 22) apply also to a hearing which is resumed under this provision.

In requesting an adjournment the representative should be aware of the emotional stress for the patient, especially if the delays are lengthy. Adjournments should therefore be avoided unless they are absolutely necessary. He should therefore ask the tribunal to resume the proceedings at the earliest possible date, and wherever possible, the date should be set prior to the adjournment.

10.4 The decision

The tribunal's decision is reached by a majority vote, the president having a second or casting vote where necessary (r 23(1)). The tribunal normally makes its decision in private directly after the hearing is concluded; in any case the decision *must* be made and communicated to the patient within seven days of the hearing (r 24(1); see below). The tribunal's decision and its reasons must be recorded in writing and signed by the tribunal president. Where the tribunal's decision rests upon whether the relevant statutory criteria are satisfied, it must state its reasons (r 23(2)). It is not sufficient for the tribunal to reiterate the statutory grounds, eg, 'it is necessary for the patient's health and safety that he should be detained'; the rules specifically require that the tribunal give substantive reasons for its decision.

In *Bone v Mental Health Review Tribunal* [1985] 3 All ER 330 it was ruled that they must be genuine reasons and not merely rehearsals of the statutory criteria. Nolan J held that this meant that the reasons given must be adequate and intelligible, and must reasonably be said to deal with the substantial points that have been raised; see per Megaw J in *Re Poyser and Mills's Arbitration* [1964] 2 QB 467 at 468. The overriding question was that enunciated by Donaldson P in *Alexander Machinery (Dudley) Ltd v Crabtree* ([1974] ICR 120 at 122) 'Is the tribunal providing both parties with the materials which will enable them to know that the tribunal has made no error of law in reaching its finding of fact?'

In *R v Mental Health Review Tribunal ex parte Clatworthy* [1985] 3 All ER 699 (at p 703) Mann J ruled that the reasons given by the tribunal were 'a bare traverse of a circumstance in which discharge could be contemplated' which did not reveal to the applicant why the contentions of the RMO and the psychiatrist who reported on the patient's behalf had not been accepted.

In *R v Mental Health Review Tribunal ex parte Pickering* [1986] 1 All ER 99 (at p 104) Forbes J said that when a tribunal gives reasons 'one must somehow be able to read from the reasons the issue to which the reasons are directed.'

The decision may be given immediately after the hearing. In s 2 cases the decision should always be given at the end of the hearing. In any case the tribunal's written decision together with the reasons for it must be sent to all the parties within seven days of the hearing (r 24(1)). An exception may be made in cases where the tribunal considers that full disclosure would adversely affect the health or welfare of the patient or others. In such cases the tribunal may communicate its decision to the patient in any other appropriate manner (r 24(2)). For example, the tribunal may ask the patient's RMO to inform the patient of its decision; or it may send the patient a copy of its decision but may withhold some or all the reasons for it. A patient's authorised representative must receive the full recorded reasons for the decision, but the tribunal may require him not to disclose some of those reasons to the patient (r 24(2)). Although the tribunal is not required to give reasons for withholding its decision or the reasons for it from the patient, the representative should question any requirement as to non-disclosure if it is made routinely or if there is no apparent reason to believe that the patient would be adversely affected by disclosure. Non-disclosure could adversely affect a patient's confidence in the tribunal.

10.4.1 Decisions with recommendations

There appear to be two inconsistencies in the legislation relating to decisions with recommendations. First, a decision with recommendations is a decision in accordance with s 72(3)(*a*) of the Act (r 2), which does not apply to restricted patients (s 72(7)). Nevertheless, r 25(2), which relates to further consideration of a case in the event that a recommendation is not complied with, explicitly applies to restricted patients; accordingly, the rule may be *ultra vires*. This view is reinforced by the decisions in *Grant v Mental Health Review Tribunal* and *R v Mental Health Review Tribunal ex parte O'Hara, The Times*, 28 April 1986; *see also 8.5.4*.

Secondly, s 72(3)(*b*) of the Act appears to give the tribunal *discretion* to consider a case further, whilst r 24(4) implies that there is a *duty* to do so in the event that the recommendation is not complied with. (On a different reading of s 72(3)(*b*), there is no inconsistency with r 24(4): s 72(3) states that if a tribunal does not make a direction for discharge it may make a recommendation and, it could be argued, once it has made a recommendation, it is to consider the case further in the event that the recommendation is not complied with.) The duty to consider the case further implied by r 24(4) represents a more constructive approach from the patient's perspective. However, the *Grant* ruling has made these questions largely academic. The most likely situation where a tribunal would wish to make a recommendation is where they consider that a patient should be transferred from a special hospital to a local hospital or Regional Secure Unit. A significant number of special hospital patients are subject to restrictions. Yet in restriction order cases tribunals have no power to make recommendations which they can back up by exercising a legal power to reconvene the hearing in the event that the recommendation is not complied with. Nevertheless, the power to make recommendations remains important for non-restricted patients in special hospitals and elsewhere. The tribunal may recommend transfer into guardianship, transfer from a RSU to a local hospital, or that leave of absence is granted.

Where the tribunal makes a decision with recommendations, which may only be done under s 72(3) when the patient is not subject to restrictions, a period must be specified at the end of which the tribunal will consider the case further if its recommendations have not been complied with (r 24(4)). At the end of the specified period the tribunal must make appropriate enquiries of the responsible authority to discover whether its recommendation has been complied with (r 25(2)). This may not always be readily apparent. Where a tribunal has recommended that a patient should be transferred from a special to a local hospital and the recommendation is opposed by the patient's RMO, it will be apparent if the recommendation has not been acted upon, but the position will be less clear where the transfer has been accepted in principle but is dependent on the agreement of a local hospital consultant to accept the patient. In the latter case the tribunal may extend the period for further consideration of the case (r 26(2)) in order to allow more time to obtain the local consultant's consent. If, after the extended period, the patient has not been transferred the tribunal will probably regard this as non-compliance with its recommendations and thus must reconsider the case.

In order to consider a case further the tribunal must give all the parties at least 14 days' notice of the date, time and place fixed for the hearing (r 25(2)).

Note that the tribunal is not obliged to reconvene the proceedings: it is possible for it to form a further view of the patient's case without hearing any further submissions (r 25(1)). This may have important implications for the patient, and it will be in the patient's interests that the proceedings be reconvened and that he be given the opportunity to make further submissions. There are three main reasons for this. First, the tribunal will base its further consideration of the case on information which was available to it at the initial proceedings. If there is a significant interval between the initial hearing and the tribunal's further consideration, the information available to the tribunal may be out of date. Secondly, without further submission by, or on behalf of, the patient, there may be less impetus for the tribunal to search for a positive solution. Thirdly, the tribunal will have had some communication with the responsible authority concerning the fate of its recommendation, but none with the patient. Even this informal communication may influence any further consideration given to the case. The representative is therefore advised to ask the tribunal to reconvene the proceedings in the event that its recommendation is not complied with and to ask the tribunal to require the attendance of a representative of the responsible authority(ies) to explain why the recommendation has not been implemented.

Although it is not explicitly stated in the Rules, it may be argued that the rights of the applicant and the representative regarding disclosure of any new information and the procedures to be followed at the hearing (*see 9.8.2,* and **10.2** above) apply to proceedings reconvened under this provision.

10.4.2 Provisional decisions

The term provisional decision is defined in r 2. It includes a deferred direction for conditional discharge (s 73(7)) (*see 8.5.2*), and, in the case of a patient subject to a restriction direction, notification to the Home Secretary that the patient would be entitled to absolute or conditional discharge. A decision to notify the Home Secretary in respect of a patient subject to a restriction *direction* is provisional in the sense that the decision cannot take effect until the Home Secretary gives his consent. A decision to defer conditional discharge of a restriction *order* patient is provisional in the sense that the tribunal has decided that the patient is entitled to conditional discharge provided that the conditions which the tribunal wishes to impose can be met. The decision will not be given final effect until the necessary practical arrangements have been made, such as hostel placement and the identification of a supervising psychiatrist, which will enable the patient to comply with the conditions.

Where a tribunal has made a provisional decision it may make any further decision without holding a hearing (r 25(1)). In *Campbell v Secretary of State for the Home Department*, [1988] 1 AC 120 at pp 127–128, Lord Bridge said that:

> when the tribunal have deferred a decision for the conditional discharge of the patient, the words of subsection (7) which reserve to the tribunal the further decision as to whether 'the necessary arrangements have been made to their satisfaction' are wholly inapt to indicate a deferment of the decision as to whether the tribunal can be satisfied, as required by subsection (2) of the matters on which a decision in favour of conditional discharge depends.

The tribunal cannot therefore use a reconvened hearing directly to re-open the question of the patient's suitability for discharge. However, Lord Bridge (at p 128) suggested that they might do so indirectly by expressing themselves dissatisfied with the arrangements that have been made, or that the Secretary of State should refer the case under s 71 where a deterioration in the patient's condition is brought to his attention.

Lord Bridge also criticised the tribunal in *Campbell* for deferring the conditional discharge to a fixed date when the hearing would be reconvened. He said, in an *obiter* passage, that:

> The decision should simply indicate that the direction is deferred until the necessary arrangements have been made to the satisfaction of the tribunal and specify what arrangements are required, which can normally be done, no doubt, simply by reference to the conditions to be imposed. Whoever is responsible for making the arrangements should then proceed with all reasonable expedition to do so and should bring the matter to the attention of the tribunal as soon as practicable after it is thought that satisfactory arrangements have been made. Pursuant to rule 25 the tribunal may then decide that the arrangements are to their satisfaction without a further hearing.

This is likely to prove a recipe for drift, since there is no provision for keeping the tribunal informed of the progress of after-care arrangements. Thus, unless the tribunal adopts its own monitoring system or the responsible authority undertakes to keep the tribunal informed, it is conceivable that the case will be forgotten. The representative is therefore advised to ask the tribunal at regular intervals for information concerning the patient's aftercare. If, after a reasonable period, the patient has not been conditionally discharged or his discharge does not appear likely in the foreseeable future, the representative should ask the tribunal to reconvene the proceedings so that he may put further submissions to it.

The power to direct deferred discharge can be particularly useful in non-restricted cases, especially where the tribunal considers that detention would not be necessary if adequate professional support and other facilities were available. The discharge can be deferred until the relevant arrangements have been made.

10.5 Expediting the proceedings

The tribunal has a general duty to ensure that an application is determined speedily, and that the administrative procedures cause minimal delay. Accordingly the tribunal has a number of powers by which it may expedite the proceedings:

(1) the tribunal may reduce the intervals at which the responsible authority and, in the case of a restricted patient, the Home Secretary, send their statements. It may not, however, reduce

any period of notice of proceedings required under the Rules (r 26(2)) unless the parties consent (rr 16(4), 20, 25(2)).

(2) the tribunal has a general power to give any direction to ensure the speedy and just determination of the application (r 13). Such directions may be given before, during or after the hearing.

In *Van der Leer v The Netherlands* (1990) 12 EHRR 567, the European Court of Human Rights pronounced upon the requirement in Art 5(4) of the Convention on Human Rights that 'everyone ... shall be entitled to take proceedings by which the lawfulness of his detention shall be decided *speedily* by a court.' The delay in question had been five months from the institution of the proceedings until the court's decision, and the Court held that this was an excessive lapse of time. In *Barclay Maguire v United Kingdom* (App No 9117/80, admissibility decision 9 December 1981) the applicant complained that a delay of 18 weeks was a breach of Art 5(4). The UK government, seeking a settlement from the Commission, suggested 13 weeks as a reasonable target figure. This case was withdrawn following the introduction of r 13 which gives the tribunal the power to 'make such directions as it thinks fit to ensure the speedy and just determination of the application.' However, with the advent under the 1983 Act of entitlement to MHRT hearings for patients admitted for 28 days for assessment, the introduction of a power to direct discharge of restricted patients, the halving of the duration of periods of detention of patients admitted for treatment or under hospital orders, and provision for automatic references, there has been a dramatic increase in tribunal case load.

In 1986 the Council on Tribunals reported a case of delay referred to them by the Mental Health Act Commission where, due to difficulties in securing the services of a judge president, a MHRT hearing originally listed for November 1985 did not take place until May 1986 over a year after the patient's original application, (*Annual Report of the Council on Tribunals 1985–6*), (1986) HMSO, paras 4.27–4.30). In 1988, the Council Annual Report contains a trenchant reference to the problem and expresses its firm opinion that this is largely due to understaffing in the MHRT offices (*Annual Report of the Council on Tribunals 1987–8*, (1988) HMSO, paras 4.5–4.9):

Last year ... we reported that average waiting times ... were between 12 and 19 weeks for non-restricted cases and between 16 and 26 weeks for restricted cases. In June 1988 the average periods for delay were 16 weeks for (non-restricted) patients and 24 weeks for (restricted) patients. This means that a patient challenging the first 6 months of his confinement for treatment under section 3 might have to wait 4 months from the time he made his application. Restricted patients, who have the right to challenge the second 6 months of their confinement and thereafter every 12 months, might have to wait 6 months for their appeal to be determined. We regard this as wholly unacceptable. Parliament has decided that patients should be able to challenge their detention regularly, yet delays of this kind can render their rights almost nugatory.

The Council recorded that it had agreed with the Department of Health and the MHRT Chairmen that hearings for non-restricted patients should be held within eight weeks and restricted cases within 12 weeks, and urged that satisfactory staffing levels be provided to attain these targets. In the 1990 Report, the Council remained concerned that the efforts of the Department of Health had failed to achieve any appreciable reduction in delays (*Annual Report of the Council on Tribunals* (1989–90) (1990) HL 64, para 2.72).

As to causes of these delays, evidence suggests that they include staffing levels, lack of judge time in restricted cases, and, in all categories of case, late submission of the RMO's report. Rule 6 of the Mental Health Review Tribunal Rules places a duty on the responsible authority to send a statement, including the RMO's report to the tribunal as soon as practicable, and in any case within three weeks of receipt of the notice of application. No mechanism is provided expressly to enforce this duty, but r 13 provides that the tribunal may give such directions as it thinks fit to ensure the speedy and just determination of the application. This broad power, which appears to have been sparingly used by tribunals, must include directing doctors who are late in submitting reports to do so forthwith. It is submitted that if greater use of this power were made by tribunals, although in the short term it might increase the workload on tribunal staff, in the long term it would have an important effect on a significant source of delay. The latest report of the Council on Tribunals gives the results of a monitoring exercise by the Department of Health (*Annual Report of the Council on Tribunals* (1990–91) (1991) HL 97 para 3.60). It also targeted late RMO reports as a significant source of delay and called upon the Department of Health to develop a strategy to speed these reports up (paras 3.62–3.65).

If the reports are not submitted, the tribunal should be asked to consider using its power of subpoena under r 14. Since the ruling in *Pickering v Liverpool Daily Post and Echo Newspapers plc and others* [1991] 1 All ER 622 it is clear that the tribunals are 'courts' for the purposes of the law of contempt and, although proceedings for contempt should be viewed as a last resort, in a bad case consideration might be given to this course. For further discussion of the law of contempt as it affects MHRTs, *see* **10.8** below. An alternative, in an extreme case where a professional person persistently causes delay by breaking an obligation to provide a report or take any other step required by the rules in relation to MHRT proceedings, would be to consider reporting him to his professional disciplinary body or to be chairman of the District, Regional or Special Hospitals Service Authority.

10.6 Transfer of proceedings

Where the tribunal members appointed to hear a case have not disposed of it and the chairman considers that it is not practicable for them to do so or that it would involve unreasonable delay, he may arrange for other members to complete the case (r 17(1)). This situation may arise if a case is adjourned or where further consideration is given to a case following a provisional decision or a decision with recommendations.

If the patient moves from the jurisdiction of one tribunal to that of another while tribunal proceedings are pending, the chairman of the first tribunal may direct that the proceedings are transferred to the jurisdiction of the second tribunal; notice of the transfer of proceedings must be given to all the parties and, in the case of a restricted patient, to the Home Secretary (r 17(2)). This may occur if a patient is transferred from a special to a local hospital or from one hospital to another. It will usually be necessary for a patient to instruct a new representative.

10.7 Irregularities

An irregularity arising from failure to comply with the rules does not necessarily render the proceedings void (r 28). Where the tribunal considers that a person has been prejudiced it *must* take steps to cure the irregularity before reaching a decision. In *Campbell v Secretary of State for the Home Department* [1988] 1 AC 120, the tribunal considered that it could remedy a failure to give notice to the Home Secretary of the hearing, in consequence of which he did not appear, and a provisional decision to direct deferred conditional discharge was made. Woolf J at first instance held that since the decision was only provisional, the defect could be cured at a reconvened hearing under r 28 where the Secretary of State could make submissions. The Court of Appeal and the House of Lords held that a decision to defer conditional discharge until suitable arrangements had been made was nevertheless a decision, and r 28 could not be used after a decision had been made, especially since the defect was a fundamental breach of the rules of natural justice.

Where an irregularity is remediable under r 28, the tribunal may right it even if it does not appear that anyone has been adversely affected. The tribunal may take any step that it considers necessary, including amending a document, giving notice of an application or of proceedings and even reconvening the hearing if necessary. Failure to correct an irregularity will constitute grounds for judicial review or an appeal by case stated.

10.8 Contempt

The tribunal has no powers itself to deal with the contempt of its proceedings, eg, failure of the responsible authority or of the Home Secretary to provide the requisite reports during the specified intervals, failure of an authority or a person to obey a time direction under r 13, refusal by someone to attend the proceedings following a direction by the tribunal to this effect, disclosure of a document to the applicant or patient or to another person without the tribunal's permission. For an example of the Home Secretary being held in contempt, see *M v Home Office and another*, *The Times*, 2 December 1991.

The High Court has a residual discretion to protect inferior courts and tribunals and can punish contemnors as if they were in contempt of court (*R v Daily Herald* [1932] 2 KB 402; Borrie and Lowe *Law of Contempt* (2nd edn), 333 *et seq*; Miller, *Contempt of Court* (2nd edn), 65 *et seq*; HWR Wade, *Administrative Law* (6th edn) 1988, pp 929–30). However, a tribunal will qualify for the protection of the High Court through the law of contempt only if it has the status of a court; see *Attorney-General v BBC* [1981] AC 303 (HL). In *Pickering v Liverpool Daily Post and Echo Newspapers plc and others* [1991] 1 All ER 622, the House of Lords held that MHRTs were courts to which the law of contempt applied, and that a MHRT is, in the words of s 19 of the Contempt of Court Act 1981, 'a tribunal . . . exercising the judicial power of the state'.

Pickering had applied for an injunction restraining the defendants from publishing any information about his application to a MHRT. He relied on r 21(5) of the Rules which states that:

> Except in so far as the tribunal may direct, information about proceedings before the tribunal and the names of any persons concerned in the proceedings shall not be made public.

The House of Lords held (per Lord Bridge at p 631f–j) that the function of r 21(5) is to ensure that the protection given by the law of contempt to the proceedings generally applies to the subject matter of the hearing before the tribunal, except in so far as the tribunal may direct to the contrary. However, r 21(5) did not give rise to an action for breach of statutory duty in respect of unauthorised publication of information about the proceedings. The House of Lords ruled that it was permissible to publish the fact that an application or reference to the tribunal had been made, the fact that the tribunal would sit, had sat, or was sitting at a certain date, time or place, and any direction made by the tribunal that the patient be absolutely or conditionally discharged. It was not permissible to publish the recorded reasons for the tribunal's decision to the extent that they disclosed the evidential or other material on which it was based, nor was it lawful to publish any conditions attached to the patient's discharge (*Pickering v Liverpool Daily Post and Echo Newspapers plc and others* [1991] 1 All ER 622, 635–6). The House of Lords left open the question of whether the plaintiff would have been entitled to an injunction without the intervention of the Attorney General had the newspapers been seeking to publish protected information such as part of the evidence before the tribunal.

The ruling that MHRTs are courts for the purposes of the law of contempt means that it is open to a party to the proceedings to apply for the committal of any party who is in contempt of the tribunal under RSC Ord 52. Order 52 r 1(2) provides that 'Where contempt of court—(a) is committed in connection with ... proceedings in an inferior court ... then an order of committal may be made only by a Divisional Court of the Queen's Bench Division'. An application for leave to apply for committal must be made *ex parte* to a Divisional Court (RSC Ord 52, r 2(2)) and the Court hearing an application for an order of committal may sit in private where the application arises out of proceedings relating to a person suffering, or appearing to be suffering, from mental disorder within the meaning of the Mental Health Act 1983 (RSC Ord 52, r 6(1)(*a*)). Apart from the power to imprison for contempt there is jurisdiction to fine or take security for good behaviour. It should be remembered that it is a general principle that process by way of contempt should not be lightly employed and not in aid of a civil remedy where some other method of achieving justice is available (*Danchevsky v Danchevsky* [1974] 3 All ER 933).

10.9 Case stated and judicial review

Section 78(8) of the Act provides that a tribunal may, and if so required by the High Court, must state in the form of a special case for determination by the High Court any question of law which may arise before them. This provision entitles the representative to ask the tribunal to state a case for determination by the High Court. The court will not review findings of fact, save if no reasonable tribunal on the evidence before them could have come to the same conclusion. The court is only entitled to review matters of law which were decided by the tribunal in the course of its proceedings or judgment.

The question of law must have been brought to the attention of the tribunal. Thus the representative should make his claim early, eg, to see a particular document or as to a procedure affecting the fairness of the tribunal proceedings, by referring to the rule of law or procedure relied upon.

Order 56 of the Rules of the Supreme Court, rr 7–12, and Ord 94, r 11 set out a general code of procedure for applications for orders to state a case. The steps are:

(1) a written request must be made to the tribunal by any party to the proceedings (see Definition section) within 21 days after the decision of the tribunal was communicated to him (Ord 94, r 11(3)). The request must specify the question of law to be determined by the High Court;

(2) if the request is refused or the tribunal fails to comply within 21 days of the request being made, application must be made within 14 days after receipt of the notice of refusal or, where the tribunal simply failed to comply, within 14 days of the expiry of the 21 days allowed to the tribunal to reply (Ord 94, r 11(4)). Application is by originating motion in the Queen's Bench Division of the High Court, to be served on the tribunal and every party to the tribunal proceedings (see Definition section). The notice of motion must state the grounds of the application, the question of law, and any

reasons given by the tribunal for its refusal to state a case (Ord 56, r 8);

(3) a High Court judge will hear the application. There is no precedent indicating the principles which will govern the exercise of the power to order a case to be stated. Probably an arguable case needs to be shown, as in applications for leave to apply for judicial review;

(4) if the tribunal agrees or is ordered to state a case, then within 14 days after the case is served, the proceedings must be started before the court by originating motion. The notice of motion must set out the applicant's contentions on the question of law concerned (Ord 56, r 10);

(5) the MHRT is entitled to appear and be heard in the proceedings (Ord 94, r 11(5));

(6) if the court is of the opinion that any decision of the MHRT on the question of law raised was erroneous, the Court may give any direction which the tribunal ought to have given under Part V of the Act.

In practice the tendency since the 1983 Act has been for those aggrieved by a MHRT decision to seek judicial review, and applications for judicial review outnumber appeals by case stated. Since the passage of the 1983 Act, there have been four appeals by case stated, and more than 20 reported applications for judicial review. The explanation for this can be found in *Bone v Mental Health Review Tribunal* [1985] 3 All ER 330 at p 334b, where Nolan J ruled that a MHRT is under a duty to give reasons for its decision, whether that decision is in favour of or against discharge. He said this.

> If any further such case is to be brought before the court, an application for judicial review should be considered as an alternative to a case stated under s 78(8). I say this not only because the judicial review procedure allows a broader consideration of the issues, but also because it offers a more comprehensive range of reliefs. Here my powers, apart from answering the question as I have done, are limited by RSC Ord 94, r 11(6) to giving any direction which the tribunal ought to have given under Part V of the Mental Health Act 1983. No such direction could appropriately be made in the circumstances of the present case.

Nolan J found himself in a difficult position. The point had been decided in favour of the applicant, who was a restricted patient, on the procedural ground that inadequate reasons had been given. A direction in the applicant's favour would have been a direction to discharge, which might have posed a risk to the public. In *Bone*,

Nolan J *suggested* that the case be reheard before a differently constituted tribunal, a course which he could have *directed* had the proceedings been by way of judicial review. Since then, judicial review has been the most frequently used means of redress.

The procedure for applying for judicial review is governed by RSC Ord 53. Leave is required. An application for leave is normally made *ex parte*, and must be made within three months of the tribunal decision. The application is on Form 86A giving the name and description of the applicant, the relief sought, and the grounds for the application, and is supported by an affidavit. Where leave is granted, the Notice of Motion, a copy of the Form 86A, and the affidavit are served on the tribunal. The tribunal then has 56 days within which to file in the Crown Office and serve on the applicant an affidavit in reply. In *R v Lancashire County Council ex parte Huddlestone* [1986] 2 All ER 941 (per Parker LJ at p 947) it was held that whilst the granting of leave did not entitle an applicant to embark on a fishing expedition for grounds of review, when challenged, an authority or tribunal 'should set out fully what they did and why, so far as is necessary, fully and fairly to meet the challenge.' The application then proceeds to a hearing unless it is conceded or withdrawn.

One of the difficulties facing an applicant for judicial review is that he may become entitled to make a fresh application to the tribunal before his application for leave to seek judicial review is heard. In some such cases the High Court has refused to grant leave, even though it might be some time before the case is heard by a tribunal (*see* **10.5** above, and the unpublished outline of a talk by Diana Babar (Treasury Solicitor's Department) to London MHRT legal members 6 November 1991).

Chapter 11
Section 2 Hearings and References

11.1 Assessment applications

The proceedings in relation to s 2 tribunals are governed by rr 30–33 inclusive. In general terms the differences between the proceedings in s 2 tribunals and those in other applications as discussed in the previous two chapters relate to the need to expedite the proceedings. The procedural modifications applying to s 2 tribunals are considered below.

11.1.1 Applying to the tribunal

The patient or someone authorised by him (including a representative) may apply to the tribunal; the application must be made in writing and signed by the patient or the person authorised by him (r 30(1)). The application must indicate that it concerns a patient admitted for assessment and wherever possible should contain the following information:

(1) the patient's name;
(2) the address of the hospital or home where he is detained;
(3) the name and address of the patient's nearest relative and his relationship to the patient;
(4) the name and address of any representative authorised by the patient, or, if he has not yet authorised one, whether he intends to do so or wishes to conduct his own case.

As with other applications, failure to provide this information does not invalidate the application (*see* **9.1**); if any of the information is not included in the application it must be provided as far as is practicable by the responsible authority at the tribunal's request (r 30(3)).

A patient who is detained for assessment should apply to the tribunal as early as possible after admission (he is eligible to apply at any time during the first 14 days of admission (*see* **7.2**)). Although, as will be seen below, the proceedings are very much expedited, there may nevertheless be ten days between receipt by the tribunal of the application and its decision. A patient who applies to the tribunal immediately after the order is made and who subsequently changes his mind may withdraw his application in the same way as patients detained under any other section of the Act, and does not lose his right to re-apply to the tribunal (rr 33, 19; s 77(2)); he must, however, do so within 14 days of admission.

11.1.2 Appointment of the tribunal, hearing date and notice

It may be recalled that, for other applications, there is no specified maximum period within which the case must be determined, although the tribunal is required to conduct the proceedings speedily (*see* **9.5**). With s 2 tribunals the date of the hearing must be no later than seven days from the date on which the application was received by the tribunal (r 31(*a*)). The date must be fixed by the tribunal when it receives the application.

Rules 4, 7 and 20 relating to notice of the application, proceedings and hearing do not apply to assessment applications. On receipt of an application from a patient detained for assessment the tribunal must give notice to the patient of the date, time and place fixed for the hearing (r 31(*b*)). The tribunal must also give notice to the responsible authority, the nearest relative where practicable and any other person who the tribunal considers should have an opportunity of being heard (r 31(*c*)). The representative may inform the tribunal of any person who he considers should have an opportunity of being heard and accordingly to whom notice should be given; alternatively, he may ask that person to attend the proceedings as a witness.

On receiving the application the tribunal must appoint the tribunal members to hear the case in accordance with r 8 (r 31); this is discussed in **9.3**.

Since the hearing date must be fixed within seven days of receipt of the application (r 31(*a*)) it will not normally be possible to allow the representative further preparation time. Although it is extremely rare to do so the tribunal may, if necessary, adjourn to allow further preparation by the representative (r 33(*b*); *see 11.1.4* below).

11.1.3 Information for the tribunal, and disclosure

On receiving notice of the application or upon request from the tribunal, whichever is earlier, the responsible authority must provide for the tribunal the following information (r 32(1)):

(1) Copies of the admission papers. The admission papers consist of an application made by an approved social worker or the patient's nearest relative (Form 1 or 2), two medical recommendations or a joint medical recommendation (Form 3 or 4), a record of admission made by the hospital managers (Form 14) and a record of receipt of the medical recommendations (Form 15). Copies of the appropriate forms are in the Mental Health (Hospital, Guardianship and Consent to Treatment) Regulations 1983 (SI No 893). The representative should pay particular attention to the following information: the legal category of disorder from which the patient is suffering, the reasons why the patient should be detained and why informal admission was not appropriate.

(2) The information specified in Sched 1 Part A of the Rules *as is within the knowledge of the responsible authority*. This information was discussed in *9.7.1* in relation to other applications.

(3) Such of the reports specified in Sched 1 Part B of the Rules *as can reasonably be provided in the time available*. These reports, which were discussed in *9.7.1*, include an up-to-date medical report and a social circumstances report. However, unlike other applications, an up-to-date medical report need not be submitted and the tribunal may determine the case without it. Where it appears to the representative, on the basis of the information available to him that the patient's condition has significantly improved, he should bring this to the attention of the tribunal and if necessary, ask the tribunal to adjourn so that a responsible medical officer's report or an independent psychiatric report may be obtained.

Note that, in cases where the nearest relative has made the application for the patient's admission, the hospital managers have a duty under s 14 of the Act to obtain from the responsible social services authority, as soon as is practicable, a report on the patient's social circumstances (*see 1.5.1*). This report should be provided to the tribunal if it is available; where the report is not provided in circumstances where it should reasonably have been available, the representative should bring this to the tribunal's attention.

It is apparent that the information submitted to the tribunal in a s 2 case may be minimal, although in practice tribunals do expect within reports and the presence of the relevant professionals. Nevertheless, reports are often handed to the representative on the day of the hearing. It is therefore important to attend early to give sufficient time to discuss them with the patient. Therefore, to ensure that the tribunal's decision is made on the basis of as much of the relevant information as possible, and because of the need for speed in these proceedings, the representative may make more than usual use of oral evidence; eg, where the patient's home circumstances are crucial but no report upon them is available to the tribunal, the representative should ask the tribunal to call a social worker from the relevant social services authority to give oral evidence on the patient's home and social circumstances. The nearest relative may have valuable up-to-date information about the circumstances of the admission and the alternatives to hospitals.

As with other applications the responsible authority must indicate any part of the information which it has supplied to the tribunal and which, in its opinion (the authority must give its reasons), should be withheld from the patient on the grounds that its disclosure would adversely affect the health of the patient or others (r 32(2)). These are the same provisions that apply to other applications under r 6(4) and the representative is referred to **9.8** for further discussion. The tribunal must send all other papers and documents to the patient (r 32(3)).

Thereafter, r 12 pertaining to the disclosure of information by the tribunal to the patient and to his representative, applies to assessment applications as if a reference to a withheld document under r 6 was a reference to a part of a document or admission papers withheld in accordance with r 32 (r 33(*a*)). It follows that the tribunal must make an independent decision regarding disclosure of information to the patient; it must, in any case, disclose all information to the patient's authorised representative. The representative is referred to **9.8** for a full discussion of disclosure.

11.1.4 Adjournment

Rule 16 relating to adjournment applies in relation to s 2 tribunals except that, where the hearing is resumed the tribunal need only give such notice as is reasonably practicable (as compared to 14 days' notice in other applications and references) (rr 33(*b*), 16; *see* **10.3**).

11.1.5 The decision

Rule 24 relating to the communication of the decision applies in relation to s 2 tribunals except that the tribunal's decision and its reasons must be communicated to the patient and to the responsible authority within *three* (as opposed to seven) days of the hearing (r 33(*d*) *see* **10.4**). The decision should be communicated to the patient orally at the end of the hearing.

11.1.6 The application of the Rules to s 2 tribunals

The following rules do not apply to s 2 tribunals (r 33):

(1) rr 4, 7 and 20 which concern notice of the application, the proceedings and the hearing. Notice of a s 2 tribunals is given in accordance with r 31 as discussed in *11.1.2* above;

(2) r 6 which concerns the statements by the responsible authority and the Home Secretary. This rule is replaced by r 32 which is discussed in *11.1.3* above;

(3) r 3 which concerns the making of an application. This is replaced by r 30 which is discussed in *11.1.1* above;

(4) r 9 concerning postponement. The purpose of the power of postponement rests on the need to delay consideration of a case if it has already received recent consideration by a tribunal. This does not apply to s 2 tribunals as a case can only be considered once during the duration of the order and that is by application by the patient.

All other rules apply to s 2 tribunals as they do to other applications *in so far as the circumstances permit* and subject to the modifications specified in *11.1.1* to *11.1.5* above. The need to expedite the proceedings will be the primary factor determining any modification which may be necessary in the application of the Rules to s 2 tribunals. For example, the tribunal may generally be more reluctant to adjourn an s 2 tribunal than any other application. Where further information which is relevant to the case is needed the tribunal may direct that the information be presented to it orally rather than that the proceedings be adjourned for written reports. However, the tribunal cannot suspend the rights under the Rules nor under the rules of natural justice for the sake of expedition. The representative must use his best endeavours to ensure that the tribunal's decision is based on a full and fair consideration of the case.

11.2 References

The tribunal must consider a reference to a tribunal (whether automatic or by the Secretary of State) as if it had been an application by a patient except that:

(1) the following rules do not apply (r 29(*a*)):

   (a) r 3 which concerns the making of an application;

   (b) r 4 which concerns notice of the application. On receipt of the reference the tribunal must send notice of it to the patient and to the responsible authority; if the case has been referred by the authority (ie, in accordance with the duty of the hospital managers to refer a case under s 68(1)), instead of giving notice of the reference the tribunal must send the authority a request for its statement (r 29(*b*)). The other rules which concern notice of the proceedings (r 7) and notice of the hearing (r 20) apply to references as they do to applications;

   (*c*) r 9 which concerns postponement of the consideration of an application. This rule does not apply to references (whether automatic or discretionary). Automatic references cannot be postponed because, as a matter of law, a case must be determined at specified intervals. A reference which is made in accordance with the Secretary of State's discretion cannot be postponed because, in theory, the Secretary of State would only refer a case to a tribunal if he had good reason to do so;

   (d) r 19 which concerns withdrawal of an application. Thus a case which is referred to the tribunal cannot be withdrawn at the request of the patient. However a case which has been referred by the Secretary of State in accordance with his discretion (ie, not automatically) may be withdrawn *by the Secretary of State* at any time before the hearing; the tribunal must inform the patient and other parties of the withdrawal (r 29(*c*)).

(2) Rules 5 (the performance of preliminary and incidental matters by the chairman), 6 (statement by the responsible authority and the Home Secretary) and 7 (notice to other persons of the proceedings) apply as if r 6(1) referred to notice of the reference or request for the responsible authority's statement as the case may be, instead of notice of the application (r 29(*c*)). This rule takes into account the changes

regarding the giving of notice of a reference as discussed in paragraph (1)(b) above.

11.3 Representation for automatically referred patients

The Law Society has established a panel of legal representatives to assist all patients whose cases have been referred to the tribunal under the provisions for automatic reference (*see* **7.7**). The assumption is that such patients may need special assistance in obtaining representation. In order to ensure that solicitors, legal executives, trainee solicitors and articled clerks who appear on the panel are competent to assist and represent patients, the Law Society operates a selection procedure. The current criteria for selection are:

(1) willingness to prepare cases and to represent patients before a MHRT hearing personally;

(2) either:

  (a) representation of at least five clients before a tribunal in the last 12 months; or

  (b) attendance at two tribunal sittings covering a minimum of three cases where patients are represented, one of which is a restricted case, one an unrestricted case, and the third either restricted or under s 2 of the 1983 Act;

(3) attendance at an approved course (MIND, the Legal Action Group, and North West Law Conferences run approved conferences, and details may be obtained from these organisations; for addresses see Appendix 8); and

(4) attendance at an interview at which the applicant satisfies the interviewers of his suitability for membership of the Panel.

The panel is supervised by the Professional Standards and Development Directorate of the Law Society, and membership is reviewed every three years. Any inquiries about the operation of the panel should be sent to: The Panel Administrator, Professional Standards and Development Directorate, The Law Society, Ipsley Court, Berrington Close, Redditch, Worcestershire B98 OTD, Tel 071 242 1222.

The Law Society circulates the list of solicitors on the panel to hospitals, Tribunal offices, Social Services Departments, voluntary organisations and advice agencies. It is also available at each area legal aid office. Hospitals may pass the list on to the patient or may contact a solicitor on the panel on behalf of the patient. There is no rota or other system for choosing solicitors from the panel. Note that the list may be used to assist all patients seeking representation; it is not limited to patients who are automatically referred.

Members of the panel are not restricted to representing clients within the county boundaries under which their firms appear. Members may travel within a reasonable distance outside the county boundary to represent clients from another county.

The panel may not include all solicitors, legal executives, trainee solicitors and articled clerks who have experience of MHRT cases. A patient's choice of solicitor need not be restricted to those on the panel, and the availability of legal aid (both green form and ABWOR; *see* chapter 12 below) for representation is not affected by the absence of the solicitor's name from the panel. Nevertheless, the presence of a representative's name on the panel is a reliable indication that the person concerned has the necessary skill and experience to carry out MHRT work.

11.4 Difficulty in taking instructions

The sources of authority for a representative at a MHRT is, as for any representative/client relationship, the instructions of the client. This assumes that the patient is competent to help the representative in the conduct of the case and to have a minimum understanding of the proceedings. If a patient is wholly incapable in these areas, then technically the representative should step down and ask for the appointment of a guardian *ad litem* (eg, the Official Solicitor). However, the Official Solicitor has not traditionally become involved in MHRT hearings and this was one of the reasons behind the establishment of the Law Society's panel. Such incapacity used to be quite exceptional since, under the Mental Health Act 1959, a patient was required positively to apply for a tribunal; a patient doing so had himself formed a judgment concerning his continued residence in hospital and therefore had obtained the necessary information to make a valid application. Since under the 1983 Act patients' cases may be automatically referred to a tribunal, some patients may not wish for their cases to be examined; while others may not even be aware that their cases are coming before the tribunal and what it means (although it must be stressed that this situation is still going to be quite exceptional). Where it occurs, the representative is advised as follows. If the patient does not wish his case to come before a tribunal he has the right to decline to appear need not instruct a representative. If he is incompetent to handle his affairs and a representative is appointed for him, it is submitted that the representative should seek as best he can to take instructions. The representative should then marshall the evidence on behalf of the patient as he would in any other case, defending primarily the patient's interest in liberty and treatment in the least restrictive setting. It is for the tribunal to decide whether the evidence is sufficient for them to make an order discharging the patient. It would seldom serve any constructive purpose to step down in favour of a guardian *ad litem*; such a guardian will not be in any better position to determine the interest of the patient. The use of a representative on the Law Society's panel together with the general oversight of the tribunal is likely to be a sufficient safeguard in most cases.

Chapter 12

Finance

Few applicants to MHRTs are able to meet the costs of legal assistance and representation from their own resources. The majority are eligible for assistance in accordance with the legal advice and assistance provisions of the legal aid scheme. This chapter examines these provisions and other means of assistance.

12.1 Terminology

(1) Legal advice and assistance (more commonly known as 'green form') refers to preliminary help provided to a client in accordance with s 9 of the Legal Aid Act 1988, not including representation at the proceedings. Assistance by way of representation (ABWOR) refers to assistance provided to a client by representing him. For the sake of clarity, advice and assistance and ABWOR are considered separately, even though ABWOR is an extension of advice and assistance as such shares the same income eligibility and contribution limits; it differs from advice and assistance in that approval must be sought from the legal aid authorities before costs are incurred.

(2) In this chapter the term applicant, unless otherwise stated, refers to the applicant to the MHRT (whether patient or nearest relative) or, in the case of a reference to the tribunal, the patient.

(3) References to *the Act* are references to the Legal Aid Act 1988 and sections are sections of that Act. References to regulations are to the Legal Advice and Assistance Regulations 1989 (SI No 340) as amended.

12.2 Statutory background

The scheme of funding legal advice and assistance was established by the Legal Advice and Assistance Act 1972. The Legal Aid Act 1974 consolidated enactments relating to advice and assistance and legal aid. Prior to amending legislation in 1979, these provisions enabled a solicitor to provide advice and assistance to a client, but did not cover any step that the solicitor might take in the institution or conduct of proceedings. Thus a solicitor assisting an applicant to a MHRT could recover the cost of preparing the applicant's case, but not the costs of representing him before the tribunal. The Legal Aid Act 1979 provided for the extension of legal advice and assistance to ABWOR. In 1982 ABWOR was extended to MHRTs following strong representations from MIND, the Law Society, and other bodies that this should be done because of the fact that MHRT decisions directly affect individual liberty, and because of the difficulties facing a psychiatric patient seeking to represent himself. The Legal Aid Act 1988 transferred the administration of the legal aid system from the Law Society to the Legal Aid Board, and regulations made under the 1988 Act have vested extensive decision-making powers in Area Directors appointed by the Legal Aid Board. The availability of ABWOR for MHRTs is continued by the Legal Advice and Assistance (Scope) Regulations 1989 (SI No 550, reg 9(*a*)).

12.3 The 'green form' scheme

The advice and assistance or 'green form' scheme is governed by Part III of the Legal Aid Act 1988, and the Legal Advice and Assistance Regulations 1989 (SI No 340). The Legal Aid system is administered by the Legal Aid Board. The relevant legislation and notes for guidance are published in the *Legal Aid Handbook* (Sweet and Maxwell revised annually).

12.3.1 Scope

The green form scheme is intended to cover preliminary advice and assistance given by a solicitor to a client, and is wide in scope. 'Advice' means 'oral or written advice on the application of English law to any particular circumstances that have arisen in relation to the person seeking the advice and as to the steps which that person might appropriately take having regard to the application of English law to those circumstances' (s 2(1)). Assistance means taking these steps on behalf of the person concerned, or assisting him to take them on his own behalf (s 2(2)). Under s 9(1) a solicitor may advise or assist a financially eligible client on any question of English law, but s 8(3) enables the Lord Chancellor by regulation to exclude from the scheme either advice or assistance of all descriptions, or advice or assistance of a prescribed description throughout the country or in any prescribed area; see the Legal Advice and Assistance (Scope) Regulations 1989 (SI No 550). Most conveyancing is excluded (SI No 550, reg 3). The making of wills is also excluded, except for certain cases involving children or unless the client is aged 70 or over, is blind, deaf, dumb or suffering from mental disorder, or is substantially and permanently handicapped by illness, age or congenital deformity (SI No 550, reg 4). A solicitor cannot provide representation under the green form provisions. For this approval must be sought for ABWOR.

In the majority of cases patients appearing before MHRTs want representation at the tribunal and so remuneration under the ABWOR provisions will be appropriate. Use of the green form provisions should be limited to the initial preparatory steps only. ABWOR rates for MHRTs have recently been increased without a corresponding increase in green form rates, so solicitors acting under green form are paid at a lower hourly rate than if they were acting under ABWOR (Law Society's Gazette 6 November 1991, p 16). Initial preparation normally includes obtaining the responsible authority's statement and interviewing the patient. The solicitor is expected to undertake the initial preparation within the green form limit. Where the solicitor anticipates that the costs of initial work will exceed that limit, he may seek authority to incur extra costs (*see 12.3.3* below).

There may be circumstances where representation is not wanted but help is needed to prepare the case and to obtain independent psychiatric advice. The solicitor may then do all the preparation for the case under the green form scheme with extensions as appropriate (*see 12.3.3* below).

12.3.2 Applications and eligibility

An application for advice and assistance is normally made by a client in person (Legal Advice and Assistance Regulations 1989 (SI No 340), reg 9). The regulations posit the normal solicitor/client relationship where the client personally attends the solicitor. In most MHRT cases the patient, because he is detained, cannot attend the solicitor and it is usual for the solicitor to visit the patient in hospital and have the application signed and completed at the initial interview. If, for good reason, this is not feasible, it may be possible for the patient to authorise someone on his behalf to attend the solicitor for these purposes (Legal Advice and Assistance Regulations 1989 (SI No 340), reg 10).

It should be emphasised that a solicitor may not accept a postal application from a person unless he resides outside England and Wales and prior permission has been obtained from the Area Director appointed by the Legal Aid Board who must be satisfied that acceptance is reasonable in all the circumstances (Legal Advice and Assistance Regulations 1989 (SI No 340) reg 15).

A person may not be given advice and assistance on the same matter by more than one solicitor (unless the advice is being given in a magistrates' court or a police station, see Legal Advice and Assistance Regulations 1989 (SI No 340), regs 6, 7 and 8), without obtaining the prior authority of the Area Director, and the Area Director may impose such terms and conditions on the giving of advice and assistance as he thinks fit (reg 16). It is the solicitor's responsibility to try to discover whether the client has received advice and assistance from another solicitor. The tribunal office will be able to inform the solicitor whether a copy of the responsible authority's statement has been forwarded to any other solicitor.

The regulations make special provision in the case of the person who, by reason of mental disorder within the meaning of the Mental Health Act is incapable of managing and administering his property and affairs (Legal Advice and Assistance Regulations 1989 (SI No 340), regs 3 and 14). An application on behalf of such a person may be accepted from his nearest relative or guardian within the meaning of Part II of the 1983 Act, from his receiver within the meaning of Part VII of the 1983 Act, from the person acting as next friend or guardian *ad litem* for the purpose of any proceedings, or from any other person with the prior approval of the Area Director (reg 14). The Area Director will give authority to 'any other person' if there is:

(1) a good reason why the nearest relative, guardian or receiver cannot make the application;
(2) sufficient connection between the patient and the other person to ensure that the other person is likely to act responsibly in the interests of the patient; and
(3) the other person has sufficient knowledge of the patient, the problem and the financial circumstances, to give proper

instructions to the solicitor (*Legal Aid Handbook*, Notes for Guidance, para 2.12).

This regulation applies to all patients whose property and affairs are being administered by the Court of Protection under Part VII of the Mental Health Act. It may also be applied to patients whose affairs have not been placed under the supervision of the Court of Protection but whose disabilities are so severe that they are unable to give instructions or understand the nature of the proceedings. Some patients whose cases have been referred automatically to the tribunal under s 68 or 71 of the Act fall into this category.

It should be noted that there is nothing in the regulations which expressly precludes a patient, even if incapable of administering his own property and affairs, from signing the application for advice and assistance himself. Provided that the patient understands the purpose and intent behind the application it is likely that the signature will be accepted by the Area Director. For patients who lack even this minimal understanding it is advisable to obtain the signature of a person authorised under reg 14. For difficulty in taking instructions from a patient *see* **11.4**.

Financial eligibility and the extent of contribution, if any, is determined by the solicitor (Legal Advice and Assistance Regulations 1989 (SI No 340), reg 13) by completing the green form (GF1). At the time of writing advice and assistance are available to a person if his weekly disposable income is not greater than £145 and his disposable capital does not exceed £1,000 (Legal Advice and Assistance Regulations 1989 (SI No 340), reg 11 and Sched 3, as amended by SI 1990 No 486). Where a client's disposable income exceeds £75 per week he is liable to pay contributions which the solicitor is responsible for collecting (reg 28). Schedule 3 of the 1989 Regulations sets out the maximum contributions payable according to the client's disposable income. Where the client is in receipt of income support, family credit or disability working allowance, the solicitor is to treat the disposable income as not exceeding the lowest sum specified in Sched 3. Most patients have little or no capital and no private income and are eligible for advice and assistance without contributions. Representatives should, however, note that where a patient has between £1,000 and £3,000 disposable capital, he will not be eligible for advice under the green form scheme, but he will be eligible for ABWOR (*see* **12.4**). Therefore he may have to pay solicitor's costs for the first unit, unless these are waived.

12.3.3 Financial limit and eligibility

A solicitor may give up to two hours' worth of advice and assistance at the current green form rates (or three hours' worth in respect of matrimonial work involving the preparation of a petition) in respect of costs and disbursements without further authorisation. If it appears to the solicitor that the cost of giving advice and assistance is likely to exceed that limit, approval of an extension must be sought by an application on Form GF3 with supporting information to the Area Director before incurring additional expenditure; Legal Aid Act 1988, s 10(1) and reg 21. In assessing an application, the Area Director must consider whether it is reasonable for the advice to be given, and whether the estimated amount required is fair and reasonable (reg 21).

As discussed in *12.3.1* above, where an application is to be made for ABWOR, the solicitor is expected to undertake initial preparatory work only under the green form provisions. This should normally be done within the limit. Extension would only be necessary where travelling expenses are high, or where, for other reasons, the costs of initial preparatory work are likely to exceed the limit. If ABWOR has already been granted in relation to the MHRT application an extension will not be granted but the bill for the required advice and assistance will be paid under ABWOR (Notes for Guidance, para 2.20(*d*)). If ABWOR has already been applied for but not granted, the extension may still be granted if there is likely to be delay before the application is determined and further work needs to be done (*Legal Aid Handbook*, Notes for Guidance, para 2.20(*f*)).

The cost of giving advice and assistance consists of any expenses incurred by the solicitor or his firm in connection with the giving of advice or assistance and any charges or fees properly chargeable by the solicitor's firm in respect of the advice or assistance (Legal Aid Act 1988, s 10(3)).

12.4 Assistance by way of representation

The main provisions which cover ABWOR are ss 1, 2 and 8–13 of the Legal Aid Act 1988, regs 22–27 of the Legal Advice and Assistance Regulations 1989, and reg 9 of the Legal Advice and Assistance (Scope) Regulations 1989. Notes for Guidance are provided in the *Legal Aid Handbook* (Sweet and Maxwell revised annually).

12.4.1 Scope

ABWOR is defined as assistance given to a person by acting on his behalf in the institution or conduct of proceedings before a court, tribunal or statutory inquiry. This may include obtaining the report of an expert, tendering the expert's evidence, instructing counsel and any other steps which are necessary in the institution of proceedings. The demarcation between steps which constitute advice and assistance and those which constitute ABWOR is not a rigid one. As noted in *12.3.1* and *12.3.3* above it is envisaged that a solicitor representing a person in respect of MHRT proceedings will undertake all but the initial preparatory work under the ABWOR provisions. Initial preparatory work will normally consist of obtaining the responsible authority's statement and an interview with the applicant or patient.

12.4.2 Applications and eligibility

A solicitor must apply to the Area Director for approval of ABWOR (reg 22(3)). The solicitor completes the green form GF1 to determine the client's financial eligibility and the amount of contribution, if any. The limits on disposable income for ABWOR are the same as for advice and assistance, but the upper limit for disposable capital is set at the higher figure of £3,000. The contribution rates are the same as those which apply to advice and assistance (reg 11(2) and Sched 3; *see 12.3.3* above). The solicitor then completes form ABWOR 1A for ABWOR and sends this to the nearest legal aid office for approval. After completion of the work, the solicitor claims payment of costs from the Area Office on form ABWOR 3.

The Area Director must apply specific criteria when deciding whether to approve applications for ABWOR. Regulation 22(5) provides that an application shall be refused unless it is shown that the client has reasonable grounds for taking, defending, or being a party to the proceedings to which it relates (reg 22(6)), or if it appears unreasonable for approval to be granted in the circumstances of the case. This is the legal merits test, and it does not apply to ABWOR for MHRTs. Regulation 3(2) of the Legal Advice and Assistance (Amendment) Regulations 1990 (SI No 486) specifically disapplies reg 22(5) to ABWOR for MHRT. The fact that a patient is exercising his legal entitlement to apply for discharge from detention will always amount to reasonable grounds (Notes for Guidance, para 3.11). An application may be refused if it appears unreasonable that approval should be granted, but this is unlikely to apply in a case involving a MHRT. In 1982 the Lord Chancellor acknowledged that under the criteria for assistance by way of representation, there would 'rarely, if ever, be circumstances in which this type of assistance would be refused to a patient' (Memorandum on behalf of the Lord Chancellor, Special Standing Committee on the Mental Health (Amendment) Bill, Second Sitting HC Debs, cols 3–5, 22 April 1982). Further, the Lord Chancellor's Advisory Committee:

> were unable to envisage any situation in which the approval of an application for assistance by way of representation in such cases could be regarded as unreasonable ... In particular, the fact that previous applications had failed should not be regarded as grounds for refusing authorisation. Not only would refusal involve a prejudgment of the medical evidence, but also, where the Mental Health Act had laid down appropriate periods between applications, it was not for the legal aid authorities effectively to frustrate the intentions of that Act by questioning the appropriateness of those periods.

(32nd Annual Reports of the Law Society and of the Lord Chancellor's Advisory Committee (1981–2 (HMSO 1983).)

ABWOR is available to 'a person in proceedings before a MHRT under the Mental Health Act 1983 whose case or whose application to the tribunal is or is to be the subject of the proceedings' (Legal Advice and Assistance (Scope) Regulations 1989 (SI No 550), reg 9). This means that ABWOR may be granted to the patient and to the nearest relative if the latter is the applicant whether or not there is a conflict of interest. This was confirmed by the Legal Aid Board in Note for Guidance 36, *Legal Aid Handbook* (1990). Other parties to the proceedings are entitled to be represented under the MHRT Rules (r 10; **8.6**). Such persons are not entitled to ABWOR but may be assisted under the green form scheme with extensions as necessary.

The Area Director may grant an application for ABWOR in whole or in part or may impose conditions upon the conduct of the proceedings (reg 22(7)). Solicitors must obtain prior permission from the Area Director to obtain the report or the opinion of an expert, to tender expert evidence or to do anything that is by its nature or expense unusual, unless such permission has been included in the grant of approval (reg 22(7); *see 12.4.3* below).

A solicitor must also apply to the Area Director for approval to instruct counsel and the Director is required to grant approval if he considers that the proper conduct of the proceedings requires counsel (reg 23). However, it is generally expected that solicitors on the panel of authorised representatives will be experienced enough to provide representation themselves at MHRTs. Approval for briefing counsel is unlikely to be given except where a difficult point of law is to be argued or where, for other reasons, counsel is better able to represent the patient. Approval for ABWOR may be withdrawn under reg 25, but this is unlikely to occur before MHRTs.

12.4.3 Independent expert opinion

Under the ABWOR provisions, the opinion of an independent psychiatrist cannot be obtained without prior permission from the Area Director (reg 22(7); *see 12.4.2* above). A solicitor assisting an applicant to a MHRT would be expected to use his professional judgment to decide whether an independent psychiatric report is necessary. Nevertheless, requests for independent psychiatric reports are generally considered sympathetically. A strong case can be made for an independent psychiatric report because of the specialist nature of the evidence that has to be presented and assessed. The Notes for Guidance in the *Legal Aid Handbook* state that permission for an independent psychiatric report will usually be granted if the RMO's report contains recommendations which are not acceptable to the client. The solicitor will need to inform the Area Office of the likely cost of the report (*see* Note for Guidance 3.14, also *9.7.5* and *13.8.3*).

In appropriate cases a solicitor may ask the Area Director for permission to obtain a report from an independent social worker. The cost of such a report depends on the extent of the work required and may be considerable if visits to family members are entailed (*see 14.1.3*).

The ABWOR provisions may cover the attendance of an independent psychiatrist or social worker at the proceedings. Permission must be sought from the Area Director (reg 17(7)). The tribunal is also empowered to pay the costs of an independent expert if it considers that his attendance is necessary (*see* **12.5** below).

12.4.4 Appeal

Any refusal by an Area Director to grant ABWOR, to give permission for an expert report, or to allow for an expert to give evidence is appealable to the area committee (reg 26). An appeal is made by giving notice to the committee within 14 days of the Area Director's decision (reg 26(2)). The decision of the area committee on any appeal is final, and the committee must give written notice of its decision and the reasons for it to the client and to any solicitor acting for him (reg 27(2)).

12.4.5 The European Convention on Human Rights

The European Commission and Court of Human Rights have repeatedly emphasised the need for effective legal representation as part of the special procedural guarantees required in mental health cases (see for example *Winterwerp v The Netherlands* (Judgment of 24 October 1979, Series A Judgments and Decisions of the European Court of Human Rights No 47, 4 EHRR 288, paras 60–61, 101–2)). In *Airey v Republic of Ireland* (Judgment of 9 October 1979, Series A No 32, 2 EHRR 305 para 24) the European Court considered that the right of a person to appear in the High Court without representation would not be 'effective in the sense of whether she would be able to present her case properly and satisfactorily'. The Court concluded that publicly funded representation was required so that her rights under the European Convention were not 'theoretical or illusory', but 'practical and effective'. These cases suggest that where a patient has expressed clearly a desire to be represented, and he is prevented from being represented either because the tribunal does not ensure that someone is appointed and/or he cannot afford representation, an application for breach of Art 5(4) could be made. The case which precipitated the extension of ABWOR to MHRTs was *Collins v the United Kingdom*, app no 9729/82, which was declared admissible by the Commission, but withdrawn when the law was changed. Mr Collins was a patient at Broadmoor Hospital whose solicitor would not represent him at the tribunal hearing because there was no legal aid to pay for a representative. The Commission found his case admissible.

12.5 Payment by the tribunal to persons attending the hearing

In accordance with s 78 of the 1983 Act a tribunal may make the following payments to the applicant, a representative other than a legal representative, the nearest relative or guardian and any witness whose attendance it considers necessary:

(1) travelling expenses to the hearing by public transport or,

where the hospital is inaccessible, by taxi or private hire. A witness who uses his own car may be reimbursed;

(2) a day subsistence allowance where the person is away from home or work for more than five hours;

(3) a night subsistence allowance where it is necessary for the person to be away from home overnight;

(4) a loss of earnings allowance.

Payment to witnesses called by the applicant, the representative, nearest relative or guardian is dependent on the tribunal agreeing that their attendance is necessary. It is advisable to obtain the tribunal's agreement prior to the hearing. Where it is known before the hearing that a person is travelling to the hearing a railway warrant may be issued. Claims are normally paid out by the tribunal officer at the hearing. Information about the forms of transport available may be obtained from the tribunal officer or from the hospital. These allowances may be paid to the patient who is the subject of the proceedings, provided he is neither the applicant nor a witness.

It should be noted that payments by the tribunal relate to costs incurred in attending the hearing. The tribunal will not make payments in respect of steps taken by persons prior to or in preparation for the hearing.

Chapter 13

Medical Issues

13.1 Legal and clinical classifications of mental disorder

Mental disorder is defined in s 1 of the MHA to include mental illness, arrested or incomplete development of mind, psychopathic disorder and any other disorder or disability of mind. Mental disorder is a generic term with particular legal significance; it is not a specific medical diagnostic term. Mental disorder may encompass a multiplicity of psychiatric diagnoses. In psychiatric practice it is the specific diagnosis of a disorder which is of greater importance than the legal classification (and which forms the terms of discussion of a medical report). There follows a brief discussion of the legal categories of mental disorder and some of the clinical syndromes which may be encompassed by them.

13.2 Mental illness

The category of mental illness is undefined in the Act. In its consultative document on the 1959 Act the DHSS (now Department of Health) defined the category as including any disorder having one or more of the following characteristics:

(1) more than temporary impairment of intellectual functions shown by a failure of memory, orientation, comprehension and learning capacity;

(2) more than temporary alteration of mood of such degree as to give rise to the patient having a delusional appraisal of his situation, his past or his future, or that of others or to the lack of any appraisal;

(3) delusional beliefs, persecutory, jealous or grandiose;

(4) abnormal perceptions associated with delusional misinterpretation of events;

(5) thinking so disordered as to prevent the patient making a reasonable appraisal of his situation or having reasonable communication with others.

The illness must be of a nature or degree which warrants the detention of the patient in the interest of his health or safety or for the protection of others.

The Department's definition has no legal significance. However, it provides a useful guideline in determining the specific symptomatology which may reasonably be seen as indicative of the legal category of 'mental illness'.

There are many psychiatric disorders which show the characteristics described above. However, specifying these disorders can be difficult because of the existence of a variety of different names (nomenclature) and classification (nosology) systems in use in psychiatry. Variations in nomenclature arise from the lack of a clear and mutually exclusive definition in psychiatry; disorders are differentiated by symptom patterns (syndromes) rather than by the presence or absence of a single sign or symptom which is specific to that disorder. Similarly there is no universally agreed system of classifying the large number of psychiatric disorders. Classification systems differ according to the criteria used to group the disorders. In the following discussion the clinical terms used are based on the International Classification of Diseases, 9th revised system of classification (ICD-9). This system is widely recognised. The World Health Organisation also issues a useful glossary which consists of internationally agreed descriptions of the terms used in the ICD-9 (WHO, 1978). Another widely recognised classification system is DSM-III-R published by the American Psychiatric Association. This classification system has detailed criteria for its use by mental health professionals. New editions of both classification systems are due to be published in 1992. The World Health Organisation and the American Psychiatric Association are working to make these two systems compatible. ICD-10 (WHO, 1992) and DSM-IV (APA, 1992).

The mental disorders most likely to be grouped into the category of mental illness under the Mental Health Act 1983 are those that are classified as psychoses under the ICD-9. A psychosis is 'a mental disorder in which impairment of mental function has developed to a degree that it interferes grossly with insight, ability to meet some ordinary demands of life or to maintain adequate contact with reality.' The term does not include learning disability (mental handicap). Some psychotic disorders are less common, eg, psychoses which are associated with intracranial infection; others are more common, eg, schizophrenia.

The ICD-9 recognises two groups of psychoses: *organic psychotic conditions* and *other psychoses*. The principal disorders in the latter group are *schizophrenic psychoses, affective psychoses* and *paranoid states*. The DSM-III-R classification of psychoses differs from that of ICD-9, particularly in its groupings and nomenclature. For the representative's benefit, a brief introduction to the principal non-organic psychoses, including their treatment, is provided below.

It should be emphasised that clinical descriptions can tend to be cold and objective. The representative should not, however, lose sight of the fact that behind the clinical terminology is a unique and feeling human being.

13.2.1 Schizophrenic psychoses

The concept of schizophrenia is complicated. Criteria for its diagnosis are not fully agreed upon by the major classifications (ICD-9 and DSM-III-R). Yet it is a serious mental illness with a prevalence rate of about one per cent, and leaves many patients unable to live independently in the community. Its aetiology is unknown, but most agree that genetic, biological, social, and familial factors play roles to varying degrees in individual cases. Many suggest that 'schizophrenia' is an umbrella term for a number of separate disorders.

Symptomatology can be very varied and patients are usually described by clinicians according to type. Features common to most types include at least some of the following: social withdrawal or isolation with loss of effective functioning; markedly peculiar behaviour; lack of interest in personal appearance and hygiene; speech that is circumstantial, grandiose, vague, neologistic (using invented words), generally disorganised or displaying a poverty of form or content; odd beliefs or magical thinking; unusual perceptual experiences; loss of energy or of the ability to engage in consistent goal directed behaviour.

In the acute phase of their illness, most patients diagnosed as suffering from schizophrenia will also display evidence of delusions which may be bizarre; hallucinations of all senses, but most frequently auditory (hearing voices); incoherence of speech and so called loosening of associations where the person's train of thought is difficult or impossible to follow; 'affect' (response) which is flat (unchanging) or grossly inappropriate; catatonic stupor (immobility with muscle inflexibility but no true loss of consciousness) or catatonic excitement. All of the above symptoms are unlikely to be present in one patient, but delusions (false beliefs that are unshakable despite incontrovertible evidence to the contrary and are not normally held in the patient's culture) and hallucinations (sensory perceptions not caused by external stimuli) are characteristic.

It should be remembered that drugs, toxins, dementia, brain lesions, and dissociative disorders can produce some or all of the symptoms described above and thus can be misdiagnosed as schizophrenia by the clinically inexperienced.

Particular types of schizophrenia include the following:

Simple: No markedly bizarre symptoms. Some would describe such patients as having a personality disorder rather than a psychosis.

Hebephrenic or disorganised: Grossly disorganised behaviour, thought patterns, affect, and speech are characteristic.

Catatonic: Stupor or excitement, negativism, echolalia (repeating what is said like an echo), echopraxia (mimicking observed behaviour of other persons).

Paranoid: Fairly systematised delusions and auditory hallucinations without the more bizarre alterations of mood, speech, and behaviour described above.

Residual: No florid symptoms or prominent delusions or hallucinations, but the clear presence of some disturbances of behaviour, thought, or mood.

This does not exhaust the list of types of schizophrenia that have been described, and it should be repeated that in neither nosology nor nomenclature is there universal agreement. Patients are best described in detailed specific terms of their symptoms, signs and functioning.

Treatment for schizophrenia The major medications for the treatment of schizophrenia are a group of drugs known as anti-psychotics. These are sometimes referred to as neuroleptics or major tranquillisers. They are generally effective at relieving psychotic symptoms, shortening the florid psychotic episode, and reducing the recurrence of relapse. **Table I** lists the major medications, their trade names and typical dosages. While chemically very diverse, all have similar anti-psychotic effect. Their precise mode of action is unknown, but they all exert an influence on the transmission of nerve impulses from neuron to neuron. Their effectiveness is not due to a sedative effect. Some, however, are structured to provide an additional sedative quality.

Table I: Anti-psychotic agents

Drug	*Trade name*	*Drug dosage (oral) (mg)*	*Possible side effects*
Chlorpromazine	Largactil	75–300	All the neuroleptic medications present the risk of tardive dyskinesia. Other frequent side effects are hypotension, drowsiness, tremor, dystonea (abnormal body and face movements), akathisia (acute restlessness), insomnia and weight change.
Thioridazine	Melleril	150–600	
Trifluoperazine	Stelazine	5–50	
Haloperidol	Haldol Dozic Serenace Fortunin	2–100	

Dosages vary widely. Patients exhibit great variability of response, and require different levels of medication during different phases of their illness. High levels are often prescribed initially; maintenance doses prescribed when the florid phase is over may be much lower. Generally, these medicines should be prescribed at the lowest dose possible which still affords the patient freedom from the most intrusive symptoms.

Some anti-psychotics may be given intramuscularly, either to achieve rapid effectiveness in the case of an acutely psychotic patient, or to achieve a long acting result when the patient is reluctant or unable to take daily oral doses. **Table II** indicates some of the more commonly prescribed medicines administered in injection form, and their dosage and duration of effectiveness.

Table II: Neuroleptics administered by depot injections—long acting

Drug	*Trade name*	*Drug dosage (mg)*	*Duration of effect*
Fluphenazine Decanoate	Moditen	12.5–100	14–40 days
Flupenthixol Decanoate	Depixol	20–400	2–4 weeks
Haloperidol Decanoate	Haldol-Decanoate	12.5–25	3–4 weeks
Zuclopenthixol Decanoate	Clopixol	100–600	2–4 weeks

Anti-psychotic medicine may have significant side effects, most notably symptoms vaguely resembling those associated with Parkinson's disease (pseudo-Parkinsonism). These include tremor, dystonia (abnormal body and face movements) and akathisia (general restlessness). These conditions can develop after only a few doses. Long-term use of the neuroleptics can lead to the much more severe, and irreversible, condition of tardive dyskinesia. Tardive dyskinesia manifests in shaking of extremities, involuntary movements of the face and tongue, a mask-like gaze and lethargy. To reduce the pseudo-Parkinsonism, the prescribing physician may adjust the dosage or choose another anti-psychotic; much depends on the particular patient's response to the various medications. Anti-Parkinsonian drugs may also be prescribed; these also can have side effects (eg, dryness of the mouth). Frequently prescribed medicines and their dosages are listed in **Table III.**

Table III: Anti-parkinsonian agents

Drug	*Trade name*	*Dosage (mg)*	*Side effects*
Benzhexol Hydrochloride	Artane, Bentex Broflex	5–15	gastro-intestinal disturbances, dry mouth, dizziness, nervousness
Benztropine Mesylate	Cogentin	1–4	same, but may cause sedation
Orphenadrine Hydrochloride	Biorphen, Disipal	150–400	same as Benzhexol, insomnia
Procyclidine	Kemadrin	5–30	

Clozapine (trade name Clozaril or Leponex) is a relatively new anti-psychotic drug. Clozapine appears effective in controlling psychotic symptoms, especially for some patients whose symptoms are resistant to standard anti-psychotic treatment. Clozapine rarely causes pseudo-Parkinsonism or tardive dyskinesia. It does, however, occasionally cause agranulocytosis, which is a serious condition characterised by a pronounced drop in certain white blood cells necessary to fight infection. There have been fatalities from clozapine-induced agranulocytosis. Accordingly, the manufacturer of clozapine (Sandoz) requires rigorous monitoring of the white-cell count, even after years of continuous use (C Salzman, 'Mandatory Monitoring for Side Effects: The "Bundling" of Clozapine', *N Engl J Med* 1990; 323:827–829).

Proper prescription of anti-psychotic medication, and when necessary, further medication to alleviate side effects, is in part a process of trial and error. It is not uncommon for several medications to be tried before the proper combination is found for any individual. A typical medical record for a patient with schizophrenia may indicate several changes in prescription, with varying medications and dosages. For chronic schizophrenia, particularly in patients closely supervised, maintenance drug therapy can periodically be stopped for a limited period of time (the so called 'drug holiday'). This must be done under careful surveillance so that treatment can be quickly restarted if necessary. These 'holidays' provide an opportunity to assess the baseline behaviour and the necessity of continuing drug treatment. The seriousness of side effects such as tardive dyskinesia is a strong reason for using as little anti-psychotic medication for as short a period of time as possible.

Medication is not the only means of treating a patient. The disturbing side effects make many patients reluctant to co-operate with the treatment programme. Where consent to treatment is part of the wider issue of treatability and discharge (eg, refusal of consent is given as a ground for using compulsory powers), the representative should enquire as to what alternative treatment may be appropriate and acceptable to the patient. The representative should also be aware that long-acting neuroleptics may be administered to a person living in the community, provided that legally effective consent is given and adequate back-up services are available. The need for medication is not of itself a justification for detention in hospital. Medication may control unacceptable behaviour and ameliorate schizophrenic symptoms without treating the 'causal' components of the patient's illness. Medication, in the absence of a more complete therapeutic programme, can seldom be considered to be an adequate treatment. Most patients require other forms of psychiatric and social support such as individual, family or group psychotherapy or a behaviour modification programme. Electro-convulsive therapy (see below for further discussion) rarely may relieve certain schizophrenic symptoms that drugs cannot. However, it is generally less effective than the medication described above and its use in the treatment of schizophrenia is controversial.

13.2.2 Affective psychoses (ICD-9) *Mood disorders (DSM-III-R)*

Mania and depression are the two principal disorders of mood or affect.

A *manic episode* is characterised by a mood that is distinctly abnormal and is persistently elevated, expansive, or irritable. Also usually present are grandiosity, decreased need for sleep, altered libido, uncharacteristic talkativeness, flight of ideas (thoughts racing faster than can be fully expressed), distractability, agitation, and excessive involvement in goal directed or pleasurable activities, usually with ineffective results or painful consequences. In true mania social and occupational functioning are markedly impaired. When this is not the case, the disorder is called hypomania.

Depression may range from a state of mild sadness to a disorder of psychotic proportions. *A major depressive episode* will usually be manifested by a persistent depressed mood in the absence of a precipitant or, if one is present, be out of all proportion to its expected effect. In adolescents the mood disorder can present itself as irritability rather than depression. Other common features include anhedonia (loss of pleasure in usually enjoyed activities), unintended weight loss or gain, decreased libido, increase or decrease in time spent sleeping, agitation or psychomotor retardation (slowing of physical or emotional reactions), ennui (feelings of guilt or unworthiness that may be of delusional proportions), somatic delusions (the idea that some bodily function is abnormal in the face of an adequate demonstration to the contrary), inability to concentrate, uncharacteristic indecisiveness, and thoughts of dying including planning or attempting suicide. A severe form of depression that, in addition to the above symptoms, usually displays early morning wakening, diurnal variations (depression regularly worse in the morning), and anorexia (loss of appetite), is sometimes called melancholia.

The term *manic depressive psychosis* (ICD-9) is used to describe patients who have an episode of mania (*manic type*) or of depression as described above (*depressed type*). It is also applied to patients who have had at least one episode each of mania and depression (*circular type*). The term *bi-polar disorder* (DSM-III-R) is similar to manic depressive psychosis except that patients with a major depression who have never had a manic or hypomanic episode are not called bi-polar disorder depressed; they are diagnosed as *major depression*.

Other mood disorders which are not regarded as psychoses include cyclothymia (mood swings less drastic than in manic depressive psychosis or bi-polar disorder), dysthymia or neurotic depression, most cases of reactive depression, and pathological grief reaction.

The term *endogenous depression* is no longer in either ICD-9 or DSM-III-R, but some clinicians may still use it. It is roughly the same as major depression with no clear precipitant.

Treatment for affective psychoses Manic states are usually treated by long term use of lithium carbonate or lithium citrate. The therapeutic dose is fairly close to the toxic dose, so regular clinical observation and blood lithium levels are necessary to titrate the dose correctly. Nausea, diarrhoea, malaise, fine hand tremor, thirst and fatigue are early signs of toxicity. Some psychiatrists include lithium in a maintenance regimen for major depression as well as for bi-polar disorder, but this use is controversial.

The drugs prescribed for affective disorders characterised by depression may be grouped into the following categories: the heterocyclic anti-depressants, the monoamine oxidase inhibitors (MAOIs), compound anti-depressants, and other new drugs.

The heterocyclic drugs are most effective for treating moderate to severe depressions with symptoms such as loss of appetite and sleep disturbances. Since there may be an interval of two to four weeks before the anti-depressant action takes affect, some psychiatrists prescribe electroconvulsive therapy for severe depression when delay is hazardous or intolerable. Approximately 10–20 per cent of patients fail to respond to heterocyclic anti-depressant medication.

The MAOIs are much less frequently used than heterocyclic anti-depressants because of the dangers of dietary and drug interactions. The MAOIs may have serious side effects when used in combination with other medications and a variety of foods, such as cheese, meat extracts, broad bean pods, and red wine.

Compound anti-depressants are combinations of heterocyclics and are generally not recommended except for short-term use.

Fluoxetine hydrochloride (trade name Prozac) has been widely prescribed since its introduction into the market in North America, but is less often used in Great Britain. Prozac is not grouped into any of the major categories of anti-depressant listed above. Prozac can be effective when other anti-depressants are not. Infrequent adverse effects include tremor, dizziness, nausea, vomiting and convulsion. Furthermore, some anecdotal reports suggest a link between suicidal ideation or attempts and the use of this drug. However, no scientific evidence exists to support this association.

While anti-psychotic medication is primarily indicated for the treatment of schizophrenia, it is sometimes prescribed for depression (eg, Fluoxetine Hydrochloride). Minor tranquillisers are more often prescribed for anxiety and phobic states than for depression. Minor tranquillisers include Chlordiazepoxide (Librium), Diazepam (Valium) and Nitrazepam (Mogadon). Minor tranquillisers can cause dependence, especially when taken over long periods.

As with the drugs used in the treatment of schizophrenia, the effects (both beneficial and adverse) of the anti-depressant and anti-manic drugs vary widely among patients. Similarly, anti-depressants may control symptoms, without affecting underlying causes. Psychotherapy and forms of supportive therapy (eg, cognitive or behaviour modification) are normally required. The representative may question the prolonged use of medication or its administration in unusually high doses, especially if not accompanied by a plan of treatment and support services.

Table IV: Anti-depressant medications

Drug	*Daily dosage (mg)*	*Side effects*
Heterocyclics		
Imipramine (Tofanil)	75–150	Dryness of mouth, drowsiness, difficulties, in vision, constipation, sweating.
Amitriptyline (Tryptizol)	75–150	
Dothiepin (Prothiaden)	75–150	
Trimipramine (Surmontil)	75–150	
Desipramine (Pertofran)	75–150	
Gamanil (Lofepramine)	140–210	
Mianserin (Norval)	30–90	
MAOIs		
Phenelzine (Nardil)	45–90	Dizziness, weakness, fatigue, severe reactions in combination with certain foodstuffs, (including alcohol).
Isocarboxazid (Marplan)	10–20	
Trianylcypromine (Parnate)	10–40	
Other Anti-depressants		
Fluoxetine Hydrochloride (Prozac)	20–40	Anxiety, insomnia, nausea, chills, weight loss, dizziness
Lithium Carbonate (Liskonum)	Dosage varied to achieve proper plasma concentra tion; typically 500–900	Gastro-intestinal disturbances, tremor, weight gain and oedema. If blood level too high, blurred vision, CNS disturbances, weakness, nausea, potentially very harmful

Electro-convulsive therapy (ECT): ECT is the passing of a current of electricity through the front part of the brain sufficient to produce a convulsion. The patient is first anaesthetised and then given a muscle relaxant in order to minimise the possibility of physical damage during the convulsion. ECT is usually given in a course of six to 12 sessions administered once or twice weekly. Research has indicated that it is an effective treatment of the more severe depressions. When compared to anti-depressant medication, ECT is at least as effective as the most effective anti-depressant and exerts its effects more rapidly. ECT is not indicated for neurotic depression. It has been used in the past for the treatment of schizophrenia, and was thought to speed recovery in the florid phase of illness; nowadays this is regarded as controversial and it is rarely if ever used for this purpose today.

Mania has been treated with ECT, although there is no indication that it is any more effective than the drugs ordinarily prescribed. Any case where maintenance ECT is used (ie, over a long period) should be carefully scrutinised. Side-effects may include slight headache, confusion and short-term memory loss. ECT does not necessarily require in-patient treatment but may be given in day hospitals when relatives and friends are able to provide appropriate care at home.

Despite its demonstrated efficacy in the treatment of severe psychotic depression, the reasons for its clinical effect are unknown. Its administration has some risks, particularly associated with the use of anaesthetic. Some patients regard its administration as frightening and aversive.

In 1989, the Royal College of Psychiatrists published a guide to the use of ECT, and the representative may refer to it for a more detailed description of the process and recommended procedures for its use.

Psychosurgery: This term describes surgical techniques in which particular nerve fibres or areas in the brain are destroyed. The most modern methods have been successful in the treatment of severe unrelieved tension states, obsessional and depressive illnesses. However, results are difficult to predict and permanent changes to the patient's personality may result, particularly with the older methods. For those reasons psychosurgery is used with extreme caution and in a very small number of selected cases where a long-term, severe and debilitating illness has proved resistant to all other forms of treatment. The patient's consent *and* a second opinion are required before psychosurgery can be performed. The patient's case should be referred to the Mental Health Act Commission prior to his transfer to the neuro-surgical centre for the operation. The

Commission will usually visit and interview the patient at the referring hospital at an early stage in the procedure (Code of Practice, para 16.7).

Other treatments: Patients recovering from depressive illness require extensive psychotherapy, support and supervision. This may be provided on an out-patient or day patient basis or may be available at home through the services of community psychiatric nurses.

13.2.3 Paranoid states

Paranoia is a relatively rare psychosis although the term is in common but incorrect lay use. Its principal and usually only symptom is non-bizarre delusions. Except as affected by the content of the delusional system, appearance and behaviour are normal and personality is intact. In this respect it differs from schizophrenia, paranoid type. Treatment, which is not always effective, is similar to that of schizophrenia.

13.2.4 Code of Practice

The Code of Practice (paras 15.4–15.6) strongly recommends that all patients (both informal and detained) should have an individual plan of treatment. Consultants should co-ordinate the formulation of the treatment plan in consultation with the multi-disciplinary team. The treatment plan should also be discussed with the patient and (with his consent) appropriate family members. The plan should be recorded in the patient's clinical notes, and should be available to the representative.

The treatment plan should include a description of the immediate and long-term goals for the patient with a clear indication of the treatment, care, and support. The treatment plan should be based upon a careful, multi-disciplinary assessment of the patient's needs; the patient's progress and the achievement of clinical and behavioural goals should be periodically assessed; and changes to the plan should be made at regular intervals.

The tribunal is not the appropriate forum to question the treatment plan in detail. However, the treatment plan is critical to the tribunal's determination as to the need for continued detention. The tribunal should satisfy itself that the patient is not simply stagnating in hospital. It should ensure that the hospital has realistic and ethically appropriate goals for the patient, and that it is making genuine progress in achieving those goals. The tribunal, moreover, should inquire whether the legitimate therapeutic goals could not be achieved as, or more, effectively in the community.

The Mental Health Act and the Code of Practice (paras 16.1–16.38) also make detailed provision for treatment without the consent of the patient. Since the Mental Health Act Commission, not the tribunal, is charged with the oversight of consent to treatment, it will not be covered here. The reader is referred to L Gostin, *Mental Health Services: Law and Practice* (London, Shaw & Sons, looseleaf, updated regularly). Where the patient is given medication without his consent after three months (s 58), the RMO should indicate on the certificate the drugs proposed, by the classes described in the British National Formulary (indicating the dosages if they are above the BNF advisory maximum limits) and the method of their administration. All treatments (whether or not they are given with consent) should be reviewed regularly and the patient's treatment plan should include details of when this will take place (Code of Practice, para 16.19).

13.3 Learning disability (mental handicap), mental impairment and severe mental impairment

Learning disability (mental handicap), 'mental impairment' and 'severe mental impairment' are terms which are used in different contexts to describe a state of 'arrested or incomplete development of mind'. Mental retardation is the term used in North America, and is also widely used in other English-speaking countries. The term 'learning disability' is a clinical and not a legal term. It refers to significantly below average general intellectual functioning together with difficulty in adaptive behaviour and it is manifested during the developmental period. The following terms may also be used to describe the same clinical state: subnormality, mental deficiency and mental retardation. Like 'mental handicap' these terms have come to carry stigmatising connotations, and the term preferred by client groups and and the Department of Health is 'learning disability'.

The terms 'mental impairment' and 'severe mental impairment' are legal terms. Mental impairment is a state of arrested or incomplete development of mind (not amounting to severe mental impairment) which includes significant impairment of intelligence and social functioning and is associated with abnormally aggressive or seriously irresponsible conduct on the part of the person concerned. Severe mental impairment is defined in the same way except that there is *severe* impairment of intelligence and social functioning (s 1(2)). Thus the only difference between mental impairment and severe mental impairment is one of degree of impairment.

The categories of mental impairment and severe mental impairment in the 1983 Act replace the categories of subnormality and severe subnormality in the 1959 Act. The major difference is that mental impairment must be associated with 'abnormally aggressive or seriously irresponsible conduct'; a person could have been classified as subnormal without any evidence of aggressive, irresponsible or otherwise dangerous behaviour. As discussed in **1.1**, a person cannot be detained under the provisions authorising long term detention (that is, more than 28 days) unless he is suffering from one of the four specific forms of mental disorder. Thus the effect of replacing subnormality by mental impairment is to restrict long-term detention to those learning disabled persons whose condition is associated with 'abnormally aggressive or seriously irresponsible' behaviour. Two further points may be noted: first, the definition of mental disorder is unchanged and includes 'arrested or incomplete development of mind'; thus learning disabled people continue to be subject to short-term compulsory detention under those provisions which require the person only to be suffering from mental disorder. Secondly a learning disabled person suffering from a concomitant mental illness may be detained under the provisions relating to long-term detention even if there is no evidence of aggressive, irresponsible or otherwise dangerous behaviour.

13.3.1 Cause, effect and treatment

The provisions relating to long-term detention under the Act no longer apply to the majority of learning disabled people. This went some way towards satisfying those who claimed that the Act was inappropriate for people with learning disabilities. Nevertheless the inclusion of mentally handicapped under *any* of the provisions relating to detention implies that learning disability, like mental illness, is a temporary disorder which may be alleviated or cured by treatment. This is not so. Learning disability is a permanent disability which is detectable from an early age and is often associated with genetic disorder or perinatal damage. The sudden onsets and temporary or recurrent nature of mental illness are not characteristics of learning disability. Learning disability cannot be cured; however, behavioural problems associated with the disability may be significantly improved by training, education, socialisation and care. This has important implications when representing learning disabled people (*see 13.8.3* below).

13.4 Psychopathic disorder

Psychopathic disorder is defined as a persistent disorder or disability of mind (whether or not including significant impairment of intelligence) which results in abnormally aggressive or seriously irresponsible conduct on the part of the person concerned (s 1(2)). The category includes learning disabled patients who are suffering from psychopathic disorder.

The legal category includes a wide variety of clinical diagnoses such as severe forms of personality disorder, sociopathic disorder, character disorder, inadequate personality, emotionally unstable personality, psychopathic behaviour and conduct disorder. The phrase 'persistent disorder' in the legal definition is significant. It means that the disorder must be a long-standing one; a person who has committed an isolated offence or displayed aggressive or irresponsible conduct on one occasion only cannot be categorised as psychopathic under the Act. In practice, psychopathic disorder is not regarded as a specific clinical condition; rather, the presence of a disorder is inferred from evidence of antisocial behaviour. Thus the definition is circular in that it infers a disease from antisocial behaviour, while purporting to explain the behaviour by the disease. The result in practice is that the category has been applied to a wide variety of people whose only common feature is some sort of antisocial behaviour. There is no clear, consistent and rational distinction between offenders who are labelled psychopaths and sent by the courts to a psychiatric hospital and those who offend repeatedly who are sent to prison without any psychiatric label.

13.4.1 Treatment

The Committee on Mentally Abnormal Offenders (the Butler Committee; Cmnd 6244, 1975) concluded that psychiatry was unable to provide any effective treatment for psychopathic disorder. The legislators of the 1983 Act responded by restricting the admission of psychopathic patients under provisions relating to long-term detention to cases where treatment is expected to benefit or prevent a deterioration of the patient's condition (ss 3(2)(*b*), 37(2): *see* **1.6**, and **2.4**). In view of the medical evidence concerning treatment of psychopathy and the findings of the Butler Committee, the burden of demonstrating that a psychopathic disorder is treatable should rest on the hospital authorities; there should be a specific treatment programme referable to clear behavioural goals and a time scale (albeit approximate) for meeting these goals.

13.5 Any other disorder or disability of mind

This phrase is not a legal category. It is an umbrella term which may be used to include any mental disorder which does not fall within one of the four specific categories. A person who is suffering from 'any other disorder or disability of mind' can be detained under short- or medium-term detention orders (ss 2, 4, 5, 135 and 136) but cannot be detained under sections of the Act providing for long-term detention (*see* **1.3** to **1.5**).

The disorders which may be categorised as 'any other disorder or disability of mind' may in some cases be less serious than those within the other subcategories. They include neuroses, personality disorders, behaviour disorders, disability resulting from head injuries and transient mental disturbances.

13.6 Treatment and treatability

Under s 145(1) medical treatment includes nursing and care, habilitation and rehabilitation under medical supervision. It follows that, once a patient is admitted to hospital and assigned to the care of a particular medical and nursing team, he may be considered to be receiving medical treatment. The wide definition of medical treatment has important implications for any consideration which a tribunal might give to a patient's treatability. Nevertheless, medical treatment must be of a certain standard to demonstrate that there is a likelihood that it will alleviate or prevent a deterioration in the patient's condition.

Unlike the 1959 Act, the 1983 Act, explicitly authorises the tribunal in certain circumstances to consider whether it is necessary for a patient to receive treatment and whether treatment will alleviate or prevent a deterioration in his condition; eg in considering the criterion specified in s 72(2)(*a*) in relation to the discharge of non-restricted patients. This does not mean that the tribunal can review the merits or side-effects of a particular treatment programme for the purpose of making recommendations for a change in treatment, but since the tribunal must, in certain circumstances, have regard to treatability, the representative may legitimately question the nature of the patient's treatment programme, the progress he has made since admission, the prognosis and the future treatment programme. This is strictly for the purposes of determining whether the treatability criterion has been fulfilled, ie, whether on the evidence before the tribunal, the RMO's programme of treatment is likely to alleviate or prevent a deterioration in the patient's condition. It is reasonable to assume that the longer the patient has been in hospital without making any particular therapeutic progress, the more difficult it is to argue that his condition is treatable. Where the only treatment the patient is receiving is nursing care or general supervision the representative should ascertain whether this requires detention in hospital and whether it can be provided in a less restrictive setting.

The representative should not accept a refusal by an RMO to discuss fully with the tribunal issues relating to treatment and treatability, as long as the discussion is relevant to the discharge criteria.

13.7 Medical information available to the tribunal

13.7.1 The nature of medical information

The term 'medical information' implies that the information required is of an expert nature and hence cannot be readily understood or properly assessed by a lay person. This is not so. A person cannot be detained on the basis of a mental disorder alone; in addition to the presence of mental disorder it must also be necessary either for his own health or safety or for the protection of others that he should receive treatment (or, in the case of a patient admitted for assessment, that he should be so detained). These are not judgments that are the exclusive preserve of psychiatry. They depend on issues such as whether the patient understands the purpose of his detention and treatment; whether he would be able to care for his physical needs if he were to be discharged; whether his discharge poses a danger to other persons; whether the treatment and care he needs could be given in any other less restrictive setting; whether he has benefited from treatment and is likely to make any further gains. These are commonsense judgments that require considerably less medical expertise than is generally supposed.

13.7.2 The responsible medical officer's report

As discussed in *9.7.1* the responsible authority is required in accordance with r 6 and the Schedule to the Rules to provide an up-to-date medical report including a relevant medical history and a full report on the patient's mental condition. The authority normally asks the RMO to provide this report. There are no guidelines for the RMO as to details which the tribunal requires. This means that in practice the quality of up-to-date medical reports is variable. For instance, some reports may provide a comprehensive account of the patient's psychiatric history and current treatment; on the other hand, where a patient has made a previous application to the tribunal, the up-to-date report may be very brief and may simply refer back to the previous report. Research has shown that the RMO's report is a very influential factor in determining the tribunal's decision, so that the representative must endeavour to ensure that its contents and scope are thoroughly examined; this is discussed further in **13.8** below.

13.7.3 Medical member's opinion

The medical member of the tribunal must examine the patient in order to form an opinion of his mental condition (r 11; **9.9**). This opinion is normally conveyed orally to the other tribunal members. Although the medical member's opinion is not formally disclosed to the parties his views may become apparent during the proceedings. It has been argued that, because the findings and opinion of the medical member are so important (in effect, they provide the tribunal with an independent psychiatric assessment of the patient), natural justice requires that they are disclosed to the parties. The argument for non-disclosure is that the findings of the medical member are part of the deliberative process of the tribunal and not part of the evidence. In **9.9** it is suggested that the information on which the medical member's opinion is based (but not the opinion itself) should be disclosed to the parties. However, it is not common practice to disclose this information and there is likely to be wide variation in the ways that requests for it are dealt with by tribunals.

13.7.4 Case and nursing notes

The tribunal will usually have before it the patient's case notes. These normally include notes made by doctors at various times, nursing notes which are routinely made, reports by other professionals such as psychologists, social workers, occupational therapists, and copies of letters written about the patient to other doctors (such as the patient's GP), relatives and administrators; these letters are useful because they summarise views held at particular times. The representative may not automatically be given access to the case notes. The tribunal does not usually examine the care notes, but often relies on the medical member to have examined them and extracted the relevant information which can be put to the parties during the hearing. The notes are usually at the hearing. If they are to form part of the evidence, the representative may argue that case notes should be disclosed under r 12(1),(3) (*see 9.8.2*). Even if the representative is denied direct access to them they must be made available to an independent psychiatrist instructed by him. The representative should bear this in mind and ask the independent psychiatrist to look in the notes for relevant information, eg correspondence regarding transfer to other hospitals. This is discussed further in *13.8.2* below.

13.7.5 Other medical reports

The statement provided by the Home Secretary to the tribunal in accordance with r 6 (*see 9.7.2*) normally contains the medical reports on the patient which were provided to the sentencing court and any other medical, psychological or other reports which had been submitted to the Home Secretary; it may also include reports made by the RMO for the purposes of previous tribunal hearing(s). These reports are provided in addition to the up-to-date report by the RMO.

13.8 Obtaining information: the representative's role

13.8.1 Interviewing the patient

On the first visit, the representative should interview the client to take instructions, and, if relevant, complete an application for ABWOR. Examination of the authority's statement and taking instructions may be done under the Green Form Scheme, but it should be remembered that the Green Form should be signed immediately on the first visit as it will not be backdated to cover work done before (*see* Chapter 12). After reviewing the written records, the representative should prepare a list of questions in preparation for interviewing the patient. The following information should be obtained from the patient:

(1) names, addresses and phone numbers of people whom the patient feels are significant. The representative should interview these people as soon as possible to determine what support they may provide in the community for the patient if he is discharged;
(2) names, addresses and phone numbers of social workers or therapists within the community with whom the patient has had contact in the past. These professionals may have experience of the patient and his abilities to maintain stability;
(3) the patient's account of both his history and the immediate events which lead to his hospitalisation;
(4) the patient's account of any major events before or during a patient's stay in hospital—eg, alleged difficult, abnormal or dangerous behaviour. It is not uncommon that widely disparate accounts will be discovered, and the patient's version should by no means be discredited. Errors in recording occur, and the stress of work in the setting of a psychiatric hospital occasionally diminishes the reporter's objectivity;
(5) the patient's expectation of his living situation if he is released. Any issue of continuing treatment needs to be discussed in detail.

The interview itself should take place in a private area, away from open wards and with no member of the hospital staff present, in order to allow the patient to speak freely. Fear or tension on the part of the representative or patient will impede an effective interview. While it is rare that patients present a real physical danger, if a particular patient's history indicates a genuine need for caution, the representative should inform hospital staff of the possible need for their assistance, and perhaps conduct the interview in a more open location which allows for privacy.

The representative should introduce himself clearly and simply, and ask if the patient is willing to speak together in the designated room. A genuine attempt by the representative to gain the patient's trust should be successful, bearing in mind that the most common complaint by patients regarding their legal representatives is the failure of the representatives to listen and to advocate their point of view. The representative should initially refrain from taking notes. If after a few minutes, the question is put to the patient 'Do you mind if I write some of these things down?', he will usually consent, and this small gesture of courtesy will lessen any feeling the patient has of being subject to yet another observation. If the patient expresses doubt about the role of the representative, the representative should reassure the patient, and stress that the sole intention and obligation of the legal representative is to help the patient express his case to the tribunal. It is possible that the patient may have resentment towards the representative, associating him with the procedures of law which bring about compulsory admission to hospital.

13.8.2 The RMO's report

Where an RMO opposes a patient's discharge or transfer he will support his opinion by reference to past or current behaviour. If his report consists of a list of difficult or dangerous behaviour or past offences, which will inevitably influence the tribunal's opinion of the patient, the representative should assess:

(1) the accuracy of reporting of the alleged behaviour. In reporting on a patient's behaviour on the wards the RMO may rely on notes made by nursing or other staff; a report on behaviour outside the hospital may be based on comments by friends or relatives or newspaper reports. All this information is second- or third-hand. The representative should investigate the source of any allegations in order to confirm that the behaviour was accurately and fairly reported. Any inaccuracies should be brought to the tribunal's attention;

(2) the context of the alleged behaviour; incidents may be reported briefly or out of context, thus distorting the true picture;

(3) the seriousness of the alleged behaviour. The representative should point out the distinctions between verbal threats of intended dangerous behaviour, behaviour which may be disruptive but not dangerous, behaviour which results in damage to property but not to persons, and behaviour which is truly harmful to the patient or to other persons;

(4) relevance of alleged dangerous behaviour to the patient's current and future behaviour. Dangerous acts are often specific to a particular social context or to a particular series of events; for example, a person who murdered his spouse may commit a further violent offence if he becomes involved in another close and emotionally demanding relationship, but he may pose no risk in any other social setting. Stress created by confinement, lack of privacy and the constant observation and assessment by hospital staff can give rise to violent behaviour which while antisocial in itself, is not

necessarily an indication of a patient's future conduct in the community.

Past events and offences are important only to the extent that they affect the patient's current and future behaviour, and part of the function of the representative may be to promote the development of an aftercare programme which controls the social circumstances which may give rise to violence, and which has a reasonable degree of support and supervision.

When the RMO submits a statement which argues the case against discharge rather than presents a balanced picture of the patient, the representative should try to redress the balance as much as possible, by presenting to the tribunal details of the patient's progress, positive relationships with other patients, staff and relatives, occupational progress and so on.

The representative must pay particular attention to the RMO's reports of behaviour and the social context of that behaviour, and to the fairness of the argument employed. On what evidence does the RMO reach his opinion that the patient is mentally disordered and requires hospital treatment, or that he is a danger to the public? If the evidence is established, do the RMO's conclusions follow logically?

In addition to making a thorough review of the RMO's report of the patient's behaviour, the representative should examine in detail the record of the patient's treatment. At a minimum, the following questions should be asked: What are the reasons for changes in medication? Do they follow or precede changes in behaviour? Is medication given purely for therapeutic benefit or is there an element of control or restraint? (*See* Code of Practice, paras 18.11–18.12.) Is the patient also receiving medication for physical ailments which may affect mood or behaviour? Does it appear that dosages have been varied, or have unusually high dosages been prescribed? Is the patient receiving drugs to counter the side effects of other medications? Is the patient seen regularly by the RMO, or does it appear that medication is re-prescribed 'automatically'? If more than one doctor has been involved in treatment, is there consistency in diagnosis and prescribed medication? Is there any indication that the diagnosis is tentative, or based on earlier records rather than current observations? How much time has been spent in seclusion or restraint? Are treatment goals indicated that can be achieved in a less restrictive setting? The representative may discuss these issues with the tribunal at the hearing or alternatively may submit to the tribunal a written statement in accordance with r 12(1) (*see 9.8.1*). While the purpose of the tribunal is to review the necessity for continued detention, rather than the treatment plan, it must be remembered that the patient is in hospital for treatment. The treatment itself should be perceived as fair as well as effective. Inappropriate restraint or punishment in the name of treatment can often promote resentment and, ultimately, inappropriate or even dangerous behaviour in the hospital.

13.8.3 Independent psychiatric opinion

Under s 76(1)(*a*) a doctor authorised by a patient or a nearest relative applicant may visit the patient at any reasonable time and examine him in private; he is also authorised to inspect any records relating to the patient's detention or treatment in any hospital (s 76(1)(*b*).

As discussed in *13.3.1* a representative should give careful consideration to whether expert opinion is required and if so, whether it should be provided by an independent social worker or an independent psychiatrist. An independent psychiatric opinion may be helpful for the following purposes:

(1) to assess the likely benefit of further psychiatric treatment;
(2) to assess whether further treatment can be given in any less restrictive setting and to suggest alternative arrangements for care and treatment;
(3) to assess the possibility of future dangerous behaviour;
(4) to provide details which have been omitted from the RMO's report;
(5) to examine the case and nursing notes in order to check the nature of incidents which have been reported by the RMO or to advise the representative on any other matter which may be detailed in those notes;
(6) to explain to the representative the meaning and implication of any technical diagnoses, prognoses and treatments which have been discussed in the RMO's report.

The MHRT places considerable importance on the professional medical opinions submitted to it. They give the MHRT more evidence on which to base a discharge decision or transfer recommendation, particularly in difficult cases. An independent report may sometimes be appropriate even in cases where the RMO is agreeing to discharge or transfer but the Legal Aid authorities may need to be persuaded that it is necessary before granting authority to meet the costs.

Where an independent psychiatrist supports the patient's discharge or transfer it is often helpful for the tribunal to discuss his report with him. The psychiatrist may be asked to attend the hearing by the representative or by the tribunal. Where the request is made by the tribunal it will probably be prepared to meet his costs. Where the representative asks the psychiatrist to attend, he may, with the special permission of the Area Director, cover the costs under the ABWOR provisions; alternatively, he may ask the tribunal to meet the costs (*see* **12.4** and **12.5**).

Choosing an appropriate psychiatrist to provide the independent report is important. Independent advice should be sought from a consultant or other senior psychiatrist and his particular expertise taken into consideration; although in cases where transfer is proposed it may be more important to instruct a psychiatrist who might be prepared to take clinical responsibility for the patient when he is transferred. There is no official register of independent psychiatrists (cf independent social enquiry reports in *14.4.1*), but organisations such as MIND and MENCAP may be able to advise on names of psychiatrists prepared to give independent reports. The Law Society's Legal Practice Information office also keeps a register of independent experts.

In choosing an expert witness, and in the lengthy discussions that will ensue, it is important to be aware of the nature of the relationship that is being formed. The Court of Appeal in *W v Egdell* [1990] 1 All ER 835, held that a doctor providing an independent medical opinion, just like any other doctor in a therapeutic relationship, has a duty to maintain the patient's confidences. The Court of Appeal, however, said that, under Rule 81(g) of the General Medical Council's Advice on Standards of Professional Conduct and Medical Ethics, 'rarely, disclosure may be justified on the ground that it is in the public interest . . .' Bingham LJ delineated the allowable exception to the duty of confidentiality:

> Where a man has committed multiple killings under the disability of serious mental illness, decisions which may lead directly or indirectly to his release from hospital should not be made unless a responsible authority is properly able to make an informed judgment that the risk of repetition is so small as to be acceptable. A consultant psychiatrist who becomes aware, even in the course of a confidential relationship, of information which leads him, in the exercise of what the court considers a sound professional judgment, to fear that such decisions may be made on the basis of inadequate information and with a real risk of consequent danger to the public is

entitled to take such steps as are reasonable in all the circumstances to communicate the grounds of his concern to responsible authorities.

The report of the independent psychiatrist, therefore, should be regarded as confidential. The independent psychiatrist may not, under any circumstances, disclose confidential information to the media, in a professional journal, or to friends or associates without the patient's informed consent. The doctor, however, could decide to disclose the information to the tribunal if he held a good faith, and well founded, professional belief that the patient would pose a serious danger to the public if he were discharged by the tribunal. See also *R v Crozier* [1991] Crim LR 138.

13.8.4 Learning disability and independent expert advice

It is now well accepted that the primary needs of learning disabled people are social, educational and caring, as well as medical, and that social workers, psychologists, teachers of special education and nurses can play an important part in the assessment, care and aftercare of people with learning disabilities. Patients should not be classified as mentally impaired or severely mentally impaired in the absence of a formal psychological assessment as evidence of severe or significant impairment of intelligence. This assessment should be part of a complete appraisal by medical, nursing, social work and psychology professionals, preferably professionals who are experienced with learning disabled people (Code of Practice, paras 28.3–28.4). Many learning disabled clients in local and special hospitals could be discharged if appropriate aftercare arrangements were made.

The medical components in the case of a learning disabled person are usually limited to instances where there is a specific accompanying mental or physical illness. It is very important to examine the major issues facing the MHRT in the case of a learning disabled person. If the issue relates to a mental or behavioural disorder it may be appropriate to choose as an independent expert a psychiatrist (or psychologist) experienced with learning disabled people. However, where the issue relates to the person's ability to guard against exploitation, or his future education, care or aftercare, a member of another appropriate profession may be useful. Psychologists sometimes specialise in assessment of intelligence and behaviour modification, while social workers can often give the most appropriate view as to a person's social situation.

13.8.5 Hospital social worker or nurse as witness

Social workers or nurses may provide first-hand accounts of the patient's behaviour on the ward and any incidents that have been reported by the RMO. While they may be willing to provide factual information to the tribunal they may be reluctant to present an opinion as to whether or not the patient should be discharged or transferred. It is becoming increasingly common for nurses to appear before tribunals. Often the patient's key worker is a nurse who submits a written report and gives evidence to back it up. Nurses are in the best position to respond to questions about what the patient is like in daily life on the ward.

13.8.6 Patient as witness and the problem of confidentiality

A representative should encourage a patient to discuss his case before the tribunal. Any attempt by the representative to 'hide' the patient will be noted by the tribunal and weaken his case. The patient should be asked to discuss his attitude to the hospital, his views on the treatment he has been receiving, the gains he thinks he has made, and he may also comment on any incidents reported by the RMO. The patient should be presented as a person with genuine strengths and weaknesses, and the latter, including, for example, past dangerous behaviour, should be openly discussed. It is important to get a sense of what the tribunal regards as most relevant, and to deal with problems directly.

Tribunal members often look at whether the patient has 'insight' into his own illness and experiences (J Peay, *Tribunals on Trial: A Study of Decision-Making Under the Mental Health Act, 1983*, Clarendon Press, Oxford, 1989). 'Insight' means the self-awareness of the patient, specifically his recognition that he was ill at the time of his offence or admission, and that his stability may be due to the effectiveness of medication. For those patients who will continue to require medication, the tribunal must be assured that the patient recognises this need and will continue to take the medication or other treatment after discharge. The patient's acknowledgement of his illness, and understanding of the need for continued treatment, is often a fragile construction. The tribunal will be concerned about the patient's relapse after discharge and (possible subsequent harm to himself or others. The representative should help the patient to recognise the tribunal's concerns. The representative should present his case emphasising evidence which demonstrates the stability of the patient's condition, the availability of supervision and support in the community, and the patient's understanding of the need for ongoing treatment and care after discharge.

The rules of procedure allow certain information in the reports to be withheld from the patient but not the representative (*see 9.8.1* and *9.8.2*). The representative may have difficulty in taking instructions and preparing a case where he cannot discuss with the patient all the relevant information and evidence, and should examine critically any assumption that it is in the patient's interests not to know relevant information (*9.8.1*). If the representative is barred from sharing information with the patient, he should use his judgment as to the extent to which he can verify certain relevant information and might reasonably choose to question the patient in a non-leading way. The representative should not disclose confidential information either directly or indirectly to the patient (r 12(3)), but it would be contrary to established legal principles and social ethics not to allow the patient to give his point of view on events of which he is aware and which may be significant to the tribunal's decision.

13.8.7 Cross-examination

Many of the most effective techniques for examination or cross-examination of witnesses hold good for MHRTs. However, it should be emphasised that persistently hostile questions put to the RMO are not often effective, since one of the objectives of MHRTs may be to gain the agreement of the RMO to a course of action; avoidance of undue aggression is likely to make implementation of the decision or recommendation more effective. Further, the rules explicitly require the tribunal to adopt an informal approach; the purpose is to encourage all parties, and particularly the patient, to discuss the case openly with each other and the tribunal, and the latter will discourage formal cross-examination if it is associated with an overly legalistic approach. It should also be remembered that the medical member of the MHRT is usually also an RMO who himself has an interest in the way evidence is obtained. He and the other tribunal members are unlikely to look kindly on a destructive line of questioning. Nevertheless, the RMO must be called upon to justify his expert opinion with clear and objective evidence (medical, social and behavioural), and to give reasons for his opinion which are open to rational scrutiny by laymen and within the legal process.

13.8.8 Subpoena, adjournment and obtaining further information

Where the medical information available to the tribunal is inadequate or in any way incomplete, it has powers to obtain further information. The representative is referred to **9.10** for the discussion of these powers.

Chapter 14

The Patient's Circumstances after Discharge

14.1 The need for information: An individual plan of aftercare

Information concerning the patient's circumstances after discharge is known as social circumstances or aftercare information. It may be comprised of details of accommodation (in the family home or with relatives or friends or, alternatively, accommodation which may be provided through the statutory authorities or voluntary bodies), the support of the patient's relatives or friends, community facilities such as day centres, and facilities for continuing care such as out-patient or day patient services or community nursing.

The patient's circumstances after discharge are often the most important factors influencing the tribunal's decision. The tribunal must have a clear picture of where and how the patient would live if he were to be discharged. (One exception to this principle is when a patient wishes to be transferred from a special to a local hospital and where it is clear that such a move will precede any consideration of discharge, but the representative must be careful not to anticipate the tribunal's decision. The representative is referred to Chapter 15 for consideration of transfer.)

A patient's social circumstances following his discharge from hospital are at the core of the tribunal's concerns. An individual plan of aftercare providing for treatment and support following discharge is the most effective means of assuring the tribunal that the patient is likely to maintain stability within the community. Ideally, the individual plan of aftercare should be prepared with the patient's participation, together with the advice of trained mental health professionals including a psychiatrist and social worker. It should include the following.

14.1.1 Medication

The plan should specify the psychiatrist or general practitioner who will be responsible for devising and monitoring the patient's treatment plan in the community following discharge. Often the key person is a Community Psychiatric Nurse (CPN). If the medication is to be administered by injection, a regularly scheduled appointment calendar, covering perhaps the first six months after discharge, will be advantageous. In the case of a patient who will receive oral medication, a general practitioner, social worker or other community mental health professional may be willing to observe and supervise the patient in taking his medication. This can be helpful even if done only a few times weekly or monthly, as long as it is on a regular basis. The patient gains encouragement by the interest of a mental health professional, and is periodically given fresh impetus to maintain co-operation with the treatment plan.

14.1.2 Treatment and counselling

The plan should specify which mental health professionals in the community will provide treatment, care, and social support. Evidence of a previous relationship or a recent meeting between the patient and the mental health professional is valuable; the willingness of known people within the community to assume responsibility for the care of the patient militates strongly for discharge. The patient benefits from a variety of caring professionals, due to the corresponding increase in social interaction and the inherent value of an inter-disciplinary approach. This also ensures that the patient does not develop a disproportionate dependence on one person; nevertheless the plan must specify one person or group of people who will serve to co-ordinate the entire aftercare plan and prevent its fragmentation.

14.1.3 Support network

Self-isolation is a major factor leading to the failure of patients to make the transition to community living. The aftercare plan must clearly identify family, friends, neighbours and volunteers who will form the patient's social web. It should provide for regular activities and outings and, if appropriate, home visits. Many people are quite willing to offer their support; they may in turn be given training and support by voluntary associations. A plan providing for such a 'second tier' of support is particularly good. Employment, including sheltered employment, should also be considered a part of the patient's social support, as its primary value in many cases is not only economic, but also the opportunities created for social interaction and integration.

14.1.4 Financial concerns

The patient's source of income and projected expenses after discharge must be set forth. If necessary, a guardian or other responsible person able to oversee the patient's budget should be identified. Ensuring that the patient receives all of the social benefits to which he is legally entitled is important to his quality of life and stability.

14.1.5 Housing

Housing is discussed in detail in **14.5** below.

14.1.6 Drug or alcohol abuse

Drug and alcohol abuse is sometimes a part of a patient's history. The time following discharge from hospital is a vulnerable period for those with drug or alcohol problems, and when necessary, the aftercare plan should provide for participation in counselling or support groups.

Tribunals almost invariably endorse the recommendations made to them (Peay 1989). A strong and detailed presentation of the patient's aftercare information is absolutely crucial if the representative is successfully to advocate for discharge. The advice of RMOs is not always based on the most current or accurate facts concerning a patient's circumstances. A comprehensive plan, prepared by the representative in conjunction with an independent social worker, may provide the tribunal with a genuine opportunity for discussion, rather than a mere rubber-stamping of the RMO's opinion.

14.2 Aftercare information available to the tribunal

In applications other than assessment applications and in references, the responsible authority must provide the tribunal, insofar as is reasonably practicable, with an up-to-date social circumstances report in accordance with Part B of Sched 1 to the Rules (r 6(1)(*c*)). The representative is referred to *9.7.1* where the duty to provide the report and the information contained in it is discussed in detail. The representative should note that, unlike a medical report which must be provided in every case, the social circumstances report may not be provided if it is impracticable to do so.

In assessment applications a social circumstances report must be provided to the tribunal if it is reasonable to do so in the time available (r 32(1), Sched 1, Part B). The representative is referred to *11.1.3* for discussion of this provision.

Note that where the nearest relative has made an application for the patient's admission for assessment or for treatment, the hospital managers are required under s 14 to obtain a report on the patient's social circumstances from the responsible social services authority (*see* **1.5** and *9.7.1*). There is no explicit duty on the responsible authority to provide a s 14 report to the tribunal; however, it may be argued that where such a report is available and is relevant to the patient's discharge the responsible authority should send it to the tribunal.

Normally the responsible authority asks the social services authority which would be responsible for the patient's care if he were to be discharged to provide the social circumstances information to the tribunal. The responsible social services authority is that for the area in which the patient is normally resident. In the case of a patient who has been in hospital for many years there may be no apparent residence in any area; the hospital managers must then persuade a social services authority to accept responsibility for him and so a report to the tribunal on his social circumstances may, in this instance, be unobtainable.

Some information concerning the patient's social circumstances may be included in the RMO's report. However, this should not be regarded as a substitute for a comprehensive account of such circumstances by the responsible social services authority. Unless the responsible authority can provide proper reasons to show that it is impracticable, the social circumstances report provided to the tribunal should be provided specifically for the purposes of the proceedings and should directly address the issue of the patient's discharge; a social circumstances report provided for some other purpose will not normally be sufficient. Some hospitals issue the relevant social services authority with a questionnaire concerning home circumstances and other facilities, which is then submitted to the tribunal.

Although since the 1983 Act there has been a marked improvement in the provision of good quality information from social services, there are still cases where the responsible authority fails to provide the tribunal with a comprehensive account of the facilities which would be available to the patient if he were to be discharged. There are a number of reasons for this. First, under the Rules the authority has wide scope to argue that an up-to-date social circumstances report could not practicably be obtained. Secondly, the social services authority may be reluctant to devote its resources to a full investigation of the patient's circumstances if it feels that there is no realistic prospect of discharge. Thirdly, where a patient has committed an offence in his home area it can be difficult for him to be discharged there. Nevertheless, it must be emphasised that the tribunal cannot reach an informed decision as to whether a patient should be discharged unless it has a clear picture of where and how the patient would live if he were to be discharged. An important role of the representative is therefore to assess the information and to ensure that the tribunal's decision is based on an adequate knowledge of the patient's circumstances if he were to be discharged. This is discussed further below.

14.3 Code of Practice: Aftercare

Chapter 26 of the Code of Practice and circulars HC(89)5 and LAC(89)7 emphasise the importance of aftercare and of marshalling full information for authorities charged with deciding whether to discharge patients. (See also Department of Health, *Discharge of Patients From Hospitals*, 1989.) The purpose of aftercare is to enable a patient to return to his home or accommodation other than a hospital or nursing home, and to minimise the chances of his needing any future in-patient hospital care (para 26.1).

The Code of Practice recommends that health and social services authorities, together with local voluntary organisations, agree on procedures for aftercare arrangements. Proper records must be kept for all patients to whom s 117 (duty to provide aftercare) could apply. Health and local authorities, therefore, must plan jointly for aftercare, with individual responsibility resting on the mental health professionals providing care.

The RMO must take responsibility to ensure that a discussion takes place with the relevant multi-disciplinary team and health and local authorities to establish an individual aftercare plan. While the statutory duty to provide aftercare applies after a decision has been taken to discharge or grant leave to a patient, the representative should try to facilitate these discussions before the tribunal hearing.

The process of discussing aftercare with the multi-disciplinary hospital team and those responsible for health and social services in the community is itself beneficial to the patient and provides assistance to the tribunal.

The persons that should be involved in discussions about aftercare include the RMO, a nurse who cares for the patient in hospital, a social worker specialising in mental health, the general practitioner, a CPN, a representative of a voluntary organisation (where appropriate) and, if the patient wishes, with a relative or another nominated representative (Code of Practice, para 26.7). A representative of the housing authority should also be invited if housing is an issue.

The Code of Practice (para 26.9) lists a number of issues to be carefully examined in planning aftercare: the patient's own wishes and needs (the representative can ensure that the patient's voice is heard, perhaps by being present in the discussions); the views of relevant relatives, friends, supporters or advocates; the agreement of the receiving authority if different from the discharging authority; the involvement of other agencies eg, probation or voluntary organisations; an individual aftercare plan based upon proper assessment and clearly identified needs including consideration of day care, accommodation, out-patient treatment, counselling, personal support, claiming welfare rights and benefits, and assisting in managing finances; the appointment of a Key Worker to monitor the implementation of the aftercare plan and liaison; and identification of unmet needs.

All aftercare plans should not only respect the person's rights but also his culture, religion and integrity as a human being.

14.4 Obtaining information about the patient's circumstances after discharge

There are broadly two ways in which the representative may obtain further information concerning the patient's circumstances if he were to be discharged: first, he may ask the tribunal to obtain necessary information and secondly, he may obtain the information himself.

The first step is to inform the tribunal that the information on the patient's circumstances is incomplete; the representative may do so under r 12(1) which allows him to comment on the information disclosed to him by the tribunal (*see 9.8.1*).

He may remind the tribunal of the responsible authority's duty to provide information on social circumstances unless it is impracticable to do so, or, in the case of assessment applications, it is not possible to do so in the time available. The tribunal may ascertain the authority's reasons for not providing the information and, where it is not satisfied, ask it to obtain the information.

The tribunal also has extensive powers under the Rules to obtain further information. First, under r 15(1) it has a wide discretion to call for any other reports or information and may give directions as to how that information should be obtained and by whom it may be obtained. Thus, the tribunal may direct that the responsible social services authority provide a report directly to the tribunal or that a social worker from that authority gives evidence to the tribunal. Secondly, during the hearing, if it appears to the tribunal that further information is required it may, in accordance with r 16, adjourn the proceedings to allow the representative or any other person to obtain the information. Thirdly, the tribunal may, in exceptional circumstances, subpoena a person, such as a social worker, to appear before it as a witness or to produce documents (r 14). These powers are discussed in **9.10**.

The representative may himself take steps to obtain information concerning the patient's circumstances were he to be discharged. The role of the representative as the patient's active advocate entails that he actively gather his own information, rather than passively resting his case for discharge on the information gathered by the tribunal. The momentum of detention is powerful and fraught with self-fulfilling rationales which make the prospect of unjust or unnecessary confinement far too possible. The role of the representative is to argue forcefully for the patient's rights, by presenting the strongest case for discharge. He may prepare this case in the following ways.

14.4.1 Independent social enquiry reports

In appropriate cases the representative may seek a report from an independent social worker although this is rarely done. This may be in addition to an independent psychiatric report or instead of it. The representative should note, however, that the Legal Aid Board may be reluctant to fund both reports and the representative should consider carefully which report is more appropriate (*see 12.4.3* for further discussion of financing independent reports). In the past, representatives have often sought independent psychiatric reports in preference to independent social enquiry reports. To some extent this reflects a misconception of the nature and purpose of psychiatric care. In many cases the patient's detention and discharge have less to do with diagnosis, treatment or dangerousness than with the availability of community facilities as an alternative to hospital. Many government reports and inquiries have concluded that large numbers of patients in hospital could be discharged provided that appropriate accommodation, social and medical support were available, so that a report on such facilities is in many cases more appropriate than an independent psychiatric opinion.

The representative should instruct an independent social worker as to the nature of the issues which are important in the case and the issues on which advice is sought. Where necessary the representative should ask the tribunal for permission to release to the social worker any information which has been disclosed to him in confidence (r 12(3); *see 9.8.2*). An independent social enquiry report may:

(1) provide another view of the aftercare facilities;
(2) clarify any important details of the patient's home circumstances;
(3) investigate the facilities for housing, treatment, social support community care and employment that may be provided to the patient by the local authority or by voluntary bodies;
(4) comment on the appropriateness of the patient's detention in the context of less restrictive facilities that may exist in the community.

The independent social worker's report is confidential and may not be disclosed without the patient's consent. The representative should be aware, however, that the social worker may be allowed to inform the tribunal and/or the detaining authority if he has good reason for believing that the patient would pose a danger to other persons in the community. (See *W v Egdell* [1990] 1 All ER 835.)

An independent social enquiry report should not be provided by a social worker who has a connection with either the responsible authority or the responsible social services authority. MIND and the Law Society's Legal Practice Information Office maintain information about independent social workers who may be willing to provide reports for MHRTs (see Appendix 8 for addresses and telephone numbers).

14.4.2 Enquiries by the representative

The representative may often obtain helpful information from the patient's social worker in the hospital. He may establish contact with the patient's relatives or friends who may be able to provide him with accommodation or other help if he were to be discharged. It has been known that an offer of assistance from a friend or relative has been sufficient to prompt an RMO to change his opinion concerning the need for detention; in this context the hearing is a forum where not only the tribunal but also the RMO is given information which is relevant to the patient's case but of which he may have been unaware.

The representative should be familiar with the powers and duties of local social services authorities and housing authorities with respect to mentally disordered persons and to persons, whether mentally disordered or not, who may be discharged from hospital; these powers and duties are discussed in **14.5** below.

14.4.3 Social worker as witness

Where relevant information has been omitted from the responsible authority's reports or where clarification is required, the representative may ask the tribunal to call a social worker from the responsible social services authority to give evidence. Asking the social worker to attend in person may avoid having to adjourn the proceedings and is useful in assessment applications where the need for speed is particularly important. Irrespective of whether or not the social worker attends the hearing the representative should discuss the case and the social circumstances information with him before the hearing.

14.5 Statutory powers and duties to provide aftercare

The local authority and the district health authority have a number of statutory powers and duties to provide support services for mentally disordered people of which the representative should be aware. For a more detailed discussion of the law the reader is referred to L Gostin, *Mental Health Services: Law and Practice* (Shaw & Sons, London, looseleaf).

14.5.1 Duties of local social services authorities

The general duties of local social services authorities in providing social services are set out in three main statutory provisions:

(1) Residential accommodation (National Assistance Act 1948, s 21(1)) Local authorities are empowered (and in many cases required) to provide residential accommodation for persons who by reason of age, infirmity, or any other circumstance are in need of care and attention which is otherwise not available to them. The Secretary of State has directed authorities, *inter alia*, to make arrangements to provide residential accommodation for persons ordinarily resident in their area. These provisions are often used to provide accommodation for elderly people, sometimes referred to as 'Part III' accommodation, referring to Part III of the 1948 Act.

(2) Welfare services (National Assistance Act 1948, s 29(1)) Local authorities are empowered (and in many cases required) to make arrangements for the welfare of persons who suffer from mental disorder of any description, and other specified forms of handicap. The Secretary of State has directed authorities, *inter alia*, to provide a social work service and such advice and support as may be needed by mentally disordered people.

(3) Prevention of illness, care and aftercare (National Health Service Act 1977, s 21(1)(b), Sched 8) Local authorities are empowered (and in many cases required), to make arrangements for the prevention of illness, the care of persons suffering from illness and the aftercare of persons so suffering. 'Illness' includes mental disorder within the meaning of the Mental Health Act 1983. The Secretary of State directs authorities to provide residential accommodation such as residential homes, hostels, group homes and minimum support facilities, training and day centres, and social work and social support services and other domiciliary and care services to people living in their homes or elsewhere.

(4) Aftercare (MHA 1983, s 117) Section 117 of the MHA 1983 places a duty on the DHA and the social services authority to provide in co-operation with relevant voluntary organisations, aftercare services. This provision applies to patients who have been detained for treatment (s 3), under a hospital order (s 37) or under a transfer direction (ss 47, 48) and are then discharged. The duty, technically, does not apply until after the MHRT has decided to discharge the patient. Nevertheless, good professional practice would require relevant health and social services authorities to have regard to these provisions and to be in a position to provide a

full aftercare service to patients discharged by MHRTs. This aftercare provision can often be best utilised in cases where the MHRT are minded to grant a delayed discharge. In such cases the relevant authority would have a clear duty to plan and arrange adequate aftercare support and services.

14.5.2 General duties of local housing authorities

(1) Review of housing needs It is the duty of every local housing authority to consider housing conditions in its district and the needs of the district with respect to the provisions of further housing accommodation (Housing Act 1985, s 8). A housing authority, in considering the housing needs of its district, must have regard to the special needs of chronically sick, and disabled persons (Chronically Sick and Disabled Persons Act 1970, s 3(1)). The authority must periodically review the housing information brought to its notice by its own offices or otherwise (Housing Act 1985, s 8(2)).

(2) Provision of accommodation and accompanying services A local authority may provide housing accommodation by the erection of houses on land acquired or appropriated by it, conversion of buildings into houses or acquiring houses (Housing Act 1985, s 9 as amended by Local Government and Housing Act 1989, s 161). The authority can also fit out, and furnish the accommodation and provide meals and other facilities and services. However, s 161 of the Local Government and Housing Act 1989 aims to achieve a shift in the role of local authorities to be facilitators rather than service providers by stating that nothing in this Act shall be taken to require a local housing authority itself to acquire or hold any houses or other land.

14.5.3 Duties of local housing authorities towards homeless persons

A local housing authority has a duty to house homeless persons under Part III of the Housing Act 1985 if satisfied that the person is homeless or threatened with homelessness, in priority need of accommodation (mentally ill and mentally handicapped people are included) and did not become homeless intentionally. Other homeless persons may be entitled to assistance. See generally A Arden, *Homeless Persons: The Housing Act Part III* (LAG 1988);

Department of the Environment, Department of Health and Welsh Office, *Homelessness Code of Guidance for Local Authorities* (issued under s 71 of the Housing Act 1985) (3rd edn) (London HMSO 1991). The 1985 Housing Act is an important statute for mentally disordered people. There are several particular issues which arise in the construction of Part III of the 1985 Act which are reviewed below.

(1) Homelessness It is arguable that the term 'homelessness' could include patients who remain in institutional care only because there is no alternative accommodation in the community—ie, what could be called 'hidden homelessness'. However, until a patient is actually discharged he would have an express or implied licence to occupy the accommodation in the hospital and would be unlikely to be regarded as homeless under s 58 of the 1985 Act.

(2) Threatened with homelessness A patient may be regarded as threatened with homelessness if he is likely to be discharged from hospital within 28 days (Housing Act 1985, s 58(4)). Authorities should be prepared to advise and assist people where the possibility of becoming homeless is known more than 28 days in advance. This would clearly arise where tribunals have made an order for delayed discharge (*see* **8.2**). The Code of Guidance provides that housing authorities should identify a nominated homelessness liaison officer to liaise between the department dealing with housing and health authorities or departments on, eg, the rehousing of patients on discharge from NHS general, psychiatric and mental handicap hospitals and hostels (paras 6.11, 15.5 and 15.7).

(3) Intentional homelessness A reasonable justification for departure, or imminent departure, must exist in order to avoid the imputation that a person rendered himself intentionally homeless. A compulsorily detained patient is, or is threatened with, homelessness if his liability to detention is, or will be, discharged or expired. The patient would have to declare an intention not to remain in hospital on an informal basis and, arguably, the hospital would have to regard continued residence as undesirable. It would be difficult in these circumstances to conclude that the patient rendered himself intentionally homeless for it could not be said to be reasonable for a person to continue to occupy a hospital bed when the medical need for it has ended. It is for the housing authority to satisfy itself whether the person is homeless or

threatened with homelessness intentionally; the burden does not rest with the applicant to prove that he is not.

(4) Incapacity to manage affairs A mentally disordered person who has lost his home in the community, eg, for failure to pay his rent or mortgage, owing to an incapacity to manage his affairs cannot reasonably be regarded as having made himself intentionally homeless.

(5) Priority need It might be assumed that, if a patient has made sufficient recovery so as to be discharged from hospital, he cannot be considered to have a priority need due to vulnerability as a result of mental illness or handicap or other special reason. Note, however, that usually a tribunal does not make a discharge order on the basis that the person is no longer mentally disordered, but on the grounds that detention is no longer necessary for reason of health and safety. Further, it should be possible to establish that a person, even if he were no longer diagnosed as mentally ill or handicapped, was in priority need if he retained a marked social handicap resulting, eg, from prolonged residence in an institution. Housing authorities are advised in the Code of Guidance (para 6.11) that 'Many people discharged from psychiatric and mental handicap hospitals and local authority hostels into the community may be regarded as vulnerable. Health authorities have an express duty under advice contained in DH circulars HC(90)23 and LASSL(90)11 to implement a specifically tailored care programme for patients considered for discharge from psychiatric hospitals and all new patients accepted by the specialist psychiatric services.' Authorities are reminded that the liaison arrangements between housing, health and social services authorities may fall down and that they should be 'sensitive to direct approaches from discharged patients who are homeless.'

(6) Local connection A patient in hospital for many years may have difficulty establishing a local connection with any particular housing authority. A compulsorily detained patient cannot have a local connection with the authority in which the hospital is situated solely by reason of confinement in the hospital.

The local connection provisions should not pose a problem for an otherwise homeless patient: the duty to secure accommodation can be transferred to an authority where the patient has a local connection; or, in the absence of a local connection with any authority, the duty rests with authority to which the patient applies (1985 Act, s 61).

14.5.4 Function of housing associations

Registered housing associations are non-profit making bodies managed by a voluntary committee of which there are more than 3,000 nationally. They are established for the purpose of constructing, improving, managing, or encouraging the construction or improvement of houses (Housing Associations Act 1985). Registered housing associations can provide hostel accommodation that gives a substantial degree of care to tenants provided that the additional 'caring' costs above the normal hostel allowances are met by other statutory bodies or from charitable sources. Projects under these 'joint funding' arrangements, ie where local social services authorities or recognised voluntary organisations make 'topping-up' contributions in respect of management costs of a supportive nature, are eligible for housing association grant. Projects that are not eligible for a grant are those required to be registered under the Registered Homes Act 1984, or are clearly designed to provide accommodation involving an intensive degree of care and support—eg, where social services authorities are empowered to assume responsibility for the fees of individual residents under the National Assistance Act 1948 (s 21(1)) or the National Health Service Act 1977 (s 21(1)). The range of accommodation which can be provided for mentally disordered people includes hostels, group homes, individual lettings and clusters of bedsits or flatlets.

Chapter 15

Transfer from Special Hospitals

15.1 Special hospitals

A hospital is defined in s 145(1) of the Mental Health Act as '(a) any health service hospital . . . ; and (b) any accommodation provided by a local authority and used as a hospital.' The duty of the Secretary of State for Health to promote a comprehensive health service includes in s 4 of the National Health Service Act 1977 'a duty to provide and maintain establishments . . . for persons subject to detention under the Mental Health Act 1983 who in his opinion require treatment under conditions of special security on account of their dangerous, violent or criminal propensities.'

Under s 145(1) of the Mental Health Act the Secretary of State for Health is designated as the manager of the special hospitals. The Secretary of State has delegated all of his management responsibilities to the Special Hospitals Service Authority. The special hospitals have a resident population of approximately 1,700 patients. There are three special hospitals: Broadmoor Hospital, situated in Crowthorne, Berkshire; Rampton Hospital, situated in Retford, Nottinghamshire; and Ashworth Hospital (formerly Park Lane and Moss Side Hospitals), situated in Maghull, Lancashire (Special Hospitals Service Authority Development Plan 1991–96).

15.2 Regional Secure Units

In 1974 the Committee on Mentally Abnormal Offenders (the Butler Committee; Cmnd 6244, 1975) proposed the establishment of a secure unit in each RHA which would provide a transitional stage between the special hospitals and local psychiatric hospitals.

The unit would serve the needs of patients who did not require the high security of a special hospital but who required a greater degree of control than is provided by the 'open door' policy of most local hospitals. These proposals were accepted, and the government made a grant to each RHA for the construction of the units, either by adaptation of existing hospitals or by building anew. As an interim measure regions were to designate particular hospitals which would provide treatment in secure conditions until the proper regional units could be built.

As of 31 January 1991 there were a total of just under 600 beds in regional secure units (RSUs) in England.

Regional secure units usually have a regional catchment area. In addition to receiving patients from special hospitals RSUs also provide a local forensic service. They take patients from prisons and local psychiatric hospitals. Those patients are often seen as having a greater priority for admission to a RSU than special hospital patients as their need for care (or, in the case of patients in local hospitals for security) is more urgent. For information on the regional secure facilities available in a particular region the representative should contact the regional medical officer for the relevant RHA.

15.3 The purpose of transfer

Transfer serves two major purposes. First, it allows the patient to adjust gradually to increased freedoms within a comparatively controlled environment and secondly, the authorities can ensure that the patient receives any necessary treatment, and his progress can be monitored and assistance given.

There is no ready method of deciding when it is more appropriate to advocate a patient's transfer than to argue for his discharge. The decision depends on many factors: the patient's mental condition, the need for further treatment, the risk of further offences or dangerous behaviour, and the availability of hostel or other suitable accommodation in the community. In general, if a patient has been in a special hospital for a considerable period, transfer into a local hospital or RSU is likely to precede discharge (unless, of course, the criteria for discharge are satisfied). As will be discussed later in this chapter, some patients may wait for two years or considerably more on a transfer list for a bed in a local NHS hospital. It is not uncommon for a patient on a transfer list to have improved to the point that discharge is appropriate rather than transfer.

15.4 Reasons for transfer delays

Transfers to a lesser degree of security (as opposed to absolute discharge) are a common, and often preferable route by which patients leave special hospitals. Many patients in special hospitals have been detained in maximum security conditions for many years. This makes it difficult to assess how the patient would progress and behave outside of a secure facility; and it makes it difficult for the patient to adjust to the freedom of living in the community. A person's ability to cope with the complete freedom of an unstructured environment after an extended stay in a total and secure institution is limited. Empirical studies have demonstrated that institutions breed disabilities in coping with everyday life irrespective of a person's mental state.

The most effective and humane method of leaving special hospital, therefore, is often through transfer to less secure provision. Patients require a full range of facilities including regional (medium) secure units, local hospitals, and community (supportive) services (see below).

The need to find a less secure facility to allow for a gradual return to complete freedom is perhaps the greatest challenge for the representative of a special hospital patient. Inordinate delays in transferring special hospital patients have long plagued the mental health services. See L Gostin, *A Human Condition*, Part II (1977); L Gostin, *Institutions Observed: Towards a New Concept of Secure Provision in Mental Health* (The Kings Fund, 1986).

The Mental Health Act Commission in each of its four Biennial Reports has expressed serious concern with delays in transferring special hospital patients to regional secure units and local hospitals. In many instances, patients have waited two years or more *after* being placed on the transfer list, with a firm recommendation from their RMO. The Commission's Third Report contains the case of a patient who, in 1989, had been in Rampton since 1978 even though his RMO and a MHRT agreed he did not need to be there. He remained for eight years in Rampton, far from his home and detained in a level of security he did not need.

The Mental Health Act Commission regards transfer delays from one level of security to another as one of its highest priorities. If a blockage occurs anywhere in the system (at the Home Office, Department of Health, special hospitals, regional secure units (RSUs), local hospitals, or social services authorities), it can have serious consequences for patients. These delays ought not to be regarded as a mere inconvenience or an administrative problem. A person's liberty is at stake, and it is morally wrong to detain him in conditions more secure and restrictive than necessary for his condition. Nevertheless, the Mental Health Act Commission reported that many persons and authorities responsible for special hospital patients have not shown a sense of urgency in obtaining transfers.

Special hospital patients can be awaiting transfer within several different categories:

(1) some patients are on trial leave in a regional secure unit or local hospital;
(2) some patients remain in special hospitals because of the lack of suitable local facilities;
(3) some patients remain in special hospitals even though local facilities are available because they have not received the necessary Home Office approval for transfer.

Many patients are on a 'transfer list' because they have been recommended for transfer by the RMO. The transfer list is not a comprehensive list of persons who could benefit from a transfer. RMOs may not even put a patient on a transfer list because he is pessimistic about finding a less secure placement. In some areas, the RMO is highly conservative, and the tribunal may take another view about the need for early transfer.

Many reasons exist for transfer and, if the representative is to have a positive effect on speeding transfer, he needs to know what these reasons are and how to overcome each obstacle. The first reason for transfer delays is that those responsible simply do not move with the speed and urgency that the situation requires. The Commission found that delay can occur in initiating or answering correspondence among several parties: the Home Office, the Department of Health, the RMO, the local hospital or RSU consultant, or the case worker or social services authority. Identifying the persons or authorities who have neglected their responsibility for obtaining a transfer can be an important first step in removing the obstacle to progress. The representative should ask the independent psychiatrist to examine any correspondence relevant to transfer or trial leave in the course of his persual of the case notes.

A second cause of delay can occur in securing the approval of the Home Office. This is particularly so where the case is reviewed by the Advisory Board on Restricted Patients (the Aarvold Board). See the Report on the Aarvold Committee on Procedures for the

Discharge and Supervision of Psychiatric Patients Subject to Special Restrictions (Cmnd 5191, 1973). Particularly difficult cases of restricted patients are referred to the Board for its advice before the Home Secretary approves a transfer or discharge.

The Mental Health Act Commission recommended that a time limit of 90 days be set for decisions taken by the Advisory Board and the Home Office. This is by analogy with s 74(2)(*b*) of the Act which specifies the time within which the Home Secretary must notify a tribunal that he will permit the discharge of a patient who is subject to a restriction direction.

A third reason for delay in transfer is the difficulty of finding an appropriate place that is willing to receive the patient. The key to a transfer is finding an appropriate, less secure facility and a consultant who is willing to take responsibility. Many cases arise where the catchment area hospital refuses to take the patient because it lacks the facilities or the consultant refuses to accept responsibility. The local hospital may give a variety of reasons such as a lack of beds, inadequate security, insufficient nursing staff or lack of therapeutic or rehabilitative resources. Sometimes the problem arises because the hospital or local community has had negative experiences with the patient in the past, and is reluctant to have him back. The problem is particularly acute in regions without adequate medium secure facilities.

The Commission suggested a number of possible remedies. If the DHA says it has insufficient facilities, it could be asked to pay for the cost of care in another NHS hospital or in a private hospital. If the local consultant is an obstacle, the health authority, as employer, could be asked to require co-operation or seek another consultant's help. By analogy to s 39 of the 1983 Act, the Regional Health Authority could be required to advise the Secretary of State of the reasons why a bed cannot be found.

Trial leave can also be explored. In such cases, if the special hospital promises to take the patient back in the event of a problem, it can provide an incentive for co-operation.

Finally, if the health authority is negligent or simply will not co-operate, it could be construed as maladministration, and could be referred to the Health Service Commissioner for investigation. If there is a problem with aftercare services, the tribunal can be asked to supoena the Director of Social Services; if the problem is lack of a hospital bed, a representative of the appropriate health authority may be required to attend.

If the health or social services authority does not co-operate, the tribunal or RMO could consider giving notice of the intention to discharge the patient. This would invoke the 'aftercare' duties in s 117 of the Act.

15.5 Range of secure facilities

Mentally disordered offenders should be placed in the least restrictive setting commensurate with their personal and clinical needs, and the need to protect the public. This means that they should remain in a special hospital for as short a time as necessary, and should move to gradually reduced security with the goal of returning to their normal communities as soon as possible. Patients should, wherever possible, be in a local hospital or community settings near their homes and families, rather than in maximum or medium secure facilities. The best way to accomplish this goal is by providing rehabilitation and support in sustaining an independent life. *Department of Health and Home Office Review of Health and Social Services for Mentally Disordered Offenders: Report of the Community Advisory Group* (November 1991).

A perennial problem in the mental health services is the absence of a range of less secure facilities to enable special hospital patients to be treated in the least secure accommodation necessary to meet their needs. The provision of facilities 'is weighted very strongly towards the secure end, and the system is often described as an inverted pyramid,' P Fennell, 'Diversion of Mentally Disordered Offenders from Custody' [1991] Crim LR 333. While there are some 1,700 beds in special hospitals, the number of medium security beds at the regional and local level appears inadequate. As of 31 January 1991 there was a total of 597 beds in regional secure units in England, *Department of Health and Home Office Review of Health and Social Services for Mentally Disordered Offenders* (The Reed Committee, 7 November 1991). By comparison, the Butler Committee (Report of the Committee on Mentally Abnormal Offenders, Cmnd 6244, 1975) recommended 2,000 beds in medium secure units as long ago as the mid-1970s. The Report of the Hospital Advisory Group more recently recommended that Regional Health Authorities take immediate steps to plan secure hospital facilities for 1,000 per million population, *Department of Health and Home Office Review of Health and Social Services for Mentally Disordered Offenders* (November 1991). As the Mental Health Act Commission noted in its *Fourth Biennial Report* (1991, para 10.2), there is an 'acute lack of appropriate facilities' for learning disabled people who offend, resulting in patients being placed, or kept in special hospitals for want of any other, more suitable placement.

Mental Health Review Tribunals, it must be remembered, are also frustrated by the same inadequate system of secure accommodation. Tribunals are unlikely to discharge a patient who really needs to be transferred, and unlikely to transfer unless they are convinced that there is an appropriate place to go. The job for mental health campaigners is to call for more resources; while the job for the representative is to help find the proper placement for the patient and to circumvent the numerous obstacles that can delay progress toward a more independent life for the person he represents.

15.6 Law and practice

A patient may be transferred from a special to a local hospital if the following three conditions are satisfied:

(1) The Special Hospitals Service Authority (SHSA), as manager of the special hospital, gives the authority for transfer (SI 1983 No 893, reg 7(2)(*a*)). In practice the decision as to whether a patient should be transferred is normally taken by the patient's RMO in the special hospital. Where the RMO considers that a patient should be transferred he will write a transfer report to the SHSA who will normally sanction it and give the necessary authority. If the RMO supports transfer the SHSA will almost invariably authorise it. Conversely, the SHSA will rarely authorise a transfer if the patient's RMO opposes it. Nevertheless, in exceptional cases the Secretary of State may be prepared to give the authority for transfer against the advice of the RMO; however, as a general rule, the SHSA agrees to the recommendation of the patient's RMO. In the case of a restricted patient a panel of professional members of the SHSA will consider the RMOs proposal and will forward a response to C3 Division in the Home Office.

(2) The SHSA is satisfied that arrangements have been made for the admission of the patient to the hospital to which he is to be transferred within 28 days from the date on which the authority for his transfer is given (SI 1983 No 893, reg 7(2)(*b*)). Thus, even if the RMO is prepared to recommend transfer, no movement can take place unless a bed is available for the patient in a local hospital. It is the duty of the Secretary

of State for Health to provide facilities in the NHS (NHS Act 1977, s 3); this duty has been delegated by him to RHAs and may be further delegated by RHAs to DHAs. In practice any request to a RHA or a DHA to provide a place for a special hospital patient is passed to the catchment area hospital which is responsible for the patient's care. This is normally determined on the basis of the patient's place of residence.

Where the patient has retained no real links with his home area, the catchment area may be determined on the basis of other factors, such as the address of his nearest interested relative. The patient may hold strong views about where he would like to live; this may also be taken into account. The catchment area of a hospital is often further subdivided between consultant psychiatrists in the hospital (this is called 'sectorisation') with the result that for each patient there may be one consultant psychiatrist in the NHS who is responsible for his care. The request from the special hospital to accept a patient whose transfer has been proposed is normally sent to that consultant. The consultant, together with members of his staff, may visit the patient in the special hospital in order to assess his suitability for transfer into their care or may decide on the basis of the written reports from the special hospital as to whether he should be admitted. If the consultant and his staff agree to receive the patient and the SHSA has given the necessary authority ((1) above) then, subject to the Home Secretary's consent in the case of a restricted patient (see (3) below), the patient may be transferred. If the consultant and his staff decide not to admit the patient he cannot be transferred to that hospital; furthermore, it is rare for any other hospital to admit a patient when, on the basis of catchment area, it is not responsible for him. The consultant may refuse to accept a patient for any reason, eg, lack of room, objections to the patient's character or past behaviour, refusal by the staff to accept the patient, lack of security and catchment area arguments (see *Ashingdane v Secretary of State for Social Services and others*, unreported, 18 February 1980 CA, discussed in *15.8.4* below). Where the SHSA has agreed in principle to the patient's transfer but no place is available for him in a local hospital, the authority for transfer cannot be given. In these circumstances the patient is placed on a transfer list until a place in a local hospital becomes available (unless in the meantime he is discharged). It is common for patients to wait for six to twelve months for a transfer. However, some patients may wait in the special hospitals on the transfer list for two years or more because of difficulties in locating a bed in a local hospital for them.

It should be noted that under s 123(2) the Secretary of State for Health has the power to *direct* the transfer of any special hospital patient into a local hospital, irrespective of whether the local hospital has agreed to accept the patient. In practice, however, this power is never used. There are three reasons for this. First, it would not be in the patient's interests to be admitted to a hospital which did not want him. Secondly, although the Secretary of State can direct the patient's admission to the hospital it cannot force the hospital to give him treatment. Thirdly, the exercise of this power would doubtless be regarded by health authorities as an unwarranted interference by the Secretary of State in the exercise of powers delegated to them. Thus for practical purposes all transfers take place in accordance with the regulations discussed above;

(3) In the case of restricted patients, the Home Secretary gives his consent to the transfer (s 41(3)(*c*)). In practice, if the patient's RMO supports his transfer the Home Secretary normally gives his consent. He may, however, withhold consent if he receives contrary advice from the Aarvold Board (*see* **4.5**).

15.7 The tribunal's role

As discussed in *8.3.1* and *8.5.4* a tribunal may recommend that a patient is transferred from a special to a local hospital. However, as can be seen from the discussion above, in practice a patient can only be transferred if his RMO at the special hospital supports the transfer and a consultant in a local hospital is willing and able to provide the patient with a bed and the necessary care. In this context the practical role of the tribunal is the limited one of persuading the RMO at the special hospital to the opinion that the patient should be transferred. Where a tribunal makes a recommendation for transfer its advice is sent to the Secretary of State for Health; it is then forwarded to the patient's RMO for his consideration. If the RMO is persuaded by the tribunal's advice that the patient should be transferred he will report to that effect to the Secretary of State for Health; the RMO will then establish contact, either directly or through the Department of Health, with the appropriate consultant at the receiving hospital. Provided that the consultant is willing to admit the patient he can then be transferred. If the RMO remains opposed to the transfer the tribunal's recommendation cannot be implemented. The tribunal must, however, give the case further consideration (r 24(4); *10.4.1*). Although the Secretary of State for Health will not overrule the RMO, the tribunal's recommendation for transfer may prompt discussion with the RMO about his plans for the patient's treatment and rehabilitation.

It is apparent from the above that a representative who is advocating a patient's transfer must persuade not only the tribunal, but more importantly, the patient's RMO of the appropriateness of transfer. Strategies for achieving this are discussed below.

15.8 What the representative can do

15.8.1 Independent psychiatric report

An independent psychiatric report which favours the patient's transfer into a local hospital may be a powerful aid in persuading a tribunal that the patient should be moved. However, as discussed above, it is the RMO who holds the key to transfer and many RMOs are dismissive of such reports; they argue that a psychiatrist who has no responsibility for a patient's care may too readily support a transfer. It is much more persuasive if a report favouring transfer were to be provided by the consultant psychiatrist who would be responsible for the patient in the local hospital. Thus it is useful for the representative to locate the responsible consultant and to ask him to report on the patient's suitability for transfer. As discussed in **15.6** above the catchment area responsible for a special hospital patient is normally based on the patient's links with a particular area prior to his admission to the special hospital. The representative may telephone or write to the DHA to discover the hospital and the consultant psychiatrist who would be responsible for the patient's care. The patient's social worker at the special hospital may also be helpful. Where there is any doubt or dispute as to which consultant is responsible for the patient the representative may ask the regional medical officer of the relevant RHA to resolve the issue.

Where a report favours the patient's transfer the representative should ask the independent psychiatrist to attend the proceedings. This enables the tribunal to test the independent psychiatrist's opinion and to satisfy itself that the opinion is well founded. More importantly, it may initiate dialogue between the special hospital RMO and the responsible consultant in the local hospital as to the feasibility of transferring the patient. It is not unknown for the tribunal hearing to provide the first dialogue between the two doctors; such dialogue may be beneficial for the patient's immediate and subsequent care and rehabilitation.

Another strategy is to obtain an independent report from a respected psychiatrist. If the report favours transfer and, at the hearing, the tribunal appears minded that way, the representative may request an adjournment (r 16; **10.3**) for the purpose of asking the catchment area psychiatrist to examine the patient and report to the tribunal.

The cost of an independent report may be obtained under the ABWOR provisions; there may also be circumstances where ABWOR will cover a second psychiatric report. The costs of the psychiatrist's attendance at the hearing may also be covered by the ABWOR provisions or, in some circumstances, by the tribunal itself (*12.3.3* and **12.4**).

The representative is referred to *13.8.3* for further discussion of independent psychiatric advice.

15.8.2 Conditional discharge as an alternative to transfer

In cases where there are difficulties in locating a local hospital bed for a restricted patient the representative may ask the tribunal to consider the possibility of conditional discharge as an alternative to transfer. This is particularly relevant to patients who are on transfer lists and reapply to the tribunal. Changes in the patient's condition or his circumstances may mean that conditional discharge is now appropriate.

15.8.3 Duty of the RHA to provide a bed

Where a patient's transfer has been approved in principle but the transfer has been blocked by the refusal of the catchment area hospital to accept the patient the representative may ask the regional medical officer of the relevant RHA to provide him with a bed in another hospital. As mentioned previously it is rare for a consultant who, on the basis of catchment area, is not responsible for the patient, to provide him with a bed. Nevertheless, in some cases the RHA has been able to persuade another hospital within the region to accept the patient. In other cases the RHA may, by contractual arrangement with a hospital in the voluntary or private sector, provide a patient with a bed in that hospital: this hospital may be outside the region.

15.8.4 Legal action

In *Ashingdane v Secretary of State for Social Services and others* (unreported, CA 18 February 1980) a patient in Broadmoor Hospital was considered by his RMO to be ready for transfer to a local hospital. The consultant at the catchment area hospital examined the patient and confirmed that the hospital was able to provide him with a bed and the necessary care. However, the two local branches of the nursing union, the Confederation of Health Service Employees (COHSE), had resolved not to admit any restricted patients. Faced with possible strike action by the nursing staff if the patient was admitted the consultant would not agree to accept him. Nor would the Secretary of State for Health or the area health authority (as manager of the hospital at that time) take any action to force his admission or to provide him with a bed in another local hospital.

A case was brought for breach of statutory duty against the Secretary of State and the area health authority. COHSE was also joined in the proceedings. The Court of Appeal ruled that s 141 of the MHA 1959 protected the Secretary of State and the area health authority from such a claim and the case could not proceed. However, the MHA 1983 amended s 141 (now s 139) so that it expressly does not apply to the Secretary of State or the health authorities. Consideration might therefore be given to similar action in a case where it is clear that the patient should be transferred.

Appendix 1

Part V of the Mental Health Act 1983

References to Definitions are to the Definitions given on pages xvii—xx at the beginning of this book

Mental Health Review Tribunals

Constitution etc

Mental Health Review Tribunals. 1977 c 49

65.—(1) There shall continue to be a tribunal known as a Mental Health Review Tribunal for every region for which a Regional Health Authority is established in pursuance of the National Health Service Act 1977 and for Wales, for the purpose of dealing with applications and references by and in respect of patients under the provisions of this Act.

(2) The provisions of Schedule 2 to this Act shall have effect with respect to the constitution of Mental Health Review Tribunals.

(3) Subject to the provisions of Schedule 2 to this Act, and to rules made by the Lord Chancellor under this Act, the jurisdiction of a Mental Health Review Tribunal may be exercised by any three or more of its members, and references in this Act to a Mental Health Review Tribunal shall be construed accordingly.

(4) The Secretary of State may pay to the members of Mental Health Review Tribunals such remuneration and allowances as he may with the consent of the Treasury determine, and defray the expenses of such tribunals to such amount as he may with the consent of the Treasury determine, and may provide for each such tribunal such officers and servants, and such accommodation, as the tribunal may require.

'Patient' s 145(1); *see* Definitions.
See chapter 6 for the structure and administration of the Mental Health Review Tribunals.

Applications and references concerning Part II patients

Applications to tribunals.

66.—(1) Where—

(*a*) a patient is admitted to a hospital in pursuance of an application for admission for assessment; or

(*b*) a patient is admitted to a hospital in pursuance of an application for admission for treatment; or

(*c*) a patient is received into guardianship in pursuance of a guardianship application; or

(*d*) a report is furnished under section 16 above in respect of a patient; or

(*e*) a patient is transferred from guardianship to a hospital in pursuance of regulations made under section 19 above; or

(*f*) a report is furnished under section 20 above in respect of a patient and the patient is not discharged; or

(*g*) a report is furnished under section 25 above in respect of a patient who is detained in pursuance of an application for admission for treatment; or

(*h*) an order is made under section 29 above in respect of a patient who is or subsequently becomes liable to be detained or subject to guardianship under Part II of this Act,

an application may be made to a Mental Health Review Tribunal within the relevant period—

(i) by the patient (except in the cases mentioned in paragraphs (*g*) and (*h*) above) or, in the case mentioned in paragraph (*d*) above, by his nearest relative, and

(ii) in the cases mentioned in paragraphs (*g*) and (*h*) above, by his nearest relative.

(2) In subsection (1) above 'the relevant period' means—

(*a*) in the case mentioned in paragraph (*a*) of that subsection, 14 days beginning with the day on which the patient is admitted as so mentioned;

(*b*) in the case mentioned in paragraph (*b*) of that subsection, six months beginning with the day on which the patient is admitted as so mentioned;

(*c*) in the case mentioned in paragraph (*c*) of that subsection, six months beginning with the day on which the application is accepted;

(*d*) in the cases mentioned in paragraphs (*d*) and (*g*) of that subsection, 28 days beginning with the day on which the applicant is informed that the report has been furnished;

(*e*) in the case mentioned in paragraph (*e*) of that subsection, six months beginning with the day on which the patient is transferred;

(*f*) in the case mentioned in paragraph (*f*) of that subsection, the period for which authority for the patient's detention or guardianship is renewed by virtue of the report;

(*g*) in the case mentioned in paragraph (*h*) of that subsection, 12 months beginning with the date of the order, and in any subsequent period of 12 months during which the order continues in force.

(3) Section 32 above shall apply for the purposes of this section as it applies for the purposes of Part II of this Act.

'Patient' s 145(1); *see* Definitions.
'Hospital' ss 79(6), 34(2) and 145(1); *see* Definitions.
'Application for admission for assessment' ss 2, 145(1), *see* **1.5**.
'Application for admission for treatment' ss 3, 145(1), *see* **1.6**.
Nearest relative ss 26(3), 145(1); *see* Appendix 6.
This section sets out the entitlement of a patient and his nearest relative to apply for a tribunal hearing. See generally **7.2**. In *R v Wessex Mental Health Review Tribunal ex parte Wiltshire County Council, The Times* 29 August 1989, the Court of Appeal left open the question of the entitlement of a patient admitted for assessment to apply to a tribunal when the 14 days following admission have elapsed and the duration of the detention has been extended under s 29(4) of the 1983 Act. Section 29(4) allows the duration of detention under s 2 to be extended pending the hearing of an application to the county court to displace the nearest relative, in this case because he allegedly unreasonably objected to the patient's admission under s 3. Lord Donaldson MR suggested that this question be addressed by the Department of Health in compiling their 'shopping list' of reforms to the Mental Health Act 1983.

References to tribunals by Secretary of State concerning Part II patients.

67.—(1) The Secretary of State may, if he thinks fit, at any time refer to a Mental Health Review Tribunal the case of any patient who is liable to be detained or subject to guardianship under Part II of this Act.

(2) For the purpose of furnishing information for the purposes of a reference under subsection (1) above any registered medical practitioner authorised by or on behalf of the patient may, at any reasonable time, visit the patient and examine him in private and require the production of and inspect any records relating to the detention or treatment of the patient in any hospital.

(3) Section 32 above shall apply for the purposes of this section as it applies for the purposes of Part II of this Act.

'Patient' s 145(1); *see* Definitions.
'Hospital' ss 79(6), 34(2) and 145(1); *see* Definitions.
'Secretary of State' in this case the Secretary of State for Health.
See **7.8**; **11.2–11.4**.

Duty of managers of hospitals to refer cases to tribunal.

68.—(1) Where a patient who is admitted to a hospital in pursuance of an application for admission for treatment or a patient who is transferred from guardianship to hospital does not exercise his right to apply to a Mental Health Review Tribunal under section 66(1) above by virtue of his case falling within paragraph (*b*) or, as the case may be, paragraph (*e*) of that section, the managers of the hospital shall at the expiration of the period for making such an application refer the patient's case to such a tribunal unless an application or reference in respect of the patient has then been made under section 66(1) above by virtue of his case falling within paragraph (*d*), (*g*) or (*h*) of that section or under section 67(1) above.

(2) If the authority for the detention of a patient in a hospital is renewed under section 20 above and a period of three years (or, if the patient has not attained the age of sixteen years, one year) has elapsed since his case was last considered by a Mental Health Review Tribunal, whether on his own application or otherwise, the managers of the hospital shall refer his case to such a tribunal.

(3) For the purpose of furnishing information for the purposes of any reference under this section, any registered medical practitioner authorised by or on behalf of the patient may at any reasonable time visit and examine the patient in private and require the production of and inspect any records relating to the detention or treatment of the patient in any hospital.

(4) The Secretary of State may by order vary the length of the periods mentioned in subsection (2) above.

(5) For the purposes of subsection (1) above a person who applies to a tribunal but subsequently withdraws his application shall be treated as not having exercised his right to apply, and where a person withdraws his application on a date after the expiration of the period mentioned in that subsection, the managers shall refer the patient's case as soon as possible after that date.

'Patient' s 145(1); *see* Definitions.
'Hospital' ss 79(6), 34(2) and 145(1); *see* Definitions.
'Application for admission for treatment' ss 3, 145(1); **1.6**.
See **7.7**; **11.2–11.4**.

Applications and references concerning Part III patients

Applications to tribunals concerning patients subject to hospital and guardianship orders.

69.—(1) Without prejudice to any provision of section 66(1) above as applied by section 40(4) above, an application to a Mental Health Review Tribunal may also be made—

(*a*) in respect of a patient admitted to a hospital in pursuance of a hospital order, by the nearest relative of the patient in the period between the expiration of six months and the expiration of 12 months beginning with the date of the order and in any subsequent period of 12 months; and

(*b*) in respect of a patient placed under guardianship by a guardianship order—

(i) by the patient, within the period of six months beginning with the date of the order;

(ii) by the nearest relative of the patient, within the period of 12 months beginning with the date of the order and in any subsequent period of 12 months.

(2) Where a person detained in a hospital—

(*a*) is treated as subject to a hospital order or transfer direction by virtue of section 41(5) above, 82(2) or 85(2) below, section 73(2) of the Mental Health (Scotland) Act 1960 or section 5(1) of the Criminal Procedure (Insanity) Act 1964; or

(*b*) is subject to a direction having the same effect as a hospital order by virtue of section 46(3), 47(3) or 48(3) above,

then, without prejudice to any provision of Part II of this Act as applied by section 40 above, that person may make an application to a Mental Health Review Tribunal in the period of six months beginning with the date of the order or direction mentioned in paragraph (*a*) above or, as the case may be, the date of the direction mentioned in paragraph (*b*) above.

'Patient' s 145(1); *see* Definitions and *R v Mersey Mental Health Review Tribunal ex parte K* [1990] 1 All ER 694, discussed in **8.5**.
'Hospital' ss 79(6), 34(2) and 145(1); *see* Definitions.
'Hospital order' ss 37, 145(1); *see* Definitions, **2.4**.
'Transfer direction' ss 47, 145(1); *see* **2.5**.
'Nearest relative' ss 26(3), 145(1); *see* Appendix 6.
See generally **7.2, Table II**.
(2) *See* **7.2** and **7.3**.

Applications to tribunals concerning restricted patients.

70. A patient who is a restricted patient within the meaning of section 79 below and is detained in a hospital may apply to a Mental Health Review Tribunal—

(*a*) in the period between the expiration of six months and the expiration of 12 months beginning with the date of the relevant hospital order or transfer direction; and
(*b*) in any subsequent period of 12 months.

'Hospital' ss 79(6), 34(2) and 145(1); *see* Definitions.
'Patient' s 145(1); *see* Definitions and *R v Mersey Mental Health Review Tribunal ex parte K* [1990] 1 All ER 694, discussed in **8.5**.
'Restricted Patient' s 79(1); *see* Definitions.
See **7.2, Table II.**

References by Secretary of State concerning restricted patients.

71.—(1) The Secretary of State may at any time refer the case of a restricted patient to a Mental Health Review Tribunal.

(2) The Secretary of State shall refer to a Mental Health Review Tribunal the case of any restricted patient detained in a hospital whose case has not been considered by such a tribunal, whether on his own application or otherwise, within the last three years.

(3) The Secretary of State may by order vary the length of the period mentioned in subsection (2) above.

(4) Any reference under subsection (1) above in respect of a patient who has been conditionally discharged and not recalled to hospital shall be made to the tribunal for the area in which the patient resides.

(5) Where a person who is treated as subject to a hospital order and a restriction order by virtue of an order under section 5(1) of the Criminal Procedure (Insanity) Act 1964 does not exercise his right to apply to a Mental Health Review Tribunal in the period of six months beginning with the date of that order, the Secretary of State shall at the expiration of that period refer his case to a tribunal.

(6) For the purposes of subsection (5) above a person who applies to a tribunal but subsequently withdraws his application shall be treated as not having exercised his right to apply, and where a patient withdraws his application on a date after the expiration of the period there mentioned the Secretary of State shall refer his case as soon as possible after that date.

'Hospital' ss 79(6), 34(2) and 145(1); *see* Definitions.
'Patient' s 145(1); *see* Definitions and *R v Mersey Mental Health Review Tribunal ex parte K* [1990] 1 All ER 694, discussed in **8.5**.
'Restricted patient' s 79(1); *see* Definitions.
'Secretary of State' in this case the Home Secretary.
See **7.2, Table II**.
(5) See now the Criminal Procedure (Insanity and Unfitness to Plead) Act 1991, and **7.3**.

Discharge of patients

72.—(1) Where application is made to a Mental Health Review Tribunal by or in respect of a patient who is liable to be detained under this Act, the tribunal may in any case direct that the patient be discharged, and—

(*a*) the tribunal shall direct the discharge of a patient liable to be detained under section 2 above if they are satisfied—

(i) that he is not then suffering from mental disorder or from mental disorder of a nature or degree which warrants his detention in a hospital for assessment (or for assessment followed by medical treatment) for at least a limited period; or

(ii) that his detention as aforesaid is not justified in the interests of his own health or safety or with a view to the protection of other persons;

(*b*) the tribunal shall direct the discharge of a patient liable to be detained otherwise than under section 2 above if they are satisfied—

(i) that he is not then suffering from mental illness, psychopathic disorder, severe mental impairment or mental impairment or from any of those forms of disorder of a nature or degree which makes it appropriate for him to be liable to be detained in a hospital for medical treatment; or

(ii) that it is not necessary for the health or safety of the patient or for the protection of other persons that he should receive such treatment; or

(iii) in the case of an application by virtue of paragraph (*g*) of section 66(1) above, that the patient, if released, would not be likely to act in a manner dangerous to other persons or to himself.

(2) In determining whether to direct the discharge of a patient detained otherwise than under section 2 above in a case not falling within paragraph (*b*) of subsection (1) above, the tribunal shall have regard—

(*a*) to the likelihood of medical treatment alleviating or preventing a deterioration of the patient's condition; and

(*b*) in the case of a patient suffering from mental illness or severe mental impairment, to the likelihood of the patient, if discharged, being able to care for himself, to obtain the care he needs or to guard himself against serious exploitation.

(3) A tribunal may under subsection (1) above direct the discharge of a patient on a future date specified in the direction; and where a tribunal do not direct the discharge of a patient under that subsection the tribunal may—

(*a*) with a view to facilitating his discharge on a future date, recommend that he be granted leave of absence or transferred to another hospital or into guardianship; and (*b*) further consider his case in the event of any such recommendation not being complied with.

(4) Where application is made to a Mental Health Review Tribunal by or in respect of a patient who is subject to guardianship under this Act, the tribunal may in any case direct that the patient be discharged, and shall so direct if they are satisfied—

(*a*) that he is not then suffering from mental illness, psychopathic disorder, severe mental impairment or mental impairment; or

(*b*) that it is not necessary in the interests of the welfare of the patient, or for the protection of other persons, that the patient should remain under such guardianship.

(5) Where application is made to a Mental Health Review Tribunal under any provision of this Act by or in respect of a patient and the tribunal do not direct that the patient be discharged, the tribunal may, if satisfied that the patient is suffering from a form of mental disorder other than the form specified in the application, order or direction relating to him, direct that that application, order or direction be amended by substituting for the form of mental disorder specified in it such other form of mental disorder as appears to the tribunal to be appropriate.

(6) Subsections (1) to (5) above apply in relation to references to a Mental Health Review Tribunal as they apply in relation to applications made to such a tribunal by or in respect of a patient.

(7) Subsection (1) above shall not apply in the case of a restricted patient except as provided in sections 73 and 74 below.

'Hospital' ss 79(6), 34(2) and 145(1); *see* Definitions.
'Medical treatment' s 145(1); *see* Definitions.
'Mental illness' *see* **13.2**.
'Mental disorder' ss 1, 145(1); **1.1**.
'Mental impairment', ss 1, 145(1); **13.3**.
'Patient' s 145(1); *see* Definitions and *R v Mersey Mental Health Review Tribunal ex parte K* [1990] 1 All ER 694, discussed in **8.5**.
'Psychopathic disorder', ss 1, 145(1); *see* **13.4**.
'Severe mental impairment' ss 1, 145(1); *see* **13.3**.
'Restricted patient' s 79(1); *see* Definitions.
For a general discussion of the powers of tribunals *see* chapter 8.
(1) This subsection confers a general discretion on tribunals to direct the discharge of patients who are not subject to Home Office restrictions. For an explanation of restrictions, *see 2.4.4* and **2.5**. It also places a tribunal under a duty to discharge if specified criteria are met.
(1) (*a*) sets out the criteria to be met if the tribunal is to come under a duty to discharge a patient admitted under s 2 (*see* **1.5** and *8.1.1*).
(1) (*b*) sets out the criteria which must be met before a tribunal comes under a duty to discharge a non-restricted patient detained otherwise than under s 2. This includes patients detained under ss 3 or 37, and patients who have been transferred from prison who are not subject to Home Office restrictions (*see 8.1.2*).
(2) Requires the tribunal, in exercising its general discretion to discharge, to have regard to specified matters (*see 8.1.2*).

(2) (*b*) (iii) the dangerousness criterion is discussed in *8.1.2*.
(3) Empowers the tribunal to direct discharge on a specified future date, or to recommend transfer or leave of absence with a view to facilitating the patient's transfer on a future date. The tribunal may further consider the patient's case in the event of such a recommendation not being complied with (*see* **8.2** and **8.3**).
(4) Sets out the criteria to be met if the tribunal is to come under a duty to discharge a guardianship patient; *see 8.1.3*.
(5) Confers jurisdiction on the tribunal to reclassify; *see* **8.4**.

Power to discharge restricted patients.

73.—(1) Where an application to a Mental Health Review Tribunal is made by a restricted patient who is subject to a restriction order, or where the case of such a patient is referred to such a tribunal, the tribunal shall direct the absolute discharge of the patient if satisfied—

(*a*) as to the matters mentioned in paragraph (*b*)(i) or (ii) of section 72(1) above; and
(*b*) that it is not appropriate for the patient to remain liable to be recalled to hospital for further treatment.

(2) Where in the case of any such patient as is mentioned in subsection (1) above the tribunal are satisfied as to the matters referred to in paragraph (*a*) of that subsection but not as to the matter referred to in paragraph (*b*) of that subsection the tribunal shall direct the conditional discharge of the patient.

(3) Where a patient is absolutely discharged under this section he shall thereupon cease to be liable to be detained by virtue of the relevant hospital order, and the restriction order shall cease to have effect accordingly.

(4) Where a patient is conditionally discharged under this section—
(*a*) he may be recalled by the Secretary of State under subsection (3) of section 42 above as if he had been conditionally discharged under subsection (2) of that section; and
(*b*) the patient shall comply with such conditions (if any) as may be imposed at the time of discharge by the tribunal or at any subsequent time by the Secretary of State.

(5) The Secretary of State may from time to time vary any condition imposed (whether by the tribunal or by him) under subsection (4) above.

(6) Where a restriction order in respect of a patient ceases to have effect after he has been conditionally discharged under this section the patient shall, unless previously recalled, be deemed to be absolutely discharged on the date when the order ceases to have effect and shall cease to be liable to be detained by virtue of the relevant hospital order.

(7) A tribunal may defer a direction for the conditional discharge of a patient until such arrangements as appear to the tribunal to be necessary for that purpose have been made to their satisfaction; and where by virtue of any such deferment no direction has been given on an application or reference before the time when the patient's case comes before the tribunal

on a subsequent application or reference, the previous application or reference shall be treated as one on which no direction under this section can be given.

(8) This section is without prejudice to section 42 above.

'Hospital' ss 79(6), 34(2) and 145(1); *see* Definitions.
'Patient' s 145(1); *see* Definitions and *R v Mersey Mental Health Review Tribunal ex parte K* [1990] 1 All ER 694, discussed in **8.5**.
'Restricted patient' s 79(1); *see* Definitions.
'Relevant hospital order' s 79(2).
'Secretary of State' in this case the Home Secretary.
This section details the circumstances in which a tribunal comes under a duty absolutely or conditionally to discharge a restricted patient. Unlike the situation with non-restricted patients, the tribunal has no general discretion to direct discharge. It may only discharge a restricted patient when the criteria placing it under a duty to do so are satisfied; *see* **8.5**.

Restricted patients subject to restriction directions.

74.—(1) Where an application to a Mental Health Review Tribunal is made by a restricted patient who is subject to a restriction direction, or where the case of such a patient is referred to such a tribunal, the tribunal—
- (*a*) shall notify the Secretary of State whether, in their opinion, the patient would, if subject to a restriction order, be entitled to be absolutely or conditionally discharged, under section 73 above; and
- (*b*) if they notify him that the patient would be entitled to be conditionally discharged, may recommend that in the event of his not being discharged under this section he should continue to be detained in hospital.

(2) If in the case of a patient not falling within subsection (4) below—
- (*a*) the tribunal notify the Secretary of State that the patient would be entitled to be absolutely or conditionally discharged; and
- (*b*) within the period of 90 days beginning with the date of that notification the Secretary of State gives notice to the tribunal that the patient may be so discharged,

the tribunal shall direct the absolute or, as the case may be, the conditional discharge of the patient.

(3) Where a patient continues to be liable to be detained in a hospital at the end of the period referred to in subsection (2)(*b*) above because the Secretary of State has not given the notice there mentioned, the managers of the hospital shall, unless the tribunal have made a recommendation under subsection (1)(*b*) above, transfer the patient to a prison or other institution in which he might have been detained if he had not been removed to hospital, there to be dealt with as if he had not been so removed.

(4) If, in the case of a patient who is subject to a transfer direction under section 48 above, the tribunal notify the Secretary of State that the patient would be entitled to be absolutely or conditionally discharged,

the Secretary of State shall, unless the tribunal have made a recommendation under subsection (1)(*b*) above, by warrant direct that the patient be remitted to a prison or other institution in which he might have been detained if he had not been removed to hospital, there to be dealt with as if he had not been so removed.

(5) Where a patient is transferred or remitted under subsection (3) or (4) above the relevant transfer direction and the restriction direction shall cease to have effect on his arrival in the prison or other institution.

(6) Subsections (3) to (8) of section 73 above shall have effect in relation to this section as they have effect in relation to that section, taking references to the relevant hospital order and the restriction order as references to the transfer direction and the restriction direction.

(7) This section is without prejudice to sections 50 to 53 above in their application to patients who are not discharged under this section.

'Hospital' ss 79(6), 34(2) and 145(1); *see* Definitions.
'Managers' s 145(1); *see* Definitions.
'Restriction direction' ss 49, 145(1); *see* **2.5**; **8.6**.
'Restriction order', ss 41, 145(1); *see* **2.4**; **8.5**.
'Restricted patient' s 79(1); *see* Definitions.
'Relevant transfer direction' s 79(2).
'Secretary of State' in this case the Home Secretary.
This section details the powers of the tribunal regarding patients subject to a restriction direction; *see* **8.6**.

Applications and references concerning conditionally discharged restricted patients.

75.—(1) Where a restricted patient has been conditionally discharged under section 42(2), 73 or 74 above and is subsequently recalled to hospital—

(*a*) the Secretary of State shall, within one month of the day on which the patient returns or is returned to hospital, refer his case to a Mental Health Review Tribunal; and
(*b*) section 70 above shall apply to the patient as if the relevant hospital order or transfer direction had been made on that day.

(2) Where a restricted patient has been conditionally discharged as aforesaid but has not been recalled to hospital he may apply to a Mental Health Review Tribunal—

(*a*) in the period between the expiration of 12 months and the expiration of two years beginning with the date on which he was conditionally discharged; and
(*b*) in any subsequent period of two years.

(3) Sections 73 and 74 above shall not apply to an application under subsection (2) above but on any such application the tribunal may—

(*a*) vary any condition to which the patient is subject in connection with his discharge or impose any condition which might have been imposed in connection therewith; or (*b*) direct that the restriction order or restriction direction to which he is subject shall cease to have effect;

and if the tribunal give a direction under paragraph (*b*) above the patient shall cease to be liable to be detained by virtue of the relevant hospital order or transfer direction.

'Hospital' ss 79(6); 34(2) and 145(1); *see* Definitions.
'Restriction direction' ss 49; 145(1); *see* **2.5**; **8.6**.
'Restriction order', ss 41, 145(1); *see* **2.4**; **8.5**.
'Restricted patient' s 79(1); *see* Definitions.
'Relevant hospital order' s 79(2).
'Relevant transfer direction' s 79(2).
'Secretary of State' in this case the Home Secretary.
See **8.7** and *R v Secretary of State for the Home Department ex parte K* [1990] 1 All ER 704.

General

Visiting and examination of patients.

76.—(1) For the purpose of advising whether an application to a Mental Health Review Tribunal should be made by or in respect of a patient who is liable to be detained or subject to guardianship under Part II of this Act or of furnishing information as to the condition of a patient for the purposes of such an application, any registered medical practitioner authorised by or on behalf of the patient or other person who is entitled to make or has made the application—

(*a*) may at any reasonable time visit the patient and examine him in private, and

(*b*) may require the production of and inspect any records relating to the detention or treatment of the patient in any hospital.

(2) Section 32 above shall apply for the purposes of this section as it applies for the purposes of Part II of this Act.

'Patient' s 145(1).
'Hospital', ss 79(6), 34, 145(1); *see* Definitions.
See 9.7.5; **13.8** and *W v Egdell* [1989] 2 WLR 689, [1989] 1 All ER 1089 (ChD); [1990] 1 All ER 835 (CA).

General provisions concerning tribunal applications.

77.—(1) No application shall be made to a Mental Health Review Tribunal by or in respect of a patient except in such cases and at such times as are expressly provided by this Act.

(2) Where under this Act any person is authorised to make an application to a Mental Health Review Tribunal within a specified period, not more than one such application shall be made by that person within that period but for that purpose there shall be disregarded any application which is withdrawn in accordance with rules made under section 78 below.

(3) Subject to subsection (4) below an application to a Mental Health Review Tribunal authorised to be made by or in respect of a patient under this Act shall be made by notice in writing addressed to the tribunal for the area in which the hospital in which the patient is detained is situated or in which the patient is residing under guardianship as the case may be.

(4) Any application under section 75(2) above shall be made to the tribunal for the area in which the patient resides.

'Patient' s 145(1).
'Hospital', ss 79(6), 34, 145(1); *see* Definitions.
See chapter 7.

Procedure of tribunals.

78.—(1) The Lord Chancellor may make rules with respect to the making of applications to Mental Health Review Tribunals and with respect to the proceedings of such tribunals and matters incidental to or consequential on such proceedings.

(2) Rules made under this section may in particular make provision—

(*a*) for enabling a tribunal, or the chairman of a tribunal, to postpone the consideration of any application by or in respect of a patient, or of any such application of any specified class, until the expiration of such period (not exceeding 12 months) as may be specified in the rules from the date on which an application by or in respect of the same patient was last considered and determined by that or any other tribunal under this Act;

(*b*) for the transfer of proceedings from one tribunal to another in any case where, after the making of the application, the patient is removed out of the area of the tribunal to which it was made;

(*c*) for restricting the persons qualified to serve as members of a tribunal for the consideration of any application, or of an application of any specified class;

(*d*) for enabling a tribunal to dispose of an application without a formal hearing where such a hearing is not requested by the applicant or it appears to the tribunal that such a hearing would be detrimental to the health of the patient;

(*e*) for enabling a tribunal to exclude members of the public, or any specified class of members of the public, from any proceedings of the tribunal, or to prohibit the publication of reports of any such proceedings or the names of any persons concerned in such proceedings;

(*f*) for regulating the circumstances in which, and the persons by whom, applicants and patients in respect of whom applications are made to a tribunal may, if not desiring to conduct their own case, be represented for the purposes of those applications;

(*g*) for regulating the methods by which information relevant to an application may be obtained by or furnished to the tribunal, and in particular for authorising the members of a tribunal, or any one or more of them, to visit and interview in private any patient by or in respect of whom an application has been made;

(*h*) for making available to any applicant, and to any patient in respect of whom an application is made to a tribunal, copies of any documents obtained by or furnished to the tribunal in connection with the application, and a statement of the substance of any oral information so obtained or furnished except where the tribunal considers it undesirable in the interests of the patient or for other special reasons;

(*i*) for requiring a tribunal, if so requested in accordance with the rules, to furnish such statements of the reasons for any decision given by the tribunal as may be prescribed by the rules, subject to any provision made by the rules for withholding such a statement from a patient or any other person in cases where the tribunal considers that furnishing it would be undesirable in the interests of the patient or for other special reasons;

(*j*) for conferring on the tribunals such ancillary powers as the Lord Chancellor thinks necessary for the purposes of the exercise of their functions under this Act;

(*k*) for enabling any functions of a tribunal which relate to matters preliminary or incidental to an application to be performed by the chairman of the tribunal.

(3) Subsections (1) and (2) above apply in relation to references to Mental Health Review Tribunals as they apply in relation to applications to such tribunals by or in respect of patients.

(4) Rules under this section may make provision as to the procedure to be adopted in cases concerning restricted patients and, in particular—

(*a*) for restricting the persons qualified to serve as president of a tribunal for the consideration of an application or reference relating to a restricted patient;

(*b*) for the transfer of proceedings from one tribunal to another in any case where, after the making of a reference or application in accordance with section 71(4) or 77(4) above, the patient ceases to reside in the area of the tribunal to which the reference or application was made.

(5) Rules under this section may be so framed as to apply to all applications or references or to applications or references of any specified class and may make different provision in relation to different cases.

(6) Any functions conferred on the chairman of a Mental Health Review Tribunal by rules under this section may, if for any reason he is unable to act, be exercised by another member of that tribunal appointed by him for the purpose.

(7) A Mental Health Review Tribunal may pay allowances in respect of travelling expenses, subsistence and loss of earnings to any person attending the tribunal as an applicant or witness, to the patient who is

the subject of the proceedings if he attends otherwise than as the applicant or a witness and to any person (other than counsel or a solicitor) who attends as the representative of an applicant.

(8) A Mental Health Review Tribunal may, and if so required by the High Court shall, state in the form of a special case for determination by the High Court any question of law which may arise before them.

(9) The Arbitration Act 1950 shall not apply to any proceedings before a Mental Health Review Tribunal except so far as any provisions of that Act may be applied, with or without modifications, by rules made under this section.

'Patient' s 145(1).
(1) and (2) The Mental Health Review Tribunal Rules 1983 (SI No 942) are reproduced in Appendix 2.
(8) The procedure for stating a special case is set out in Rules of the Supreme Court, Order 56; *see also* **10.9**.

79.—(1) In this Part of this Act 'restricted patient' means a patient who is subject to a restriction order or restriction direction and this Part of this Act shall, subject to the provisions of this section, have effect in relation to any person who—

(*a*) is subject to a direction which by virtue of section 46(3) above has the same effect as a hospital order and a restriction order; or

(*b*) is treated as subject to a hospital order and a restriction order by virtue of an order under section 5(1) of the Criminal Procedure (Insanity) Act 1964 or section 6 or 14(1) of the Criminal Appeal Act 1968; or

(*c*) is treated as subject to a hospital order and a restriction order or to a transfer direction and a restriction direction by virtue of section 82(2) or 85(2) below or section 73(2) of the Mental Health (Scotland) Act, 1984,

as it has effect in relation to a restricted patient.

(2) Subject to the following provisions of this section, in this Part of this Act 'the relevant hospital order' and 'the relevant transfer direction', in relation to a restricted patient, mean the hospital order or transfer direction by virtue of which he is liable to be detained in a hospital.

(3) In the case of a person within paragraph (*a*) of subsection (1) above, references in this Part of this Act to the relevant hospital order or restriction order shall be construed as references to the direction referred to in that paragraph.

(4) In the case of a person within paragraph (*b*) of subsection (1) above, references in this Part of this Act to the relevant hospital order or restriction order shall be construed as references to the order under the provisions mentioned in that paragraph.

(5) In the case of a person within paragraph (*c*) of subsection (1) above, references in this Part of this Act to the relevant hospital order, the relevant transfer direction, the restriction order or the restriction direction or to a transfer direction under section 48 above shall be construed as references to the hospital order, transfer direction, restriction order, restriction direction or transfer direction under that section to which that person is treated as subject by virtue of the provisions mentioned in that paragraph.

(6) In this Part of this Act, unless the context otherwise requires, 'hospital' means a hospital within the meaning of Part II of this Act.

'Patient' s 145(1); *see also* Definitions.
'Hospital order' ss 37 and 145(1); *see* Definitions and *2.4.2.*
'Restriction direction' ss 49, 145(1); *see* **2.5; 8.6**.
'Restriction order', ss 41, 145(1); *see* **2.4; 8.5**.
'Transfer direction' ss 47, 145(1); *see also* **2.5**.

SCHEDULE 2

Mental Health Review Tribunals

1. Each of the Mental Health Review Tribunals shall consist of—
   (*a*) a number of persons (referred to in this Schedule as 'the legal members') appointed by the Lord Chancellor and having such legal experience as the Lord Chancellor considers suitable;
   (*b*) a number of persons (referred to in this Schedule as 'the medical members') being registered medical practitioners appointed by the Lord Chancellor after consultation with the Secretary of State; and
   (*c*) a number of persons appointed by the Lord Chancellor after consultation with the Secretary of State and having such experience in administration, such knowledge of social services or such other qualifications or experience as the Lord Chancellor considers suitable.

2. The members of Mental Health Review Tribunals shall hold and vacate office under the terms of the instrument under which they are appointed, but may resign office by notice in writing to the Lord Chancellor; and any such member who ceases to hold office shall be eligible for re-appointment.

3. One of the legal members of each Mental Health Review Tribunal shall be appointed by the Lord Chancellor as chairman of the Tribunal.

4. Subject to rules made by the Lord Chancellor under section 78(2)(*c*) above, the members who are to constitute a Mental Health Review Tribunal for the purposes of any proceedings or class or group of proceedings under this Act shall be appointed by the chairman of the tribunal or, if for any reason he is unable to act, by another member of the tribunal appointed for the purpose by the chairman; and of the members so appointed—
   (*a*) one or more shall be appointed from the legal members;

(*b*) one or more shall be appointed from the medical members; and
(*c*) one or more shall be appointed from the members who are neither legal nor medical members.

5. A member of a Mental Health Review Tribunal for any area may be appointed under paragraph 4 above as one of the persons to constitute a Mental Health Review Tribunal for any other area for the purposes of any proceedings or class or group of proceedings; and for the purposes of this Act, a person so appointed shall, in relation to the proceedings for which he was appointed, be deemed to be a member of that other tribunal.

6. Subject to any rules made by the Lord Chancellor under section 78(4)(*a*) above, where the chairman of the tribunal is included among the persons appointed under paragraph 4 above, he shall be president of the tribunal; and in any other case the president of the tribunal shall be such one of the members so appointed (being one of the legal members) as the chairman may nominate.

Appendix 2

Mental Health Review Tribunal Rules 1983 (SI 1983 No 942)

ARRANGEMENT OF RULES

PART I INTRODUCTION

Title and commencement

1 These Rules may be cited as the Mental Health Review Tribunal Rules 1983 and shall come into operation on 30th September 1983.

Interpretation

2—(1) In these Rules, unless the context otherwise requires—

'the Act' means the Mental Health Act 1983;

'admission papers' means the application for admission under section 2 of the Act and the written recommendations of the two registered medical practitioners on which it is founded;

'assessment application' means an application by a patient who is detained for assessment and entitled to apply under section 66(1)(*a*) of the Act or who, being so entitled, has applied;

'the authority's statement' means the statement provided by the responsible authority pursuant to rule 6(1);

'chairman' means the legal member appointed by the Lord Chancellor as chairman of the Mental Health Review Tribunal under paragraph 3 of Schedule 2 to the Act or another member of the tribunal appointed to act on his behalf in accordance with paragraph 4 of that Schedule or section 78(6) of the Act as the case may be;

'decision with recommendations' means a decision with recommendations in accordance with section 72(3)(*a*) of the Act;

'health authority' has the same meaning as in the National Health Service Act 1977;

'nearest relative' means a person who has for the time being the functions under the Act of the nearest relative of a patient who is not a restricted patient;

'party' means the applicant, the patient, the responsible authority, any other person to whom a notice under rule 7 or rule 31(*c*) is sent or who is added as a party by direction of the tribunal;

'president' means the president of the tribunal as defined in paragraph 6 of Schedule 2 to the Act;

'private guardian' in relation to a patient means a person, other than a local social services authority, who acts as guardian under the Act;

'proceedings' includes any proceedings of a tribunal following an application or reference in relation to a patient;

'provisional decision' includes a deferred direction for conditional discharge in accordance with section 73(7) of the Act and a notification to the Secretary of State in accordance with section 74(1) of the Act;

'reference' means a reference under section 67(1), 68(1) or (2), 71(1), (2) or (5) or 75(1) of the Act;

'registration authority' means the authority exercising the functions of the Secretary of State under the Nursing Homes Act 1975;

'responsible authority' means—

(*a*) in relation to a patient liable to be detained under the Act in a hospital or mental nursing home, the managers of the hospital or home as defined in section 145(1) of the Act; and

(*b*) in relation to a patient subject to guardianship, the responsible local social services authority as defined in section 34(3) of the Act;

'the Secretary of State's statement' means a statement provided by the Secretary of State pursuant to rule 6(2) or (3);

'tribunal' in relation to an application or a reference means the Mental Health Review Tribunal constituted under section 65 of the Act which has jurisdiction in the area in which the patient, at the time the application or reference is made, is detained or is liable to be detained or is subject to guardianship, or the tribunal to which the proceedings are transferred in accordance with rule 17(2), or, in the case of a conditionally discharged patient, the tribunal for the area in which the patient resides.

'Chairman' in practice there are ten chairmen covering the 14 regions.
'Health authority' National Health Service Act 1977, as amended by the National Health Service and Community Care Act 1990.
'Nursing Homes Act 1975'; *see* now the Registered Homes Act 1984.

Part II Preliminary Matters

Making an application

3—(1) An application shall be made to the tribunal in writing, signed by the applicant or any person authorised by him to do so on his behalf.

(2) The application shall wherever possible include the following information—

(*a*) the name of the patient;
(*b*) the patient's address, which shall include—
  (i) the address of the hospital or mental nursing home where the patient is detained; or
  (ii) the name and address of the patient's private guardian; or
  (iii) in the case of a conditionally discharged patient or a patient to whom leave of absence from hospital has been granted, the address of the hospital or mental nursing home where the patient was last detained or is liable to be detained; together with the patient's current address;
(*c*) where the application is made by the patient's nearest relative, the name and address of the applicant and his relationship to the patient;
(*d*) the section of the Act under which the patient is detained or is liable to be detained;
(*e*) the name and address of any representative authorised in accordance with rule 10 or, if none has yet been authorised, whether the applicant intends to authorise a representative or wishes to conduct his own case.

(3) If any of the information specified in paragraph (2) is not included in the application, it shall in so far as is practicable be provided by the responsible authority or, in the case of a restricted patient, the Secretary of State, at the request of the tribunal.

'Tribunal', r 2.
'Nearest relative', r 2.
'Responsible authority', r 2.
3(1) The formal requirements for making an application are minimal. *See* Appendix 4 for a Model application form. For entitlement to apply, see chapter 7.
Person authorised by him. The patient's authorised representative may sign the application on his behalf (r 10(4)).

(2) *See* **8.1**.
(*e*) *authorised in accordance with r 10* by the applicant. Anyone may be authorised provided he is: (a) not liable to be detained; or (b) subject to guardianship; or (c) receiving treatment for mental disorder in the same hospital or mental nursing home as the patient (r 10(1); **9.6**).

Notice of application

4—(1) On receipt of an application, the tribunal shall send notice of the application to—

(*a*) the responsible authority;
(*b*) the patient (where he is not the applicant); and
(*c*) if the patient is a restricted patient, the Secretary of State.

(2) Paragraph (1) shall apply whether or not the power to postpone consideration of the application under rule 9 is exercised.

'Tribunal', r 2.
'Responsible authority', r 2.
(1) *See* **9.5**. The responsible authority will be asked by the tribunal to verify the entitlement of the patient to a tribunal hearing.
(2) For postponement under r 9, *see* **9.11**.

Preliminary and incidental matters

5 As regards matters preliminary or incidental to an application, the chairman may, at any time up to the hearing of an application by the tribunal, exercise the powers of the tribunal under rules 6, 7, 9, 10, 12, 13, 14(1), 15, 17, 19, 20, 26 and 28.

'Chairman', r 2.
'Tribunal', r 2.
See **9.4**.

Statements by the responsible authority and the Secretary of State

6—(1) The responsible authority shall send a statement to the tribunal and, in the case of a restricted patient, the Secretary of State, as soon as practicable and in any case within 3 weeks of its receipt of the notice of application; and such statements shall contain—

(*a*) the information specified in Part A of Schedule 1 to these Rules, in so far as it is within the knowledge of the responsible authority; and
(*b*) the report specified in paragraph 1 of Part B of that Schedule; and
(*c*) the other reports specified in Part B of that Schedule, in so far as it is reasonably practicable to provide them.

(2) Where the patient is a restricted patient, the Secretary of State shall send to the tribunal, as soon as practicable and in any case within 3 weeks of receipt by him of the authority's statement, a statement of such further information relevant to the application as may be available to him.

(3) Where the patient is a conditionally discharged patient, paragraphs (1) and (2) shall not apply and the Secretary of State shall send to the tribunal as soon as practicable, and in any case within 6 weeks of receipt by him of the notice of application, a statement which shall contain—

(*a*) the information specified in Part C of Schedule 1 to these Rules, in so far as it is within the knowledge of the Secretary of State; and

(*b*) the reports specified in Part D of that Schedule, in so far as it is reasonably practicable to provide them.

(4) Any part of the authority's statement or the Secretary of State's statement which, in the opinion of—

(*a*) (in the case of the authority's statement) the responsible authority; or

(*b*) (in the case of the Secretary of State's statement) the Secretary of State,

should be withheld from the applicant or (where he is not the applicant) the patient on the ground that its disclosure would adversely affect the health or welfare of the patient or others, shall be made in a separate document in which shall be set out the reasons for believing that its disclosure would have that effect.

(5) On receipt of any statement provided in accordance with paragraph (1), (2) or (3), the tribunal shall send a copy to the applicant and (where he is not the applicant) the patient, excluding any part of any statement which is contained in a separate document in accordance with paragraph (4).

'The authority's statement', r 2.
'Responsible authority', r 2.
'Tribunal', r 2.
'The Secretary of State's statement', r 2.
The powers of the tribunal under r 6 may be exercised by the chairman (r 5).
(1)–(3) *See* **9.7**.
(4) *See* **9.8**.

Notice to other persons interested

7 On receipt of the authority's statement or, in the case of a restricted patient, the Secretary of State's statement, the tribunal shall give notice of the proceedings—

(*a*) where the patient is liable to be detained in a mental nursing home, to the registration authority of that home;

(*b*) where the patient is subject to the guardianship of a private guardian, to the guardian;

(*c*) where the patient's financial affairs are under the control of the Court of Protection, to the Court of Protection;

(*d*) where any person other than the applicant is named in the authority's statement as exercising the functions of the nearest relative, to that person;

(*e*) where a health authority has a right to discharge the patient under the provisions of section 23(3) of the Act, to that authority;
(*f*) to any other person who, in the opinion of the tribunal, should have an opportunity of being heard.

'The authority's statement', r 2.
'Health authority', r 2.
'Nearest relative', r 2.
'Registration authority', r 2.
'Responsible authority', r 2.
'Tribunal', r 2.
'Secretary of State's statement', r 2.
See *9.5.2*; this is one of the powers which may be exercised by the chairman on behalf of the tribunal (r 5).

Appointment of the tribunal
8—(1) Unless the application belongs to a class or group of proceedings for which members have already been appointed, the members of the tribunal who are to hear the application shall be appointed by the chairman.

(2) A person shall not be qualified to serve as a member of a tribunal for the purpose of any proceedings where—
(*a*) he is a member or officer of the responsible authority or of the registration authority concerned in the proceedings; or
(*b*) he is a member or officer of a health authority which has the right to discharge the patient under section 23(3) of the Act; or
(*c*) he has a personal connection with the patient or has recently treated the patient in a professional medical capacity.

(3) The persons qualified to serve as president of the tribunal for the consideration of an application or reference relating to a restricted patient shall be restricted to those legal members who have been approved for that purpose by the Lord Chancellor.

'The authority's statement', r 2.
'Chairman', r 2.
'Health authority', r 2.
'Legal member', Sched 2, para 1(*a*).
'Nearest relative', r 2.
'President', r 2.
'Proceedings', r 2.
'Registration authority', r 2.
'Responsible authority', r 2.
'Tribunal', r 2.
'Secretary of State's statement', r 2.
See generally **9.3**.

Powers to postpone consideration of an application
9—(1) Where an application or reference by or in respect of a patient has been considered and determined by a tribunal for the same or any other area, the tribunal may, subject to the provisions of this rule, postpone

the consideration of a further application by or in respect of that patient until such date as it may direct, not being later than—

(*a*) the expiration of the period of six months from the date on which the previous application was determined; or

(*b*) the expiration of the current period of detention, whichever shall be the earlier.

(2) The power of postponement shall not be exercised unless the tribunal is satisfied, after making appropriate inquiries of the applicant and (where he is not the applicant) the patient, that postponement would be in the interests of the patient.

(3) The power of postponement shall not apply to—

(*a*) an application under section 66(1)(*d*) of the Act;

(*b*) an application under section 66(1)(*f*) of the Act in respect of a renewal of authority for detention of the patient for a period of six months, unless the previous application or reference was made to the tribunal more than three months after the patient's admission to hospital or reception into guardianship;

(*c*) an application under section 66(1)(*g*) of the Act;

(*d*) any application where the previous application or reference was determined before a break or change in the authority for the patient's detention or guardianship as defined in paragraph (7).

(4) Where the consideration of an application is postponed, the tribunal shall state in writing the reasons for postponement and the period for which the application is postponed and shall send a copy of the statement to all the parties and, in the case of a restricted patient, the Secretary of State.

(5) Where the consideration of an application is postponed, the tribunal shall send a further notice of the application in accordance with rule 4 not less than 7 days before the end of the period of postponement and consideration of the application shall proceed thereafter, unless before the end of the period of postponement the application has been withdrawn or is deemed to be withdrawn in accordance with the provisions of rule 19 or has been determined in accordance with the next following paragraph.

(6) Where a new application which is not postponed under this rule or a reference is made in respect of a patient, the tribunal may direct that any postponed application in respect of the same patient shall be considered and determined at the same time as the new application or reference.

(7) For the purpose of paragraph (3)(*d*) a break or change in the authority for the detention or guardianship of a patient shall be deemed to have occurred only—

(*a*) on his admission to hospital in pursuance of an application for treatment or in pursuance of a hospital order without an order restricting his discharge; or (*b*) on his reception into guardianship in pursuance of a guardianship application or a guardianship order; or

(*c*) on the application to him of the provisions of Part II or Part III of the Act as if he had been so admitted or received following—

(i) the making of a transfer direction, or

(ii) the ceasing of effect of a transfer direction or an order or direction restricting his discharge; or

(*d*) on his transfer from guardianship to hospital in pursuance of regulations made under section 19 of the Act.

'Reference', r 2.
'Regulations made under s 19 of the Act' Mental Health (Hospital, Guardianship and Consent to Treatment) Regulations 1983 (SI No 893).
'Tribunal', r 2.
See **9.11**. This is one of the powers which may be exercised by the chairman on behalf of the tribunal at any time up to the hearing of the application (r 5).

Part III General Provisions

Representation, etc

10—(1) Any party may be represented by any person whom he has authorised for that purpose not being a person liable to be detained or subject to guardianship under the Act or a person receiving treatment for mental disorder at the same hospital or mental nursing home as the patient.

(2) Any representative authorised in accordance with paragraph (1) shall notify the tribunal of his authorisation and postal address.

(3) As regards the representation of any patient who does not desire to conduct his own case and does not authorise a representative in accordance with paragraph (1) the tribunal may appoint some person to act for him as his authorised representative.

(4) Without prejudice to rule 12(3), the tribunal shall send to an authorised representative copies of all notices and documents which are by these Rules required or authorised to be sent to the person whom he represents and such representative may take all such steps and do all such things relating to the proceedings as the person whom he represents is by these Rules required or authorised to take or do.

(5) Any document required or authorised by these Rules to be sent or given to any person shall, if sent or given to the authorised representative of that person, be deemed to have been sent or given to that person.

(6) Unless the tribunal otherwise directs, a patient or any other party appearing before the tribunal may be accompanied by such other person or persons as he wishes, in addition to any representative he may have authorised.

'Party', r 2.
'Tribunal', r 2.
For a general discussion of r 10, *see* **9.6**. For appointment by the tribunal of a representative, *see* **11.3**. For entitlement to assistance under the 'Green Form' and ABWOR (assistance by way of representation) schemes, *see* chapter 12. At any time up to the hearing of the application, the powers of the tribunal under r 10 may be exercised by the chairman on behalf of the tribunal (r 5).

Medical examination

11 At any time before the hearing of the application, the medical member or, where the tribunal includes more than one, at least one of them shall examine the patient and take such other steps as he considers necessary to form an opinion of the patient's mental condition; and for this purpose the patient may be seen in private and all his medical records may be examined by the medical member, who may take such notes and copies of them as he may require, for use in connection with the application.

'Medical member' Sched 1, para 1(*b*).
'Tribunal', r 2.
See **9.9**. *R v Mental Health Review Tribunal ex parte Clatworthy* [1985] 3 All ER 699.

Disclosure of documents

12—(1) Subject to paragraph (2), the tribunal shall, as soon as practicable, send a copy of every document it receives which is relevant to the application to the applicant, and (where he is not the applicant) the patient, the responsible authority and, in the case of a restricted patient, the Secretary of State and any of those persons may submit comments thereon in writing to the tribunal.

(2) As regards any documents which have been received by the tribunal but which have not been copied to the applicant or the patient, including documents withheld in accordance with rule 6, the tribunal shall consider whether disclosure of such documents would adversely affect the health or welfare of the patient or others and, if satisfied that it would, shall record in writing its decision not to disclose such documents.

(3) Where the tribunal is minded not to disclose any document to which paragraph (1) applies to an applicant or a patient who has an authorised representative it shall nevertheless disclose it as soon as practicable to that representative if he is—

(*a*) a barrister or solicitor;
(*b*) a registered medical practitioner;
(*c*) in the opinion of the tribunal, a suitable person by virtue of his experience or professional qualification;

provided that no information disclosed in accordance with this paragraph shall be disclosed either directly or indirectly to the applicant or (where he is not the applicant) to the patient or to any other person without the authority of the tribunal or used otherwise than in connection with the application.

'Responsible authority', r 2.
'Tribunal', r 2.
See **9.8**; *Campbell v Secretary of State for the Home Department* [1988] 1 AC 120. This is one of the powers which may be exercised by the chairman on behalf of the tribunal at any time up to the hearing of the application (r 5).

Directions

13 Subject to the provisions of these Rules, the tribunal may give such directions as it thinks fit to ensure the speedy and just determination of the application.

'Tribunal', r 2.
See **10.5** and **10.8**. This is one of the powers which may be exercised by the chairman on behalf of the tribunal (r 5). Failure to obey such a direction may be contempt of court *Pickering v Liverpool Daily Post and Echo* [1990] 1 All ER 622 (HL). For the meaning of speedy see *Van der Leer v The Netherlands* (1990) 12 EHRR 567.

Evidence

14—(1) For the purpose of obtaining information, the tribunal may take evidence on oath and subpoena any witness to appear before it or to produce documents, and the president of the tribunal shall have the powers of an arbitrator under section 12(3) of the Arbitration Act 1950 and the powers of a party to a reference under an arbitration agreement under subsection (4) of that section, but no person shall be compelled to give any evidence or produce any document which he could not be compelled to give or produce on the trial of an action.

(2) The tribunal may receive in evidence any document or information notwithstanding that such document or information would be inadmissible in a court of law.

'President', r 2.
'Tribunal', r 2.
See 9.10.1, and **10.8**.
Evidence is not normally taken on oath.

Further information

15—(1) Before or during any hearing the tribunal may call for such further information or reports as it may think desirable, and may give directions as to the manner in which and the persons by whom such material is to be furnished.

(2) Rule 12 shall apply to any further information or reports obtained by the tribunal.

'Tribunal', r 2.
See 9.10.2.

Adjournment

16—(1) The tribunal may at any time adjourn a hearing for the purpose of obtaining further information or for such other purposes as it may think appropriate.

(2) Before adjourning any hearing, the tribunal may give such directions as it thinks fit for ensuring the prompt consideration of the application at an adjourned hearing.

(3) Where the applicant or the patient (where he is not the applicant) or the responsible authority requests that a hearing adjourned in accordance with this rule be resumed, the hearing shall be resumed provided that the tribunal is satisfied that resumption would be in the interests of the patient.

(4) Before the tribunal resumes any hearing which has been adjourned without a further hearing date being fixed it shall give to all parties and, in the case of a restricted patient, the Secretary of State, not less than 14 days' notice (or such shorter notice as all parties may consent to) of the date, time and place of the resumed hearing.

'Responsible authority', r 2.
'Tribunal', r 2.
See **10.3**; *R v Nottingham Mental Health Review Tribunal ex parte Secretary of State for the Home Department, R v Northern Mental Health Review Tribunal ex parte Secretary of State for the Home Department*, QBD before Farquharson J, *The Times* 25 March 1987, where it was held that the power to adjourn cannot be used to monitor the patient's progress in the hope that his condition will improve sufficiently to enable the tribunal to direct discharge. The notice to be given under r 16(4) before resuming a s 2 hearing is such as is reasonably practicable (r 33(*b*)).

Transfer of proceedings

17—(1) Where any proceedings in relation to a patient have not been disposed of by the members of the tribunal appointed for the purpose, and the chairman is of the opinion that it is not practicable or not possible without undue delay for the consideration of those proceedings to be completed by those members, he shall make arrangements for them to be heard by other members of the tribunal.

(2) Where a patient in respect of whom proceedings are pending moves within the jurisdiction of another tribunal, the proceedings shall, if the chairman of the tribunal originally having jurisdiction over those proceedings so directs, be transferred to the tribunal within the jurisdiction of which the patient has moved and notice of the transfer of proceedings shall be given to the parties and, in the case of a restricted patient, the Secretary of State.

'Chairman', r 2.
'Tribunal', r 2.
See **10.6**.

Two or more pending applications

18—(1) The tribunal may consider more than one application in respect of a patient at the same time and may for this purpose adjourn the proceedings relating to any application.

(2) Where the tribunal considers more than one application in respect of the patient at the same time, each applicant (if more than one) shall have the same rights under these Rules as he would have if he were the only applicant.

'Tribunal', r 2.
See **9.11**.

Withdrawal of application

19—(1) An application may be withdrawn at any time at the request of the applicant provided that the request is made in writing and the tribunal agrees.

(2) If a patient ceases to be liable to be detained or subject to guardianship in England and Wales, any application relating to that patient shall be deemed to be withdrawn.

(3) Where an application is withdrawn or deemed to be withdrawn, the tribunal shall so inform the parties and, in the case of a restricted patient, the Secretary of State.

'Tribunal', r 2.
'Party', r 2.
See **9.2** and *9.7.5*; *W v Egdell* [1989] 2 WLR 689, [1989] 1 All ER 1089 (ChD); [1990] 1 All ER 835 (CA). This is one of the powers which may be exercised by the chairman on behalf of the tribunal (r 5).

PART IV THE HEARING

Notice of hearing

20 The tribunal shall give at least 14 days' notice of the date, time and place fixed for the hearing (or such shorter notice as all parties may consent to) to all the parties and, in the case of a restricted patient, the Secretary of State.

'Party', r 2.
'Tribunal', r 2.
See **9.5**. This is one of the powers which may be exercised by the chairman on behalf of the tribunal (r 5).

Privacy of proceedings

21—(1) The tribunal shall sit in private unless the patient requests a hearing in public and the tribunal is satisfied that a hearing in public would not be contrary to the interests of the patient.

(2) Where the tribunal refuses a request for a public hearing or directs that a hearing which has begun in public shall continue in private the tribunal shall record its reasons in writing and shall inform the patient of those reasons.

(3) When the tribunal sits in private it may admit to the hearing such persons on such terms and conditions as it considers appropriate.

(4) The tribunal may exclude from any hearing or part of a hearing any person or class of persons, other than a representative of the applicant or of the patient to whom documents would be disclosed in accordance with rule 12(3), and in any case where the tribunal decides to exclude the applicant or the patient or their representatives or a representative of the responsible authority, it shall inform the person excluded of its reasons and record those reasons in writing.

(5) Except in so far as the tribunal may direct, information about proceedings before the tribunal and the names of any persons concerned in the proceedings shall not be made public.

(6) Nothing in this rule shall prevent a member of the Council on Tribunals from attending the proceedings of a tribunal in his capacity as such provided that he takes no part in those proceedings or in the deliberations of the tribunal.

'Proceedings', r 2.
'Responsible authority', r 2.
'Tribunal', r 2.
See **10.1** and **10.8**. In *Pickering v Liverpool Daily Post and Echo Newspapers plc and others* [1991] 1 All ER 622 it was held that breach of r 21(5) did not give rise to an action for a breach of statutory duty.

Hearing procedure
22—(1) The tribunal may conduct the hearing in such a manner as it considers most suitable bearing in mind the health and interests of the patient and it shall, so far as appears to it appropriate, seek to avoid formality in its proceedings.

(2) At any time before the application is determined, the tribunal or any one or more of its members may interview the patient, and shall interview him if he so requests, and the interview may, and shall if the patient so requests, take place in the absence of any other person.

(3) At the beginning of the hearing the president shall explain the manner of proceeding which the tribunal proposes to adopt.

(4) Subject to rule 21(4), any party and, with the permission of the tribunal, any other person, may appear at the hearing and take such part in the proceedings as the tribunal thinks proper; and the tribunal shall in particular hear and take evidence from the applicant, the patient (where he is not the applicant) and the responsible authority who may hear each

other's evidence, put questions to each other, call witnesses and put questions to any witness or other person appearing before the tribunal.

(5) After all the evidence has been given, the applicant and (where he is not the applicant) the patient shall be given a further opportunity to address the tribunal.

'Party', r 2.
'President', r 2.
'Proceedings', r 2.
'Responsible authority', r 2.
'Tribunal', r 2.

PART V DECISIONS, FURTHER CONSIDERATION AND MISCELLANEOUS PROVISIONS

Decisions

23—(1) Any decision of the majority of the members of a tribunal shall be the decision of the tribunal and, in the event of an equality of votes, the president of the tribunal shall have a second or casting vote.

(2) The decision by which the tribunal determines an application shall be recorded in writing; the record shall be signed by the president and shall give the reasons for the decision and, in particular, where the tribunal relies upon any of the matters set out in section 72(1) or (4) or section 73(1) or (2) of the Act, shall state its reasons for being satisfied as to those matters.

(3) Paragraphs (1) and (2) shall apply to provisional decisions and decisions with recommendations as they apply to decisions by which applications are determined.

'Decision with recommendations', r 2.
'President', r 2.
'Tribunal', r 2.
See **10.4**; *Bone v Mental Health Review Tribunal* [1985] 3 All ER 330, *R v Mental Health Review Tribunal ex parte Clatworthy* [1985] 3 All ER 699, *R v Mental Health Review Tribunal ex parte Pickering* [1986] 1 All ER 99. The decision must be communicated to the patient within seven days of the hearing (r 24(1)), or within three days in the case of an assessment application (r 33(*d*)).

Communication of decisions

24—(1) The decision by which the tribunal determines an application may, at the discretion of the tribunal, be announced by the president immediately after the hearing of the case and, subject to paragraph (2), the written decision of the tribunal, including the reasons, shall be communicated in writing within 7 days of the hearing to all the parties and, in the case of a restricted patient, the Secretary of State.

(2) Where the tribunal considers that the full disclosure of the recorded reasons for its decisions to the patient in accordance with paragraph (1) would adversely affect the health or welfare of the patient or others, the

tribunal may instead communicate its decision to him in such manner as it thinks appropriate and may communicate its decision to the other parties subject to any conditions it may think appropriate as to the disclosure thereof to the patient; provided that, where the applicant or the patient was represented at the hearing by a person to whom documents would be disclosed in accordance with rule 12(3), the tribunal shall disclose the full recorded grounds of its decision to such a person, subject to any conditions it may think appropriate as to disclosure thereof to the patient.

(3) Paragraphs (1) and (2) shall apply to provisional decisions and decisions with recommendations as they apply to decisions by which applications are determined.

(4) Where the tribunal makes a decision with recommendations, the decision shall specify the period at the expiration of which the tribunal will consider the case further in the event of those recommendations not being complied with.

'Decision with recommendations', r 2.
'President', r 2.
'Tribunal', r 2.

Further consideration

25—(1) Where the tribunal has made a provisional decision, any further decision in the proceedings may be made without a further hearing.

(2) Where the tribunal has made a decision with recommendations and, at the end of the period referred to in rule 24(4), it appears to the tribunal after making appropriate inquiries of the responsible authority that any such recommendation has not been complied with, the tribunal may reconvene the proceedings after giving to all parties and, in the case of a restricted patient, the Secretary of State not less than 14 days' notice (or such shorter notice as all parties may consent to) of the date, time and place fixed for the hearing.

'Party', r 2.
'Proceedings', r 2.
'Responsible authority', r 2.
'Tribunal', r 2.
Para (2) does not apply to restricted patients.

Time

26—(1) Where the time prescribed by or under these Rules for doing any act expires on a Saturday, Sunday or public holiday, the act shall be in time if done on the next working day.

(2) The time appointed by these Rules for the doing of any act may, in the particular circumstances of the case, be extended or, with the exception of the periods of notice specified in rule 16(4), rule 20 and rule 25(2), abridged by the tribunal on such terms (if any) as it may think fit.

'Tribunal', r 2.
The powers of the tribunal under r 26 may be exercised by the chairman (r 5).

Service of notices etc

27 Any document required or authorised by these Rules to be sent or given to any person may be sent by prepaid post or delivered—

(*a*) in the case of a document directed to the tribunal or the chairman, to the tribunal office;

(*b*) in any other case, to the last known address of the person to whom the document is directed.

'Chairman', r 2.
'Tribunal', r 2.

Irregularities

28 Any irregularity resulting from failure to comply with these Rules before the tribunal has determined an application shall not of itself render the proceedings void, but the tribunal may, and shall, if it considers that any person may have been prejudiced, take such steps as it thinks fit before determining the application to cure the irregularity, whether by the amendment of any document, the giving of any notice, the taking of any step or otherwise.

'Proceedings', r 2.
'Tribunal', r 2.
See **10.7**; *Campbell v Secretary of State for the Home Department* [1988] 1 AC 120, [1987] 3 All ER 8, [1987] 3 WLR 522 (HL). The powers of the tribunal under r 28 may be exercised by the chairman (r 5).

PART VI REFERENCES AND APPLICATIONS BY PATIENTS DETAINED FOR ASSESSMENT

References

29 The tribunal shall consider a reference as if there had been an application by the patient and the provisions of these Rules shall apply with the following modifications—

(*a*) rules 3, 4, 9 and 19 shall not apply;

(*b*) the tribunal shall, on receipt of the reference, send notice thereof to the patient and the responsible authority; provided that where the reference has been made by the responsible authority, instead of the notice of reference there shall be sent to the responsible authority a request for the authority's statement;

(*c*) rules 5, 6 and 7 shall apply as if rule 6(1) referred to the notice of reference, or the request for the authority's statement, as the case may be, instead of the notice of application;

(*d*) a reference made by the Secretary of State in circumstances in which he is not by the terms of the Act obliged to make a reference may be withdrawn by him at any time before it is considered by the tribunal and, where a reference is so withdrawn, the tribunal shall inform the patient and the other parties that the reference has been withdrawn.

'The authority's statement', r 2.
'Reference', r 2.
'Responsible authority', r 2.
'Tribunal', r 2.
See **11.2.**

Making an assessment application

30—(1) An assessment application shall be made to the tribunal in writing signed by the patient or any person authorised by him to do so on his behalf.

(2) An assessment application shall indicate that it is made by or on behalf of a patient detained for assessment and shall wherever possible include the following information—

(*a*) the name of the patient;
(*b*) the address of the hospital or mental nursing home where the patient is detained;
(*c*) the name and address of the patient's nearest relative and his relationship to the patient;
(*d*) the name and address of any representative authorised by the patient in accordance with rule 10 or, if none has yet been authorised, whether the patient intends to authorise a representative or wishes to conduct his own case.

(3) If any of the information specified in paragraph (2) is not included in the assessment application, it shall in so far as is practicable be provided by the responsible authority at the request of the tribunal.

'Assessment application', r 2.
'Nearest relative', r 2.
'Responsible authority', r 2.
'Tribunal', r 2.
See 11.1.1.

Appointment of a tribunal and hearing date

31 On receipt of an assessment application the tribunal shall—

(*a*) fix a date for the hearing, being not later than 7 days from the date on which the application was received, and the time and place for the hearing;
(*b*) give notice of the date, time and place fixed for the hearing to the patient;
(*c*) give notice of the application and of the date, time and place fixed for the hearing to the responsible authority, the nearest relative (where practicable) and any other person who, in the opinion of the tribunal, should have an opportunity of being heard;

and the chairman shall appoint the members of the tribunal to deal with the case in accordance with rule 8.

'Assessment application', r 2.
'Chairman', r 2.
'Nearest relative', r 2.
'Responsible authority', r 2.
'Tribunal', r 2.
See 11.1.2.

Provision of admission papers, etc

32—(1) On receipt of the notice of an assessment application, or a request from a tribunal, whichever may be the earlier, the responsible authority shall provide for the tribunal copies of the admission papers, together with such of the information specified in Part A of Schedule 1 to these Rules as is within the knowledge of the responsible authority and can reasonably be provided in the time available and such of the reports specified in Part B of that Schedule as can reasonably be provided in the time available.

(2) The responsible authority shall indicate if any part of the admission papers or other documents supplied in accordance with paragraph (1) should, in their opinion, be withheld from the patient on the ground that its disclosure would adversely affect the health or welfare of the patient or others and shall state their reasons for believing that its disclosure would have that effect.

(3) The tribunal shall make available to the patient copies of the admission papers and any other documents supplied in accordance with paragraph (1), excluding any part indicated by the responsible authority in accordance with paragraph (2).

'Admission papers', r 2.
'Assessment application', r 2.
'Responsible authority', r 2.
'Tribunal', r 2.
See 11.1.3.

General procedure, hearing procedure and decisions

33 Rule 5, rule 8 and Parts III, IV and V of these Rules shall apply to assessment applications as they apply to applications in so far as the circumstances of the case permit and subject to the following modifications—

(*a*) rule 12 shall apply as if any reference to a document being withheld in accordance with rule 6 was a reference to part of the admission papers or other documents supplied in accordance with rule 32 being withheld;

(*b*) rule 16 shall apply with the substitution, for the reference to 14 days' notice, of a reference to such notice as is reasonably practicable;

(*c*) rule 20 shall not apply;
(*d*) rule 24 shall apply as if the period of time specified therein was 3 days instead of 7 days.

'Admission papers', r 2.
'Assessment application', r 2.
See 11.1.3–11.1.6.

SCHEDULE 1 (Rules 6 and 32)
STATEMENTS BY THE RESPONSIBLE AUTHORITY AND THE SECRETARY OF STATE

PART A

INFORMATION RELATING TO PATIENTS (OTHER THAN CONDITIONALLY DISCHARGED PATIENTS)

1 The full name of the patient.

2 The age of the patient.

3 The date of admission of the patient to the hospital or mental nursing home in which the patient is currently detained or liable to be detained, or of the reception of the patient into guardianship.

4 Where the patient is being treated in a mental nursing home under contractual arrangements with a health authority, the name of that authority.

5 Details of the original authority for the detention or guardianship of the patient, including the Act of Parliament and the section of that Act by reference to which detention was authorised and details of any subsequent renewal of or change in the authority for detention.

6 The form of mental disorder from which the patient is recorded as suffering in the authority for detention (including amendments, if any, under sections 16 or 72(5) of the Act, but excluding cases within section 5 of the Criminal Procedure (Insanity) Act 1964).

7 The name of the responsible medical officer and the period which the patient has spent under the care of that officer.

8 Where another registered medical practitioner is or has recently been largely concerned in the treatment of the patient, the name of that practitioner and the period which the patient has spent under his care.

9 The dates of all previous tribunal hearings in relation to the patient, the decisions reached at such hearings and the reasons given. (In restricted patient cases this requirement does not relate to decisions before 30th September 1983.)

10 Details of any proceedings in the Court of Protection and of any receivership order made in respect of the patient.

11 The name and address of the patient's nearest relative or of any other person who is exercising that function.

12 The name and address of any person who takes a close interest in the patient.

13 Details of any leave of absence granted to the patient during the previous 2 years, including the duration of such leave and particulars of the arrangements made for the patient's residence while on leave.

Part B

REPORTS RELATING TO PATIENTS (OTHER THAN CONDITIONALLY DISCHARGED PATIENTS)

1 An up-to-date medical report, prepared for the tribunal, including the relevant medical history and a full report on the patient's mental condition.

2 An up-to-date social circumstances report prepared for the tribunal including reports on the following—

(*a*) the patient's home and family circumstances, including the attitude of the patient's nearest relative or the person so acting;
(*b*) the opportunities for employment or occupation and the housing facilities which would be available to the patient if discharged;
(*c*) the availability of community support and relevant medical facilities;
(*d*) the financial circumstances of the patient.

3 The views of the authority on the suitability of the patient for discharge.

4 Any other information or observations on the application which the authority wishes to make.

Part C

INFORMATION RELATING TO CONDITIONALLY DISCHARGED PATIENTS

1 The full name of the patient.

2 The age of the patient.

3 The history of the patient's present liability to detention including details of offence(s), and the dates of the original order or direction and of the conditional discharge.

4 The form of mental disorder from which the patient is recorded as suffering in the authority for detention. (Not applicable to cases within section 5 of the Criminal Procedure (Insanity) Act 1964.)

5 The name and address of any medical practitioner responsible for the care and supervision of the patient in the community and the period which the patient has spent under the care of that practitioner.

6 The name and address of any social worker or probation officer responsible for the care and supervision of the patient in the community and the period which the patient has spent under the care of that person.

PART D

REPORTS RELATING TO CONDITIONALLY DISCHARGED PATIENTS

1 Where there is a medical practitioner responsible for the care and supervision of the patient in the community, an up-to-date medical report prepared for the tribunal including the relevant medical history and a full report on the patient's mental condition.

2 Where there is a social worker or probation officer responsible for the patient's care and supervision in the community, an up-to-date report prepared for the tribunal on the patient's progress in the community since discharge from hospital.

3 A report on the patient's home circumstances.

4 The views of the Secretary of State on the suitability of the patient for absolute discharge.

5 Any other observations on the application which the Secretary of State wishes to make.

Appendix 3

Steps in Representation: a Summary Chart

Step	*Statutory provisions and references in text*	*Notes*
Prehearing		
1 Apply to the tribunal	r 3; **9.1** See Appendix 4 for model application (For assessment applications r 30; *11.1.1*)	Representative may apply on patient's behalf (r 10(4); **9.6** Note advantage of nearest relative application (**7.3**)
2 Notify MHRT of authorisation and address	r 10(2); **9.6** Addresses of tribunal offices in Appendix 7	
3 Examine statements and other documents from tribunal	rr 6, 12; **9.7** and **9.8** (For assessment applications, r 32; *11.1.3*)	Representative may take instructions from applicant before or directly after receiving statement. Examination of statement and taking instructions may be done under green form scheme (*12.3.1*). It is important to ask the patient to sign the Green Form immediately, as it will not cover work done before.
4 Apply for ABWOR	Legal Aid Act 1988, (SI No 340) regs 22–27 and SI 1989 No 550 reg 9; **12.4**	All further work under ABWOR provisions including independent experts' reports (**12.4**)

Step	*Statutory provisions and references in text*	*Notes*
5 Comment on deficiencies/ inaccuracies/omissions in tribunal documents	r 12(1); *9.8.1*	Representative may ask tribunal to obtain further information from the RA or other persons/authorities (for tribunal's powers to obtain further information see step 8 below)
6 Request disclosure of withheld information to the applicant, patient, independent experts or others	r 12(3); *9.8.2*	
7 Request public hearing if desired	r 21; **10.1**	Advantages and disadvantages to be discussed with patient. Request may be made at any stage of the proceedings but preferably as early as possible to avoid unnecessary delays
8 Ask tribunal to obtain further information	rr 14, 15; **9.10**	Representative should ensure that he receives copies of all further information obtained by tribunal
9 Further investigations by representative	Chapter 14	For example, establishing contact with friends, relatives; investigation of housing and other facilities for discharge
10 Obtain independent expert opinion	s 76; Chapter 13 in relation to independent psychiatric report; *14.4.1* in relation to independent social work report;	Consider whether independent psychiatric or social work report should be obtained
	SI 1989 No 340 reg 22(7); *12.4.3* in relation to finance	Special permission must be obtained from Area Director under ABWOR

Step	*Statutory provisions and references in text*	*Notes*
11 Discussion of information with applicant or patient except information withheld under r 12(3) by the tribunal	r 12(3); *9.8.1*; *13.8.5*	Special attention to checking important facts upon which opinions are based
12 Prepare strategy	see, in particular, Chapters 13, 14 and 15	
Hearing		
1 Put to MHRT any request as to conduct of proceedings	**10.2**	For example, that applicant or patient should remain throughout proceedings Note the rights of the applicant with respect to giving and hearing evidence, questioning witnesses and final reply
2 If further information is necessary, request adjournment	r 16; **10.3**	Hearing may be adjourned so that further information may be obtained by the tribunal, the RA or the representative. Adjourn only if information cannot be obtained in any other way
3 If hearing is adjourned in accordance with step 2 above, request that it is resumed	r 16(3); **10.3**	Representative should request copies of any further information which has been submitted to the tribunal since the proceedings were adjourned

Step	*Statutory provisions and references in text*	*Notes*
Decision		
1 If provisional decision is not finalised ask tribunal to further consider the case at reconvened proceedings	r 25(1); *10.4.2*	Representative should check with tribunal at regular intervals the progress towards finalising its decision Representative should request copies of any further information which has been submitted to the tribunal since original hearing
2 If decision with recommendations is not implemented ask tribunal to further consider the case at reconvened proceedings	s 72(3)(*b*) rr 24(4), 25(2); *10.4.1*	Representative should request copies of any further information which has been submitted to the tribunal since original hearing
3 Ensure that full reasons are given for tribunal's decision and that any requirement as to their non disclosure is reasonable and complies with the statutory requirements	rr 23(2), 24(2); **10.4**	
4 In case of irregularity, ask tribunal to take necessary steps to cure it	r 28; **10.7**	
5 On any issue of law ask tribunal to state a case for determination by High Court or apply for judicial review	s 78(9); **10.9**	
6 Send claim for costs under ABWOR to Area Committee together with green form	*12.4.2*	

Appendix 4

Model Application Form for Patient Applicants

1 I, [*patient's name*], hereby apply to the Mental Health Review Tribunal

2 (*In the case of a detained patient*)
I am currently detained in [*name and address of hospital*] under [*applicable section*] of the Mental Health Act 1983.

or (in the case of a patient subject to guardianship)
I am currently subject to guardianship in accordance with s 7 *or* s 37 [*omit whichever is not applicable*] of the Mental Health Act 1983. My present address is

My guardian is [*name and address of responsible social services authority or private guardian*]

or (in the case of a conditionally discharged patient or a patient on leave of absence)
I am liable to be detained in accordance with [*applicable section*] of the Mental Health Act 1983. I am currently conditionally discharged *or* on leave of absence [*omit whichever is not applicable*] from [*name and address of hospital*] and reside at [*address of present residence*]

3 I authorise [*name of representative*] of [*address of representative*] to act as my representative for the purposes of this tribunal application

or
I intend to authorise a representative of my own choosing and will inform the tribunal of his name and address as soon as possible

or
I would like the tribunal to appoint a representative for me for the purpose of these proceedings

or
I wish to conduct my case myself without the assistance of a representative

4 I would like the following person(s) to be given notice of the proceedings so that they may attend the hearing:
[*name of person(s)*] of [*address of person(s)*]

5 I wish for the proceedings to be in public *or* private [*omit whichever is not applicable*] and wish to be interviewed by the tribunal

(*Signed*)
applicant/authorised representative
(*Dated*) day of 19

To the clerk of the Tribunal
[*address of tribunal office*]

Appendix 5

Compulsory Admission to Hospital: a Summary Chart

Table 1: civil detention and guardianship

Statutory Provision	*Criteria and Procedure*	*Maximum duration of authority*	*Right of application or reference to MHRT*
Holding powers			
Doctor's holding power: s 5(2)	Application ought to be made for admission under Part II Doctor in charge of treatment or one doctor nominated by him furnishes report to the hospital managers	72 hours	none
Nurse's holding power: s 5(4)	(*a*) patient is suffering from a mental disorder to such a degree that it is necessary for his health or safety or for the protection of others that he is immediately restrained from leaving hospital; and (*b*) it is not practicable to secure the immediate attendance of a doctor who could exercise a holding power Registered mental nurse must record in writing that above criteria are satisfied	6 hours or until the earlier arrival of a doctor who can exercise a holding power	none

Statutory Provision	*Criteria and Procedure*	*Maximum duration of authority*	*Right of application or reference to MHRT*
Short term detention			
Admission for assessment in cases of emergency: s 4	Patient must be admitted urgently for assessment and compliance with the provisions for admission for assessment would involve undesirable delay Application by approved social worker or nearest relative supported by one medical recommendation	72 hours	none
Detention by police: s 136	It appears to a constable that a person in a public place is suffering from a mental disorder and needs immediate care and control Person may be taken to a place of safety, preferably a hospital, for the purpose of a social worker interview and medical examination	72 hours	none
Warrant to search and remove patients: s 135	There is reasonable cause to suspect that a mentally disordered person is being ill treated or neglected or is living alone and is unable to care for himself Warrant by justice of the peace on application by an approved social worker	72 hours	none

Statutory Provision	*Criteria and Procedure*	*Maximum duration of authority*	*Right of application or reference to MHRT*
Medium and long term detention			
Admission for assessment: s 2	(*a*) Patient is suffering from a mental disorder of a nature or degree which warrants his detention in hospital for assessment or for assessment followed by medical treatment for at least a limited period; and (*b*) he ought to be detained in the interests of his own health or safety or for the protection of other persons Application by an approved social worker or the nearest relative supported by two medical recommendations, one given by a doctor approved under s 12	28 days, not renewable	Right of application by patient within 14 days of admission No automatic reference
Admission for treatment: s 3	(*a*) Patient is suffering from mental illness, severe mental impairment, psychopathic disorder or mental impairment and the disorder is of a nature or degree which makes it appropriate for him to receive medical treatment in a hospital; and (*b*) in the case of psychopathic disorder or mental impairment, such treatment is likely to alleviate or prevent a deterioration of his condition; and (*c*) it is necessary for the health and safety of the patient or for the protection of other persons that he should receive such treatment and it cannot be provided unless he is detained under this section	6 months, renewable for 6 months and for 1 year periods thereafter	Right of application by patient within 6 months of the order and in every subsequent renewal period Right of application by nearest relative following barring of discharge order

Statutory Provision	*Criteria and Procedure*	*Maximum duration of authority*	*Right of application or reference to MHRT*
Admission for treatment: s 3 (continued)	Application by an approved social worker or nearest relative supported by two medical recommendations, one given by a doctor approved under s 12.		Automatic reference by hospital managers at expiry of 6 months if no application or reference is made in that period or at renewal of detention if 3 years has elapsed since case was last considered by a tribunal
Reception into guardianship: s 7	(*a*) Patient is suffering from mental illness, severe mental impairment, psychopathic disorder, or mental impairment of a nature or degree which warrants his reception into guardianship; and (*b*) It is necessary in the interests of the patient's welfare or for the protection of other persons that he should be received into guardianship Application by an approved social worker or the nearest relative supported by two medical recommendations, one given by a doctor approved under s 12	6 months, renewable for 6 months and for 1 year periods thereafter	Right of application by patient within 6 months of the order and in every subsequent renewal period No automatic reference

Table 2: detention of mentally abnormal offenders

Statutory Provision	*Criteria and Procedure*	*Maximum duration of authority*	*Right of application or reference to MHRT*
Mental disorder at the time of the offence			
The insanity defence: Criminal Procedure (Insanity) Act 1964, Criminal Procedure (Insanity and Unfitness to Plead) Act 1991	M'Naghten Rules; that is, person did not know the nature and quality of the act or did not know it was wrong Decision by a jury Defence must prove insanity on a balance of probabilities	Effect is as hospital order with or without restrictions without limit of time (see below). The Crown Court may also impose a guardianship order, a supervision and treatment order, or it may discharge the dependent absolutely or conditionally (*see* **2.2**(*a*)).	Right of application by patient within 6 months of the order. Then as for hospital order with restrictions (see below) Automatic reference by Home Secretary at expiry of 6 months if no application is made in that period and when 3 years has elapsed since case was last considered by a tribunal. Patients sentenced to a supervision and treatment order are not entitled to MHRT hearing.

Statutory Provision	*Criteria and Procedure*	*Maximum duration of authority*	*Right of application or reference to MHRT*
Diminished responsibility: Homicide Act 1957, s 2	Person was suffering from such abnormality of mind as substantially impaired his mental responsibility for the killing Decision by jury Defence must prove diminished responsibility on a balance of probabilities	Reduces charge of murder to manslaughter giving the court a wide range of disposals including a hospital order	If court makes a hospital order or a hospital order with restrictions, right of application and reference is as for patients subject to such orders (see below)
Mental disorder at time of trial			
Unfit to plead: The 1964 Act as amended by the Unfit to plead: Criminal Procedure (Insanity and Unfitness to Plead) Act 1991	Defendant is unable to understand the proceedings at the trial so as to make a proper defence, challenge a juror or to understand and to give evidence Decision by a jury	Effect is a hospital order with restrictions without limit of time (see below)	Right of application by patient within 6 months of the order. Then as for hospital order with restrictions (see below)
	If defence raises the issue, on the balance of probabilities If prosecution raises the issue, beyond a reasonable doubt		Automatic reference by Home Secretary at expiry of 6 months if no application is made in that period and when 3 years has elapsed since case was last considered by a tribunal

Statutory Provision	*Criteria and Procedure*	*Maximum duration of authority*	*Right of application or reference to MHRT*
Remand for a psychiatric report: s 35	(*a*) There is reason to suspect that the accused is suffering from mental illness, psychopathic disorder, severe mental impairment or mental impairment; and (*b*) it would be impracticable for a report on his mental condition to be made if he were remanded on bail Order by Crown Court or magistrates' court on evidence of one doctor	28 days, renewable for further periods of 28 days for not more than 12 weeks in all	none
Remand for treatment: s 36	The accused is suffering from mental illness or severe mental impairment of a nature or degree which makes it appropriate for him to be detained in hospital for medical treatment	28 days, renewable for further periods of 28 days for not more than 12 weeks in all	none
Mental condition of those accused of murder: Bail Act 1976, s 3(6A)	Order by Crown Court on evidence of two doctors Conditions of bail imposed by a court	none	
Mental disorder at the time of sentencing			
Interim hospital order: s 38	Offender is suffering from mental illness, psychopathic disorder, severe mental impairment or mental impairment, and there is reason to suppose that the mental disorder is such that it may be appropriate for a hospital order to be made Order by a Crown Court or magistrates' court on evidence of two doctors	12 weeks, renewable for 28 day periods for no more than 6 months in all	none

Statutory Provision	*Criteria and Procedure*	*Maximum duration of authority*	*Right of application or reference to MHRT*
Hospital order: s 37	(*a*) Offender is suffering from mental illness, psychopathic disorder, severe mental impairment or mental impairment of a nature or degree which makes it appropriate for him to be detained for medical treatment; and (*b*) in the case of psychopathic disorder such treatment is likely to alleviate or prevent a deterioration of his condition; and (*c*) the court is of the opinion having regard to all the circumstances, including the nature of the offence and the character and antecedents of the offender and of other available methods of dealing with him, that the most suitable method of disposing of the case is by means of a hospital order Order by Crown Court or magistrates' court on evidence of two doctors	6 months, renewable for 6 months and 1 year periods thereafter	Right of application by patient and nearest relative between 6 months and 1 year from the order and in every subsequent renewal period Automatic reference by hospital managers at renewal of detention if 3 years has elapsed since case was last considered by a tribunal
Guardianship order: s 37	The offender is at least 16 years of age and is suffering from one of the four forms of mental disorder of a nature or degree which warrants his reception into guardianship; The court must be of the opinion, having regard to all the circumstances including the nature of the offence and the character and antecedents of the offender and to other methods of dealing with him, that the most suitable method of disposing of the case is by a guardianship order.	6 months, renewable for a further 6 months and for 1 year periods thereafter	Right of application by patient within 6 months of the order and in each subsequent renewal period Right of application by nearest relative within first year and in each subsequent 1 year period

Statutory Provision	*Criteria and Procedure*	*Maximum duration of authority*	*Right of application or reference to MHRT*
	Order by Crown Court or a magistrates' court on evidence of two doctors		No automatic reference
Hospital order with restrictions: s 37	A hospital order is made and it appears to the court, having regard to the nature of the offence, the antecedents of the offender and the risk of his committing further offences if set at large, that a restriction order is necessary for the protection of the public from serious harm Order by Crown Court. Evidence of one of the doctors must be given orally	For a period specified by the court or without limit of time	Right of application by patient between 6 months and 1 year from the order and in each subsequent 1 year period Automatic reference by Home Secretary when 3 years has elapsed since case was last considered by a tribunal
Psychiatric probation order: Power of Criminal Courts Act 1973, s 3	Offender over 17 years of age whose condition requires or is susceptible to treatment, but does not warrant his detention in hospital. Order by Crown Court or magistrates' court on evidence of one doctor. Offender must consent to the order.	For a period specified by the court, being not less than 6 months and more than 3 years Any admission to hospital is on an informal basis.	none

Statutory Provision	*Criteria and Procedure*	*Maximum duration of authority*	*Right of application or reference to MHRT*
Mental disorder after sentence			
Transfer to hospital of person serving sentence of imprisonment: s 47. With or without restriction direction: s 49	(*a*) prisoner is suffering from one of the four forms of mental disorder; and (*b*) the mental disorder is of a nature or degree which makes it appropriate for him to be detained in hospital for medical treatment; and (*c*) in the case of psychopathic disorder or mental impairment, treatment is likely to alleviate or prevent a deterioration in his condition; and (*d*) having regard to the public interest and all the circumstances a transfer is expedient Direction by the Home Secretary upon reports from two doctors	If no restriction order is given, 6 months, renewable for 6 months and for periods of 1 year thereafter If a restriction order is given, the restriction order expires on the earliest date of release from prison; thereafter detention as for hospital order without restrictions	Right of application by patient within 6 months of transfer; then as for hospital order with or without restrictions whichever applies Automatic reference as for hospital order with or without restrictions whichever applies

Appendix 6

Nearest Relative (s 26(1))

The nearest relative is the first surviving person of the following:

1 husband or wife
2 son or daughter
3 father or mother
4 brother or sister
5 grandparent
6 grandchild
7 uncle or aunt
8 nephew or niece

If the patient normally lives with a relative, that relative is given preference (s 26(4)). Section 26 specifies other preferred relationships and circumstances where persons are precluded from acting as nearest relatives for the purpose of the Act. 'Husband' and 'wife' include a person who is living with the patient as the patient's husband or wife (s 26(6)). A person who is not related to the patient but who has ordinarily resided with him for not less than five years may be treated as a relative for the purposes of s 26(7). The nearest relative may authorise another person to perform his functions under the Act (SI 1983 No 893, reg 14).

Appendix 7

Tribunal Addresses

Address of tribunal office	*Tribunals served*	*Special hospitals served*
Clerk to the Mental Health Review Tribunal Government Buildings Canons Park Honeypot Lane Stanmore Middlesex HA7 1AY Tel 071 972 2000	North East Thames North West Thames East Anglia	
Clerk to the Mental Health Review Tribunal Spur B, Block 3 Crown Buildings Kingston Bypass Road Surbiton Surrey KT6 5QN Tel 081 390 4166	Oxford South East Thames South West Thames South Western Wessex	Broadmoor
Clerk to the Mersey Tribunal Office 3rd Floor Cressington House 249 St Mary's Rd Garston Liverpool L19 0NF Tel 051 494 0095	North Western Mersey West Midlands	Ashworth

Address of tribunal office	*Tribunals served*	*Special hospitals served*
Clerk to the Mental Health Tribunal Spur A, Block 5 Government Buildings Chalfont Drive Western Boulevard Nottingham NG8 3RZ Tel 0602 294222/3	Northern Yorkshire Trent	Rampton
Clerk to the Mental Health Review Tribunal First Floor Crown Buildings Cathays Park Cardiff CN1 3NQ Tel 0222 825328	Wales	

Appendix 8

Other Addresses

Council on Tribunals
22 Kingsway
London WC2B 6LE
Tel 071 936 7045

LAG Education and
Service Trust Ltd
242 Pentonville Road
London N1 7UN
Tel 071 833 2931

Law Society's Mental Health
and Disability Subcommittee
50 Chancery Lane
London WC2A 2SX
Tel (Switchboard) 071 242 1222
(Direct line) 071 320 5695

Law Society's Legal Practice
Information Office
50 Chancery Lane
London WC2A 2SX
Tel (Switchboard) 071 242 1222

Mental Health Act Commission
Maid Marian House
56 Houndsgate
Nottingham
Tel 0602 504040

Mental Health Review
Tribunal Panel Administrator
Professional Standards and
Development Directorate
The Law Society
Ipsley Court
Berrington Close
Redditch
Worcestershire B98 0TD
Tel 071 242 1222
(Local calls 0527 517141)

National Association for
Mental Health (MIND)
22 Harley Street
London WIN 2ED
Tel 071 637 0741

Royal Society for Mentally
Handicapped Children and Adults
123 Golden Lane
London EC1Y ORT
Tel 071 454 0454

Values Into Action (National
Campaign for People with
Learning Difficulties)
Oxford House
Derbyshire Street
London E2 6HG
Tel 071 729 5436

Bibliography

Reference texts

L O Gostin, *Mental Health Services: Law and Practice*, (Shaw and Sons, London) (Looseleaf)

R M Jones, *Mental Health Act Manual* (3rd edn), (Sweet and Maxwell, London) 1991

Other books

L Gostin (ed) *Secure Provision* (Tavistock, London) 1985

L Gostin, *A Practical Guide to Mental Health Law*, (MIND, London) 1983

L Gostin, *A Human Condition* (2 vols), (MIND, London) 1975 and 1977

C Greenland, *Mental Illness and Civil Liberty*, (G Bell and Sons, London) 1970

B Hoggett, *Mental Health Law* (3rd edn), (Sweet and Maxwell, London) 1991

J Peay, *Tribunals on Trial: A Study of Decision-Making under the Mental Health Act 1983*, (Clarendon Press, London) 1989

Chapters and articles

D Carson, 'Mental Health Process: The Mental Health Act 1983' (1983) *J of Social Welfare Law* 195

P Fennell, 'Diversion of Mentally Disordered Offenders from Custody' (1991) Crim LR 333–348

P Fennell, 'Consent to Treatment and Mental Disorder' in Doyal and Doyal (Eds) *Legal and Moral Dilemmas in Modern Medicine* (1990) (Basil Blackwell, Oxford), pp 29–51

P Fennell, 'The Mental Health Review Tribunal: A Question of Imbalance', *British Journal of Law and Society* No 2, 1977, 186–219

L Gostin, 'Human Rights, Judicial Review and the Mentally Disordered Offender', (1982) Crim LR 779

B Hoggett, 'The Mental Health Act 1983', (1983) *Public Law* 172

J Peay, 'Mental Health Review Tribunals and the Mental Health Amendment) Act', (1982) Crim LR 794–808

L Shuman, 'Practical Hints on Representation Before a Mental Health Review Tribunal', (1983) 80 LSG 468 and 2377.

Index